HANNA OLIVAS
ALONG WITH 24 INSPIRING AUTHORS

EMPOWERHER
STORY
STORIES OF STRENGTH, RESILIENCE, AND TRIUMPH.

ISBN: 978-1-964619-06-4

Table of Contents

INTRODUCTION

Welcome to "EmpowerHer Story," an anthology that illuminates the extraordinary narratives of women from multifaceted backgrounds. Within these pages, you'll discover a tapestry of compelling tales that resonate with resilience, triumph, and empowerment.

In a world where women often face unique obstacles, this anthology serves as a beacon of inspiration, showcasing the indomitable spirit that propels them forward. Each chapter offers a glimpse into the personal odysseys of these remarkable individuals as they navigate challenges, shatter barriers, and embrace their inner strength.

From confronting adversity head-on to embarking on transformative journeys of self-discovery, the stories within these pages encapsulate the essence of female empowerment. Through candid reflections and poignant narratives, readers are invited to embark on a journey of connection, recognizing the universal themes of courage, perseverance, and hope that unite us all.

Join us as we celebrate the resilience and tenacity of women who have dared to defy the odds and carve out their own paths, leaving an indelible mark on their lives and communities. "EmpowerHer Story" is more than an anthology; it's a testament to the enduring power of the human spirit and the limitless potential of women everywhere.

Hanna Olivas

Founder & CEO of She Rises Studios

https://www.linkedin.com/company/she-rises-studios/
https://www.facebook.com/sherisesstudios
https://www.instagram.com/sherisesstudios_llc/
www.SheRisesStudios.com

Author, Speaker, and Founder. Hanna was born and raised in Las Vegas, Nevada, and has paved her way to becoming one of the most influential women of 2022. Hanna is the co-founder of She Rises Studios and the founder of the Brave & Beautiful Blood Cancer Foundation. Her journey started in 2017 when she was first diagnosed with Multiple Myeloma, an incurable blood cancer. Now more than ever, her focus is to empower other women to become leaders because The Future is Female. She is currently traveling and speaking publicly to women to educate them on entrepreneurship, leadership, and owning the female power within.

EMBRACING LIFE THROUGH LOSS: MY EMPOWERMENT JOURNEY

By Hanna Olivas

In "EmpowerHer Story," we celebrate the amazing strength and bravery of women from all walks of life. Each story in this book shows how powerful we can be when we face tough times and make positive changes. As I share my own journey, I hope it helps you find your own path to healing and strength.

Facing Hard Times and Finding Inner Strength

Women often go through unique and tough challenges. My story is about facing one of the hardest times in my life and finding the strength to get through it. When I lost my unborn baby, Mario, at eight and a half months, it felt like my world fell apart. The excitement of expecting a baby turned into deep sorrow and guilt.

Preparing for Mario's arrival was filled with joy and anticipation. My husband and I did everything to welcome him, from decorating his room to celebrating with a baby shower and taking maternity photos. Even though I had health problems and was misdiagnosed with an illness, we held onto the hope that our baby boy would soon be with us.

But losing Mario brought overwhelming grief. The nursery, which was once full of hope, became a painful reminder of our loss. I blamed myself, thinking my body had let us down, and I felt like I had failed my husband and family.

Healing and Changing Through Difficult Times

Dealing with this loss was incredibly hard, but it also connected me with other women who have faced similar challenges. The pain I felt was something many women go through, and this shared struggle helped me find a way to heal. Through the darkest days of my depression, I started to see that healing wasn't just about getting over the pain but turning it into a source of strength.

Things changed when I found out I was going to be a grandma. This unexpected joy gave me a new purpose and hope. It reminded me that even in the hardest times, there's always a way to find light and happiness again. Becoming a grandmother gave me the push I needed to rise above my sorrow and choose life.

Finding Strength in Being Open and Supported

As I worked on healing, I learned the importance of being open about my feelings and finding support. By sharing my story, I connected with other women who had gone through similar losses. Their stories of strength and recovery inspired me.

With therapy, prayer, and support from my loved ones, I started to rebuild my life. Each step forward showed the incredible strength women have to overcome their struggles. Even when I was diagnosed with a rare blood disorder and cancer, it pushed me to find even more inner strength and determination.

Choosing to Live and Find Strength

On May 28, 2017, I made a big decision to fight for my life. This marked a new beginning for me, where I focused on healing and becoming stronger. I learned to forgive myself, let go of the pain and guilt, and appreciate the good things in my life.

Every day, I choose to live with purpose. I travel, share my story, and help other women find their own paths to healing and strength. My illness does not define me; it's just a part of my journey, but not who I am.

Celebrating the Strength of Women

My story is just one of many in "EmpowerHer Story." Each chapter in this book shows the incredible strength and determination of women who have faced difficult times and found their own paths. These stories remind us of the amazing power within each of us.

As you read "EmpowerHer Story," I hope you connect with these themes of courage, perseverance, and hope. Let these stories inspire you to find your own strength and to make positive changes in your life.

Steps to Find Your Strength and Transform Your Life

Here are some steps that helped me heal and grow:

1. **Start and end your days with prayer and gratitude.** Being thankful can help you see things in a positive light.

2. **Write in a journal.** Writing down your thoughts and feelings can help you understand them better.

3. **Find a mentor or counselor.** Getting support from someone experienced can be very helpful.

4. **Trust the journey.** Every step you take, even the small ones, are part of your healing process.

5. **Focus on what you can control and let go of what you can't.** This can help reduce stress and build resilience.

6. **Don't be afraid to ask for help.** Seeking support is a sign of strength.

7. **Practice meditation, exercise, and make healthy choices.** Taking care of your body is important for overall well-being.

8. **Discover who you are now and who you want to be.** This journey of self-discovery is empowering.

9. **Try new things.** Exploring new hobbies or experiences can help you grow.

10. **Face your fears and embrace your strength.** Overcoming fear is a big step toward unleashing your potential.

Your Journey to Empowerment Starts Here

As you read "EmpowerHer Story," remember that each story celebrates the strength and power within every woman. You have the strength to overcome any challenge and create a life full of purpose and joy.

Embrace your journey, find your strength, and live the life you were meant to lead.

With love and strength,

Xoxo,
Hanna

Ammie Michaels

Founder of WolfpackHR

https://www.linkedin.com/in/ammiemichaels/
https://www.facebook.com/missammie/
https://www.instagram.com/ammie.michaels/
https://wolfpackhr.com/
https://ammiemichaels.com/

Ammie Michaels is a seasoned Human Resources and Business Consultant and the Founder of WolfpackHR, a consulting firm specializing in flat-rate services and solutions for small businesses and startups. As a certified HR professional, mediator, and facilitator, she is known for her playful professional development workshops that help individuals and teams understand and manage behaviors and emotions, enhance their communication and collaboration skills, and foster growth mindsets, creating more fulfilling relationships and a resilient, adaptive approach to both personal and professional challenges. She creates safe spaces for everyone to be seen, heard, accepted, and understood. Additionally, as a founding member of WIN: Women's Impact Network, Ammie is committed to helping female entrepreneurs and business owners achieve their goals. She is based in the scenic Black Hills of South Dakota and balances her professional life with family time spent with her husband and two children, and adventures with her two Weimaraners.

AWAKENING: EMBRACING EMOTIONAL RESILIENCE AND SELF-DISCOVERY

By Ammie Michaels

I couldn't pinpoint the exact reason, but I was in a funk—unhappy, frustrated, and unable to understand why. I'm sure you can picture it, someone always negative and complaining—a real "Debbie Downer" or energy drain, like Eeyore or a "Negative Nancy." Despite having so much to be thankful for—a loving husband, two healthy kids, and good health, somehow I had lost my spark and smile.

My husband and I had been through a lot in our marriage, putting ourselves through college while raising kids and working was incredibly challenging. We supported each other's dreams and ultimately wanted to provide our children with a lifestyle and opportunities that we never had ourselves growing up. Yet, beneath the surface, there was an undercurrent of dissatisfaction that I couldn't shake. The feeling of being stuck was like wading through quicksand. Every attempt to move forward seemed to pull me deeper into a pit of negativity and depression.

I was constantly irritable and short-fused, snapping at small inconveniences, and my patience was as thin as a thread. My family, who deserved my love and attention, often bore the brunt of my frustration. My children would approach me with their innocent requests, only to be met with a harsh tone or a dismissive gesture. My husband, my partner in all things, grew increasingly distant as he struggled to connect with the person I had become.

My mornings started with a sigh and a heaviness in my chest that never seemed to lift. I remember looking at my reflection in the bathroom mirror, barely recognizing the person staring back at me. The joy and excitement that once danced in my eyes was replaced by a dull, weary gaze. I felt like a shadow of my former self, moving through life without truly living it.

It wasn't just at home though; my negativity seeped into my professional life as well. At work, I was unaware of the toxic environment I was creating, blinded by my own dissatisfaction in life. The turning point came one afternoon when my boss called me to come to his office. As I walked down the hallway, my mind raced with possibilities. Had I missed a deadline? Did I do something wrong?

My boss's tone was serious, and my heart pounded in my chest. As I stepped into his office, he motioned for me to sit down. His expression was grave, and I felt a knot tighten in my stomach. He took a deep breath and began to speak. His words hit me like a sledgehammer, each sentence feeling heavier than the last. He didn't criticize my work or question my productivity; instead, he spoke about my attitude. He told me that my negativity was affecting the entire team and that my behavior was creating a toxic environment. His words were like a slap in the face, a harsh wake-up call that I could no longer ignore.

How could someone in my position as a human resources professional, who was supposed to be the pillar of support and positivity, be called out for having a bad attitude? I was stunned. I had always prided myself on being a hard worker, someone who was reliable and got things done. I couldn't comprehend how my attitude could overshadow my accomplishments. The realization that I was failing in the very role designed to help others was devastating.

Leaving his office, I felt a mixture of hurt, embarrassment, and utter shame. I was upset at him for pointing out my flaws and ashamed that I had let things get to this point. How could I, a person responsible for managing workplace dynamics and ensuring a positive environment, be the source of negativity? The irony was painful. I felt exposed, vulnerable, and deeply conflicted. Part of me wanted to defend myself, but another part of me knew that he was right, and that realization was even harder to accept.

This confrontation at work only made me more sad and upset at home. The stress and shame of being called out at work added fuel to the fire of my already burning frustration and negativity. I became more depressed and retreated into myself. Then came the real blow.

One evening, my husband was waiting for me with an expression I had never seen before. His eyes, usually so full of warmth and understanding, were clouded with sadness and exhaustion. He seemed totally checked out and disconnected as he began to talk to me and my heart sank. I braced myself, sensing that whatever he was about to say would change everything. He confessed that he was miserable in our marriage. He explained that my constant unhappiness was taking a toll on him and our relationship. He admitted that he wasn't sure if he was in love with me anymore. He said he felt like nothing he did would ever make me happy and that he was done trying. His words were like a dagger to my heart.

The man sitting in front of me was the only person I ever felt truly connected to in my life. He was the one who had seen me at my best and my worst, who had stood by me through thick and thin. He was the one person who I believed truly loved me and understood me. To hear that I was driving him away and that my negativity had created a chasm between us was more than I could bear. As his words sank in, it felt as if my heart was being ripped out of my chest. The pain was so intense, it was physical. I felt as if the breath had been sucked from my lungs, leaving me gasping for air. I couldn't breathe. The room started to spin, and I was overwhelmed by a sense of despair so profound, it was as if the ground beneath me had crumbled, leaving me in a freefall of anguish and hopelessness.

I stared at him, my vision blurred by tears, and I saw the man I had fallen in love with so many years ago. The memories of our shared dreams, our laughter, and our moments of pure joy together flashed before my eyes. How had it come to this? How had I allowed my negativity and emotional turmoil to drive a wedge between us? The realization that I was losing the one person who truly mattered to me, the one person who had always been my rock, was unbearable. His words echoed in my mind, each repetition amplifying the pain. I felt paralyzed, unable to move or speak. The silence stretched between us, heavy and suffocating. I wanted to reach out, to hold him, to beg for forgiveness, but I couldn't find the strength. My body felt numb as if the weight of my sorrow had anchored me in place. I didn't think I'd be able to live without him and certainly couldn't picture my life without being married to him.

In that moment, I was forced to confront the reality that my negative mindset and emotional behaviors were not only making me miserable but were also causing pain and suffering to those around me. Despite being highly educated with an MBA, I was still stuck in the limiting beliefs and mindsets that were demonstrated to me growing up. I realized I was still operating under the emotional patterns from my childhood, where scarcity and negativity ruled. It was a harsh realization that I was at the center of the turmoil in my life. My lack of self-awareness and limited emotional intelligence had blinded me to the impact I was having on my loved ones and colleagues. This double wake-up call was like being doused with ice-cold water. The weight of this realization was crushing. I felt trapped in a prison of my own making, with walls built from years of negative thinking and emotional instability.

I was at a crossroads, faced with a choice: continue on this destructive path or find a way to change. But change seemed daunting, like climbing a mountain with no clear path to the summit. I felt overwhelmed by the magnitude of what lay ahead, but deep down, I knew I couldn't continue living this way.

I began a journey of deep self-reflection. It was like peeling back the layers of an onion, each layer revealing more about the roots of my negativity. I realized I was operating on autopilot, influenced by the negative mindset and beliefs from my childhood. Raised in a controlling environment, emotional regulation was foreign to me. I was living life by default, not by design. I had to figure out who I was.

Growing up in a household filled with scarcity, limiting beliefs, and negative emotions, I absorbed these as my own and my subconscious belief system was set in my childhood. Even with a college education, I still operated under these limiting beliefs without really realizing it. I wasn't really living my life; I was letting life live me. I lacked self-confidence and didn't feel worthy of love, likely due to my upbringing in a dysfunctional household. My father was controlling and had a temper, isolating us from my mother's side of the family most of my childhood. As a child, I felt lonely most of the time, often fending for myself as a latchkey kid of teenage parents. We moved out of my childhood home and to a new area when I was about ten years old, and I had to leave my only friends, further deepening my sense of isolation.

The move to a new school district felt like being uprooted and transplanted into rocky soil, where it was impossible to take root and flourish. This sense of not belonging, of being separate, became a recurring theme in my life. This loneliness persisted, leading me to believe I was missing out on life's milestones, waiting for things to happen to me and always wishing I'd be included and invited to things by others. The loneliness felt like a heavy fog, enveloping my every move, clouding my thoughts, and suffocating my spirit. It was as if I was wandering through a dense forest with no path, no light, and no direction. The weight of unspoken words, unshared moments, and unrealized dreams pressed down on me, making each day feel like a struggle just to get by. Every missed milestone was a reminder of the life I wasn't living, the joy I wasn't experiencing. It shaped my interactions and reinforced my belief that I was unworthy of love and connection.

Realizing that no one was going to change my life for me and that I had to be the one responsible for changing my life, I decided to start empowering myself. Transitioning from a fixed mindset to a growth mindset was key. I started to find my authentic self through self-reflection and personal development. This transformation wasn't overnight and it's still an ongoing journey that continues today. I am grateful for those wake-up calls from the men in my life because they led me to discover tools and resources that help others transform their lives. I dedicated myself to helping others through my consulting firm, WolfpackHR, and as a founding member of the Women's Impact Network (WIN).

Transitioning to entrepreneurship stretched me further, revealing how much I still had to learn. Initially, I felt like a lone wolf but soon realized I needed a supportive network. Seeking mentorship and guidance was crucial. I had to learn that asking for help is a strength, not a weakness.

I began speaking up, finding my voice, and showing up authentically in my entrepreneurial journey. This openness and vulnerability brought significant shifts in my business and my personal life. Entrepreneurship is challenging, revealing areas I still needed to work on emotionally and mentally. The emotional rollercoaster of running a business taught me the importance of emotional regulation. I invested in my mental, emotional, physical, and spiritual growth. Mentally, I banned the phrase "I can't" and focused on "How can I?" Emotionally, I adopted tools like breathwork and therapy. Physically, I underwent gastric surgery, adopted healthier eating habits, and focused on daily mindful movement as a habit. Spiritually, I focused on my connection to source energy through visualization, journaling, and meditation.

Financially, I realized that even with a business, my earning potential was limited by the number of hours in a day and the number of clients I could serve at once. I sought mentorship to learn about creating multiple income streams and shifting my mindset around money. Growing up with phrases like "money doesn't grow on trees" limited my thinking and what I believed was possible in my earning potential. I began seeing money differently, understanding that it's how we view and use it that gives it meaning. Not the phrases I heard growing up. In exploring non-traditional ways to earn money, I found opportunities for passive income that aligned with my values, like supporting American-based companies and companies focused on sustainability. One opportunity didn't cost me anything extra to join; it just required changing where I shopped for everyday products I was already purchasing.

My journey taught me that we can't always control what happens in life, but we can choose to add joy to our days. As (most) parents want happiness for their kids, we should strive for our own happiness too. Through my playful professional development workshops, I aim to empower others to shift from negativity to positivity, incorporating joy, fun, play, and laughter into their lives.

Looking deeper into my childhood, my parents' relationship was a significant influence on my early development. Their dynamic was often fraught with tension. My father, burdened by his unresolved issues from his own upbringing, struggled with anger, bitterness, and control. My mother, though well-meaning, often found herself caught in the crossfire, trying to shield us from the worst of it. This created a household atmosphere that was more about survival than thriving.

I remember my father's outbursts vividly. They were unpredictable and often over seemingly trivial matters. This unpredictability led me to become hyper-vigilant, always on edge, trying to avoid triggering his temper. My mother, on the other hand, was a source of comfort but also carried her own burdens of unfulfilled dreams and suppressed emotions. Her attempts to keep the peace often meant sacrificing her own needs and desires, a pattern I would later recognize in myself.

As I grew older, these experiences shaped my worldview. I developed a belief that the world was a lonely, harsh, and unforgiving place. I adopted a defensive posture, ready to fend off any potential threat to my well-being. This mindset, while protective in my youth, became a barrier to genuine connection and growth in my adult life.

My relationship with my brother was also influenced by these dynamics. The age gap and the turmoil at home created a distance between us. We were both navigating our own challenges, often in isolation. This sense of isolation extended to my social life. Moving to a new school district during a formative period further compounded my feelings of loneliness and disconnection. The new environment, populated primarily by transient military families, made it difficult to form lasting friendships. The constant goodbyes reinforced my belief that relationships were fleeting and unreliable.

My journey through early adulthood was marked by a series of pivotal decisions and realizations. Despite the challenges at home, I was determined to carve out a better future for myself. This determination led me to pursue higher education, a path that was neither straightforward nor easy. Balancing the demands of school with the responsibilities of family life required a level of resilience and perseverance that I had to develop on the fly. My husband and I supported each other through this period, but it was not without its strains. The financial and emotional pressures of simultaneously pursuing our degrees while raising children were immense. There were moments when it felt like the weight of our aspirations might crush us. Yet, we pressed on, driven by the desire to provide a better life for our children.

This period also brought to light my struggles with self-worth and identity. Achieving academic success did not automatically translate into a sense of personal fulfillment. Instead, I often felt like an imposter, waiting to be exposed. The accolades and degrees were not enough to silence the inner critic that had taken root during my tumultuous childhood.

My professional life was similarly fraught with challenges. My initial entry into the corporate world was a stark contrast to the academic environment I had grown accustomed to. The competitive nature of the workplace, coupled with my lingering self-doubt, created a perfect storm of anxiety and stress. My tendency to wear my heart on my sleeve, a trait rooted in my emotional upbringing, often put me at odds with the stoic professionalism expected in the corporate world.

The combined wake-up calls from my boss and my husband served as a catalyst for change. It was clear that my current trajectory was unsustainable. I needed to confront the deep-seated issues that were sabotaging both my personal and professional life. This realization marked the beginning of my profound journey of self-discovery and transformation.

I immersed myself in personal development literature, seeking to understand the root causes of my behaviors and beliefs. Books on psychology, emotional intelligence, and leadership became my constant companions. I also sought out therapy, a step that was both daunting and liberating. Discussing my childhood and its impact on my adult life was painful, but it provided the clarity I desperately needed.

A significant breakthrough came when I began to understand the concept of emotional regulation. For most of my life, I had been at the mercy of my emotions, reacting instinctively to every situation. Learning to manage and channel my emotions effectively was a game-changer. Emotional regulation is the ability to manage and respond to an emotional experience in a healthy and productive manner. It involves recognizing our emotions, understanding why they arise, and finding constructive ways to express them. This was a foreign concept to me, as my upbringing had not equipped me with the tools to manage my emotions effectively.

Techniques like mindfulness and meditation became essential tools in my emotional toolkit. Mindfulness taught me to stay present, to observe my thoughts and feelings without judgment. It was like turning on a light in a dark room, revealing the hidden corners of my mind. I started with simple practices, such as focusing on my breath or paying attention to the sensations in my body. These exercises helped me become more aware of my emotional state and allowed me to respond to situations with greater clarity and calm.

Meditation was another transformative practice. It provided a space for me to quiet my mind, which is extremely difficult as an Enneagram 6 who lives fully in their head, to connect with a deeper sense of peace and stillness. Through meditation, I learned to observe my thoughts and emotions without getting caught up in them. It was as if I was sitting by the side of a river, watching my thoughts flow by like leaves on the water. This perspective helped me gain a sense of detachment from my emotional reactions, allowing me to choose my responses more consciously.

Therapy was an integral part of my journey. My therapist helped me unravel the complex web of my emotions, tracing them back to their origins. We explored my childhood, my relationships, and the patterns that had shaped my behavior. Each session was like peeling back another layer, revealing deeper insights and understanding. One of the most profound realizations was that my emotions were not inherently bad or wrong; they were signals, messages from my inner self that needed to be acknowledged and understood.

Emotionally Focused Therapy (EFT) was particularly impactful. EFT is based on the understanding that our emotions are connected to our needs and that by addressing these needs, we can transform our emotional experiences. Through EFT, I learned to identify the underlying needs driving my emotions, such as the need for connection, validation, or security. By addressing these needs, I was able to shift my emotional responses and create more positive and fulfilling interactions.

Another valuable technique was journaling. Writing down my thoughts and feelings allowed me to process and make sense of them. It was like having a conversation with myself, a way to explore my inner world without judgment. Journaling helped me identify patterns in my thinking and behavior, uncovering the beliefs that were holding me back. It also provided a release, a way to express my emotions safely and constructively.

As I gained a deeper understanding of emotional regulation, I realized that these tools and practices were not just beneficial for me; they had the potential to help others as well. My personal journey equipped me with valuable insights and experiences that could guide others on their paths to emotional well-being. This realization inspired me to develop programs and workshops focused on emotional regulation and personal development.

I dedicated myself to creating comprehensive programs that addressed the various aspects of emotional regulation. These programs were designed to help individuals understand their emotions, develop self-awareness, and learn practical techniques for managing their emotional responses. I wanted to create a safe and supportive space where people could explore their emotions, gain new insights, and develop the skills needed to navigate life's challenges with greater ease and resilience.

One of the key components of these programs was self-awareness. Self-awareness is the foundation of emotional regulation; it involves recognizing and understanding our emotions, thoughts, and behaviors. I developed exercises and activities to help participants increase their self-awareness, such as mindfulness practices, reflective journaling, and personality assessments. These tools allowed individuals to gain a deeper understanding of themselves, their triggers, and their emotional patterns.

Personality assessments were particularly enlightening. Tools like the Myers-Briggs Type Indicator (MBTI), the Big Five, and the Enneagram provided valuable insights into different personality types and how they influence our emotional responses. Understanding one's personality type can help individuals recognize their strengths, weaknesses, and tendencies, enabling them to approach emotional regulation in a way that is tailored to their unique needs.

Another important aspect of the programs was emotional intelligence (EI). Emotional intelligence is the ability to recognize, understand, and manage our own emotions, as well as the emotions of others. It involves skills such as empathy, emotional regulation, and effective communication. I incorporated EI training into the workshops, teaching participants how to develop their emotional intelligence through practical exercises and real-life scenarios.

Empathy, for example, is a crucial component of emotional intelligence. It involves understanding and sharing the feelings of others, which can enhance our relationships and communication. I developed activities to help participants cultivate empathy, such as role-playing exercises and group discussions. These activities encouraged individuals to step into others' shoes, to see the world from different perspectives, and to respond with compassion and understanding.

Communication skills were also a central focus of the programs. Effective communication is essential for expressing our emotions constructively and building healthy relationships. I taught participants techniques such as active listening, assertive communication, and conflict resolution. These skills empowered individuals to express their needs and emotions clearly and respectfully, fostering deeper connections and reducing misunderstandings.

One of the most rewarding aspects of these programs was witnessing the transformations that occurred. Participants often came in feeling overwhelmed by their emotions, struggling with self-doubt and strained relationships. Through the workshops, they gained a sense of empowerment, and a newfound ability to navigate their emotions and interactions with confidence and grace. It was incredibly fulfilling to see individuals apply the techniques they had learned, creating positive changes in their lives and relationships.

My personal journey of emotional regulation not only transformed my life but also inspired me to help others navigate their emotional landscapes. The programs and workshops I developed became a way to share the knowledge and insights I had gained, providing others with the tools and support they needed to thrive. It was a reminder that our struggles can become a source of strength and wisdom, and that by embracing our own healing, we can light the way for others.

Through these programs, I aimed to create a ripple effect of positive change. Each individual who learned to regulate their emotions and develop self-awareness had the potential to influence their families, workplaces, and communities. Emotional regulation is not just about managing our own well-being; it is about creating a more compassionate, understanding, and connected world, especially in today's environment of the increasing adoption and use of artificial intelligence. By helping others on their journeys, I hoped to contribute to a broader cultural shift towards emotional intelligence and resilience.

Reflecting on my journey, I see that emotional regulation was a cornerstone of my transformation. It enabled me to break free from the cycles of negativity and reactivity that had held me back. It taught me that we have the power to shape our emotional experiences and that by doing so, we can create a life filled with deeper connections, joy, and fulfillment.

My commitment to emotional regulation continues to shape my work and my life. I am dedicated to ongoing learning and growth, continually seeking new insights and techniques to enhance my emotional well-being and support others. The journey of emotional regulation is an ongoing process, one that requires patience, compassion, and a willingness to explore the depths of our inner worlds.

Emotional regulation is a transformative practice that has the power to change lives. My personal journey from negativity and reactivity to self-awareness and emotional intelligence has been a testament to this power. Through my programs and workshops, I strive to share this knowledge and empower others to navigate their emotions with confidence and grace. By fostering emotional regulation and self-awareness, we can create a more compassionate and connected world, one where individuals are empowered to thrive and live their fullest, most authentic lives.

Anisa Crespo

Founder of My Mompreneur Studio

https://www.linkedin.com/in/anisacrespo/
https://www.facebook.com/anisacrespo
https://www.instagram.com/keepingupwiththecrespos/
https://linktr.ee/anisacrespo
https://bit.ly/winwithnis

Anisa Crespo, Founder of My Mompreneur Studio, passionately champions women's empowerment. She amplifies women's voices as a podcast host and shares her own transformative journeys as a published author, turning her traumas into triumphs. Anisa serves as a dedicated coach, guiding women towards fulfillment and true happiness in life by helping them define and fund their purposes. Balancing her roles as child of God, Mompreneur, and mother of twins, she embodies values of faith, family, health, wealth, and freedom. Anisa courageously left her six-figure job of over ten years in a male-dominated industry in 2024 to carry out her own mission to empower and encourage women, aspiring to help 1,000 moms become Mompreneurs by 2030. With unwavering determination, she leads by example, envisioning a world where women embrace their potential and forge long lasting legacies. Join Anisa on this extraordinary journey of pursuing dreams and living authentically by one's values.

FROM WORKING MOM TO EMPOWERED MOMPRENEUR

By Anisa Crespo

Seven deadly daggers pierced the silence that morning, each word a searing blade aimed directly at my heart. "Momma, why don't you love us anymore?" Did my baby really believe that to be true?

"What, why would you say that, Avianna?" Overcome by an overabundance of devastating emotions, that was the only response I could muster up to reply to this sweet, innocent child.

"Well Momma, you just always love to work and you don't love to play with me and Gio." My reality set in like bricks laid to build a house, each one adding more and more weight to the realization that the foundation of my life was shifting beneath me, leaving me stranded in a maze of uncertainty. I knew something would eventually have to change. It was true; not the part about me not loving my children or not wanting to play with them, of course, but the part about loving to work. Except it was more than just a love of work. I had let my work consume me like a voracious flame, leaving little room for anything else in my life.

I had been classifying myself as an entrepreneur when in reality I was actually a "hybridpreneur." You might be wondering what exactly a hybridpreneur is. It's a term that was coined to describe an individual who is becoming an entrepreneur but has not yet fully transitioned out of their role as a full time employee. It's a commonly known fact in the business world that entrepreneurs, especially solopreneurs who are starting completely on their own, put in countless hours in an attempt to chase their dreams and build an empire. Mix this with a cup of being a mom to toddler twins, sprinkle in a dash of being a wife, toss in a few spoonsful of household chores coupled with a demanding, full-time job, and you've got the perfect recipe for a high-stress situation. The stress isn't just confined to the mom putting in all the effort; it affects everyone around her whom she deeply cares for and who inspired her to begin this venture in the first place.

As I extracted each of those daggers from the depths of my heart, with each crimson drop spilled, a metamorphosis took place. I shed the skin of corporate ambition and embraced the nurturing spirit of motherhood. Strength was found in vulnerability, and the resilience cultivated through adversity. I surrendered to the pain, letting it flow freely, an outpouring of emotions as raw as the wounds themselves. In that transformative moment, the hybridpreneur within me met its demise, and from its ashes emerged a resilient phoenix, reborn as an empowered mompreneur.

Over the course of the next week, as the echoes of the old identity faded into oblivion, a sense of liberation washed over me, freeing my spirit to soar to new heights, unencumbered by the chains of societal expectations and corporate demands. With each breath, I embraced the boundless possibilities of this new chapter, guided by the steady rhythm of a mother's love. For years, I juggled the roles of business owner and employee, but it seemed like my business aspirations always took a back seat to the security of a steady job. There's a certain comfort in the ongoing routine of traditional employment that can hinder our growth. Fear of the uncertain often looms, clouding our judgment and keeping us from seizing opportunities. As long as we remain trapped in the repetitive cycle of trading time for money, true progress feels forever out of reach.

I spent what seemed like infinite hours in prayer, seeking answers and solace in the sanctuary of my devotion to God. Every whispered plea resounded through the corridors of ambiguity, each word a lifeline tethering me to hope amidst the tempest of doubt. In the quietude of introspection, I found refuge - a sacred space where faith blossomed like a resilient flower in the harshest of deserts. A breathtaking spiritual awakening came over me with the calmness of a tranquil dawn breaking over the horizon. I experienced serenity, a profound peace that transcended the tumultuous waves of existence. Finally, I managed to silence the cacophony of doubts echoing in my mind. *What will others think? How do I break the news to my husband? What will I say to my boss with whom I had shared a mutual loyalty for the past decade? What if things don't go as planned?* The relentless stream of worries seemed never-ending. My mantra "faith over fear" had never been so prevalent. I was enveloped by this impenetrable armor of joy. Harmony was my breastplate, and peace was my shield. I was going to take the leap and reclaim my 40-50 hours per week that I had been accustomed to complacently exchanging for a false illusion of security for the past two decades. It was time for this phoenix to soar.

This spiritual awakening came with more than an enlightening, "ah ha moment" to just up and quit my job to pursue my dreams. Having been in the field of logistics for ten years, it was not something that was going to happen overnight. It would require grace and a strategic blueprint to execute a successful exit and transition. So, I continued to plan and pray, and pray and plan, and pivot often! The true transformation commenced once I recognized that despite my significant contributions to male-dominated industries throughout the better half of my career, a deep-seated urge to empower women emerged within me. Specifically, I felt compelled to support women akin to my younger self from two decades prior. I literally woke up one morning with profound clarity, opened my eyes, thanked God for another twenty-four hours, and then said to myself, "I have to help women."

At that moment, an unyielding conviction surged within me, and ever since that bright morning, the universe has orchestrated a series of events, aligning people, opportunities, and circumstances in my direct route to fulfilling this very purpose. By the way, I am a staunch advocate of the law of attraction and the influence of positivity in our universe. I strongly believe that people shape their realities based on their beliefs. However, to be perfectly clear, I also strongly believe that people must take action to turn their dreams into reality and accomplish the manifestation of their aspirations. So, as it became abundantly clear that God's purpose for me was to help women, I started to phase out anything in my world that was incongruent with that narrative. Sequentially, the universe aided me along the way, affirming my path forward.

One platform materialized almost instantaneously in the form of a community of like-minded, entrepreneurial women. In my determined commitment to empowering women, I quickly and proudly began to serve as a founding member of the leadership team at WIN, The Women's Impact Network. Throughout this book, you will have the privilege, as I have had, of encountering the voices of numerous, remarkable ladies from WIN including the brilliant, visionary founder herself, Janet Clark. It's truly an honor to intersect with such extraordinary women, all united by our shared mission and core values. Collaborating with these inspiring souls in our collective pursuit of women's empowerment is nothing short of invigorating and a true testament to the power of unity and purpose.

Another pivotal moment for me was when I joined forces with She Rises Studios, a movement dedicated to women's empowerment. As I linked arms with the exceptional leaders in this company, I was overcome by a profound sense of gratitude. It was remarkable to discover yet another platform where women were uniting, collaborating, and passionately pursuing a mission that resonated deeply with my own. I had the privilege of attending the first annual "Empower Her Content Day" in Las Vegas where I was overwhelmed by astonishing keynote speakers, each one a powerful, passionate woman speaking eloquently about their meaningful missions. I had the pleasure of meeting one of my role models, Hanna Olivas, whom I had been following for some time. While it was likely just a quick hello, hug, and photo for her (given her incredibly busy schedule as the driving energy behind the logistics of the day), it was a dream come true for me and an impactful moment I will never forget. Hanna is a beacon of inspiration and a force to be reckoned with. Now, as I write these very sentences, I realize that my words will be published alongside hers in this book. This is a testament to my belief in the power of faith and shaping my reality. Vegas wasn't initially in my plans, but I made it happen because I knew that being in the presence of all the exquisiteness that Content Day had to offer could potentially open doors for me, continuing to form my future in alignment with my mission to help women, and I was absolutely correct.

The next serendipitous occurrence I brought to life was the launch of my "She Swaps" podcast where women are given a platform to amplify their voices and share their stories. I call this my happy accident because I never intended to start a podcast. One day, during a Zoom call with a fellow member of WIN, we had a brilliant idea: record our stories and swap them within our networks. Acting on our inspiration, we did just that. Soon after, I was inundated with an overwhelming response from women who resonated with the concept and expressed their eagerness to participate. It was at that vital moment that "She Swaps" was born. Now, I am privileged to engage in conversations with women from diverse backgrounds worldwide, all of whom resonate deeply with my mission of empowering women. Ladies often inquire about the qualifications needed to join me as a guest on my podcast. My response remains simple yet consistent: the only qualifying factor is to be a woman with a story to share. I want to hear your stories, and the world needs to hear your voices. Whether it's about a challenge you've conquered, a business endeavor you've pursued, or even a lighthearted anecdote, I am honored to be in the company of women who are eager to share their God-given voices with the world through my platform.

During this spiritual journey, another simultaneous blessing unfolded in my life. For years, I had struggled with my relationship with food and alcohol, subjecting my body to detrimental abuse causing physical, emotional, and spiritual turbulence. In an effort to live a vibrant, long-lasting, and healthy life, and lead by example for our children, my husband and I embarked on a transformative weight loss journey together. We shed a collective total of over 300 pounds from the birth of our twins in 2020 to the time that I write these words, four years later. We encountered numerous trials and triumphs, a narrative worthy of its own book which will soon follow and grace the shelves. As I witnessed the life-altering changes I was experiencing unfolding before my eyes and embraced my five core values of faith, family, health, wealth, and freedom, it dawned on me with astonishing clarity that I could no longer fulfill my purpose while maintaining my unhealthy relationship with alcohol.

Thus, I resolved to become and remain completely alcohol-free, committing wholeheartedly to this pivotal decision. I thought it would be an insurmountable challenge that I would struggle with from day to day, but what I hadn't realized was I had already begun the work years before, laying the foundation for freedom; I just had to commit to my decision. Once more, doubts danced through my mind like restless spirits. *Would life lack joy without alcohol? Would others perceive me differently? How would I unwind and find solace?* These questions swirled relentlessly, testing my resolve and challenging my newfound path of sobriety. Nonetheless, my cherished mantra once again took root, and I allowed faith to guide me through any and all fear. Upon making the decision to liberate my body and mind from the grip of alcoholic toxins, my spirit soared, unfettered, and unencumbered. In this newfound freedom, I found myself living my most vibrant and blessed existence.

All the doubts and uncertainties that once plagued me now seemed inconsequential, and life unfolded before me in a tapestry of joy and fulfillment unlike any I had known before. Indeed, there are myriad facets to this traumatic turned blissful journey that I yearn to delve into further. However, as you may anticipate, these tales are destined for the pages of a forthcoming book. So, I extend to you an invitation to stay tuned for the unfolding chapters yet to come!

My struggles with food and alcohol merely scratch the surface of the formidable obstacles I have overcome in my thirty-nine years on this magnificent planet. Though trauma and adversity have woven their threads into the fabric of my life's journey, I will recognize that this is not a forum for a pity party, so I will leave it at that and save some of my exhilarating stories for solo books better suited for "The Anisa Show." What I would like to emphasize is that I have never let any challenge stand in my way of championship. Every setback I ever had, however daunting, has been surpassed by a comeback of monumental proportions, each an innovative authentication of my resilience and determination.

As I mentioned previously, I had been planting seeds of recovery in my brain and body for years before I saw results. Transformative changes had been a goal I pursued, but it wasn't until I made shifts in my spirituality and mindset that I began to see the real results. Prioritizing my spirituality allowed me to tap into a deeper sense of purpose and inner strength. It provided me with the motivation and resilience needed to journey toward physical change.

Additionally, shifting my mindset was crucial. Adopting a positive mindset helped me embrace challenges as opportunities for growth. I reframed setbacks as learning experiences and cultivated a strong belief in my ability to achieve my goals. This shift in mindset empowered me to overcome obstacles and persevere through the ups and downs of my revolutionary journey. In essence, my experience highlights the interconnectedness of the mind, body, and spirit. By nurturing my spirituality and cultivating a positive mindset, I created a solid foundation for achieving real and sustainable results in my physical transformation efforts. This holistic approach fostered greater overall well-being and set the stage for continued growth and self-discovery through healing in all aspects of my life.

My journey into entrepreneurship began long before my physical transformation, with tentative steps in 2016 when my then-fiancé, now husband, Jason and I ventured into real estate investment. While we experienced success, it was accompanied by costly mistakes, highlighting the steep learning curve of free enterprise. However, it wasn't until 2020, amidst the global pandemic and the birth of our twins, that I fully immersed myself in entrepreneurship, or what I would eventually come to understand as "hybridpreneurship." The onset of the pandemic brought unforeseen challenges. Expecting assistance, I found myself alone with two newborns as safety concerns prevented family and friends from visiting. Residing in New Jersey with Jason working as an essential worker, I faced the daunting task of managing both my newborns and entrepreneurial ambitions single-handedly. This period demanded rapid adaptation and resilience as I navigated the intricate balance between nurturing my babies and pursuing entrepreneurial endeavors.

Financially, the pandemic brought significant changes. Despite prior financial stability, we faced uncertainty with multiple income sources halted, and the responsibility of providing for our growing family became increasingly challenging. Determined to secure our future, I decided to explore self-education, learning essential online skills to generate income independently. Teaching myself how to start and run a business became a rigorous process. It involved mastering various tasks, both front and back-end, and understanding the complexities of running a business.

Through this experience, I realized the misconception many have about the entrepreneurial journey; it's not just about starting a business but also about continuous learning, growth, and perseverance. Reflecting on my journey, I recognized the importance of mentorship and coaching. While my self-taught approach shaped me into the person I am today, I now advocate for seeking guidance to streamline the process, avoid pitfalls, and accelerate success. It's this insight that fuels my passion for supporting women in their entrepreneurial endeavors now. I acquired diverse skills and knowledge from building brands to navigating the intricacies of digital marketing. Alongside raising twins and a demanding full-time job, I ventured into real estate even further, understanding its potential for creating long-lasting, generational wealth, and ultimately, a legacy I could leave for my children.

In 2022, amidst the explosive housing market conditions, my husband and I made the bold decision to move to Florida despite the uncertainties. Again, my mantra of "faith over fear" had taken the wheel. We had always discussed the idea of moving to Florida, envisioning it as something we would do in our golden years. However, I've always believed in seizing opportunities rather than waiting for them to come to me. So, when the opportunity presented itself, I didn't hesitate to take massive action. Instead of waiting for the perfect moment in the distant future, I recognized the chance before me and made the decision to materialize it. Within a few months, we made it happen. We sold our house, packed up our family, and embarked on a journey of over 1000 miles to our new home and life in sunny Florida. Miami has a special place in our hearts with countless memories, but with twin toddlers, we chose to be close to Orlando. We settled near the most magical place on Earth, and indeed, it was a dream come true. Shortly after our move to the Sunshine State, life took an unexpected turn. I received a diagnosis of melanoma, and the doctors advised me to stay out of the sunshine, which felt ironic given our new location. This news shook me to the core. Suddenly, my mortality became undeniably real, and it was a pivotal turning point in my life.

Over the next several months, my commitment to personal growth and development became an obsession. I immersed myself in an expansive array of transformative experiences from informative masterminds and enriching workshops to intensive courses, enlightening coaching programs, and powerful summits. Each opportunity was a stepping stone in my quest for self-discovery and evolution. In my relentless pursuit of purpose, I threw myself into my work within both my corporate role and in my real estate ventures. However, amidst this fervent activity, I failed to realize a crucial truth: chasing my purpose was akin to grasping at straws. I was already engaging in manifestation work, but my approach was misguided. Instead of allowing things to flow naturally, I found myself trying to force outcomes, neglecting the fundamental work needed within myself, particularly in terms of nurturing my mindset and spirituality. It became evident that true transformation required a holistic approach, one that encompassed not only external pursuits but also internal exploration and alignment. As I embarked on this inward journey, I began to understand that my "why" couldn't be found externally; it resided within me all along, awaiting recognition and cultivation.

For a considerable time, I held the belief that my reality could be shaped by my beliefs - a concept often touted but far more challenging to implement. Undoing the years of conditioning inflicted by ingrained poor habits proved to be an arduous task. Among the many hurdles, one of the most intimidating was transitioning from a mindset of scarcity to one of great, abundant possibilities. My upbringing was steeped in financial struggle where every dollar was carefully hoarded, and uncertainty shadowed our financial future. We lived in a perpetual state of scraping by, constantly reminded of the necessity to cling tightly to our resources lest we find ourselves without means.

This mindset of scarcity became deeply entrenched, permeating every aspect of my life and shaping my perception of the world. Breaking free from this scarcity mindset required a profound shift that challenged the core of my beliefs and perceptions. It demanded a radical reevaluation of my relationship with abundance and a willingness to challenge the narratives instilled in me from a young age. I discovered that abundance was not merely a concept to be grasped intellectually but a state of being to be nurtured from within. It required a fundamental rewiring of my thoughts, beliefs, and behaviors - a process that demanded patience, perseverance, and firm self-reflection. I would also have to repeat my dearly beloved mantra over and over through this process, faith over fear. When I was finally able to come to terms that this universe was incredibly abundant, and God always had and always would provide, that is when the magic really happened.

This series of events eventually led to my spiritual awakening to help women, stop trading my time for money, and start enjoying every moment of my life, especially with my loved ones. Thus, My Mompreneur Studio was born. This is my studio - a sanctuary where I pursue what truly brings me joy. It's a space where creativity flourishes, and I craft products with meaningful messages while empowering women along the way. Through my mentorship program, Becoming HER: Unveiling Your True Self Aligned with Your Divine Purpose, I create self-confident women by guiding them to uncover their true desires, set goals, and attain peace and fulfillment, ultimately helping them define and fund their missions. Additionally, initiatives like the Women's Impact Network (WIN) allow me to aim to create amplification of women's voices and foster collaboration. Similarly, my podcast serves as a safe platform I have created for women to share their stories with the world. I wear a lot of hats, but aside from my two most important roles which are being a child of God and a mother of twins, everything I do, all multifaceted aspects of my company and career, are tied to the same mission of helping women.

I didn't have much guidance or support growing up, aside from my mom, a single parent, who did her best to raise my brother and me on her own. Despite the challenges life threw her way, she taught me invaluable lessons that shaped who I am today. Her strength and resilience are the pillars of my own independence. Experiencing an unplanned divorce when I was just a baby and my brother a young boy, my mom was unprepared for the curveballs life hit her with. Yet, she persevered, showing me that it's okay to have a partner in life as long as they treat you with respect, and this encouraged me to find a great love. However, she emphasized the importance of being self-sufficient and prepared to support oneself and any children, if need be.

Those lessons have stayed with me, guiding my decisions and actions as I navigated life and all of its challenges. Growing up without many inspiring female role models made navigating adulthood particularly challenging, especially when I was searching to discover my true identity. Without guidance, I found myself entangled in relationships and situations that weren't conducive to my growth, and in fact, did nothing but hinder it. Trouble seemed to follow me everywhere, and I couldn't understand why. It wasn't until later that I was introduced to the concept of the law of attraction. I had no idea that I had been unknowingly creating my own drama through my thoughts and actions. This is one of the main reasons I need to inspire other females, particularly those who haven't yet discovered their purpose.

Through my coaching program, I guide women on a profound journey to uncover their true desires and find genuine happiness. Many women find themselves trapped in the monotonous cycle of daily routine, unable to discern what truly brings them joy amid life's chaos. I help them break free from this cycle and discover the beauty of the world around them. Once they are able to understand their purpose, they can define their mission, and together, we explore personalized strategies to fund their mission, empowering them to achieve genuine happiness and fulfillment. Through my journey of transformation, I've gained a profound understanding of the impact of self-discovery through healing. Experiencing the liberation that comes with embracing one's true self has been nothing short of miraculous and life-changing. Witnessing other women undergo this metamorphosis, shedding layers of societal expectations to reveal their authentic selves, fills me with an indescribable sense of gratification. It reaffirms my unwavering passion for guiding others on their path to fulfillment and inner peace.

Reflecting on my personal evolution, I recognize the pivotal role that guidance and support play in the process. Had I had someone to lean on during my journey, someone to offer insights, perspective, and encouragement, the road to self-discovery would have been far less daunting. This realization fuels my commitment to not only assisting others in their personal development but also their entrepreneurial pursuits. Indeed, personal and professional growth are deeply intertwined. Every aspect of our lives is interconnected and sewn together, each thread contributing to the material of our existence. When one aspect is out of alignment, it can throw the entire tapestry into disarray. Recognizing this interconnectedness, I strive to offer comprehensive guidance that addresses both personal and business challenges. By fostering harmony and balance across all aspects of life, I empower women to unlock their full potential and lead fulfilling, purpose-driven lives.

My personal and professional journey, from trauma to triumph, fuels my passion for supporting others, especially women, in realizing their total potential. I firmly believe that every woman deserves the opportunity to break free from limitations, gender biases, and societal norms. Yet, it's crucial to acknowledge that our own limiting beliefs can also serve as obstacles to reaching our highest potential. We have the opportunity to reverse engineer the lives we desire to live by believing we can accomplish every goal we set out to achieve.

A wise person once said, "Whether you think you can, or think you cannot, you are correct." With dedication, resilience, and support, my mission is abundantly clear. I'm committed to empowering 1000 moms to become mompreneurs by 2030, shaping a future where women embrace their authenticity, live based on their own core values, terms, and moral compasses, and thrive in business and beyond. If you resonate with my story, I invite you to help me help you. I am here to guide you every step of the way. Let's create opportunities, fulfill dreams, and make a lasting impact together. I am devoted to making this world a happier place, one empowered woman at a time!

Anna Condinho

CEO of High Ticket Sales

https://www.linkedin.com/in/anna-condinho-6a51902a0/
https://www.facebook.com/anna.behling.14
https://www.instagram.com/annacondinho/

Anna Condinho, Owner and CEO of two successful businesses, is passionate about helping women find their inner strength, fulfill their dreams and boldly know their worth. Anna coaches women in finding financial and time freedom while showing that living the rat race and daily 9-5 grind is not our calling. Anna is a first time published author and will use this platform to glorify God above all else. Aside from all these accomplishments, Anna's primary role is not only being a child of God but also a homeschool, single mom of two. Anna is determined to teach others to find balance, pursue dreams, and break generational curses in order to live the life they were meant to live. We were all given one life, let's use it wisely. "Those dreams were planted in your heart for a reason girl, go and chase those things that set your soul on fire."

BECOMING A FEARLESS MOMPRENEUR

By Anna Condinho

I was blessed enough to be able to grow up in a loving, Godly home. My parents were always very supportive and gave excellent guidance throughout my life, and I truly believe that is one of the main reasons I am where I am today! My goal with this chapter is to encourage and bring out the realness of what it's like being a single mompreneur and how to shift your thought processes from "How could I possibly do this?" to "I am strong, I can do this, and I want to help others get there too!" It doesn't matter what your upbringing was, where you came from, or what your current circumstances are; you can become a fierce leader and break the cycle of feeling stuck and unworthy. When you think you can't, know you can.

I can clearly remember watching my mom, who was a part of a few, low-ticket businesses, during my younger years. She loved what she did, and I would go to many events with her. The biggest thing that stuck out to me was her passion for helping other people, her love and knowledge for the products, and the network of people she created along the way. My dad was a hard worker, and yet he made time for his family, so I guess you could say being an entrepreneur with a strong work ethic has always been a part of who I am. This is my story of how I started in search of financial freedom. It's not for the faint of heart, but I can guarantee you it's worth the investment. It's worth your time and effort to create something beautiful. You'll learn and grow so much personally, and for that alone, it's worth it.

I started my journey in the low-ticket business when I was in my 20s. I mostly started because I wanted a discount on the products I was already using and loved in hopes I could simply pay for my product addiction. That mindset of wanting to make money changed through the years but the most drastic shift happened when I had my first child. I quickly realized that I wanted to be home and raise my kids instead of putting them in a daycare with someone else raising them while I worked to pay for someone else to raise my child. I believe there's a time and place for that, but it wasn't for me, and I simply refused to let it be an option. I tried several different businesses and hardly made anything in each one. It wasn't a lack of work on my end but the structure and comp plans were just not making it possible. I became very frustrated but still believed in my soul that this could happen for me, believed something existed that could fulfill my dreams of being financially stable and bringing in passive income.

When I say I've tried a lot of low-ticket businesses, I mean it! Makeup, dishes, bags, health and wellness products, you name it, and I tried selling it! Now, don't get me wrong, there is usually a need for all those things, but to make money? It just wasn't working. I know the letters MLM freak people out and they immediately say "Pyramid Scheme!!!" For all the naysayers out there, I would like to point out that a 9-5 is the real pyramid scheme here. Think about it. You work all day, you are away from your family, you carry stress and who knows what else depending on the job, you barely get a raise, and sometimes it takes years for that to happen. Meanwhile, the owners, CEOs, and higher-up management seem to be sitting around, working less but making more…does that sound right to you? Seriously! If that doesn't make you want to become your own boss, then I don't know what will. Working for someone else lets them have the time and financial freedom that you so longingly desire. Why not do that for yourself? If you have to call off work, you don't make money, plain and simple. You build a legacy and passive income, you can take a month off and not even bat an eye. We are conditioned to think that a 9-5 is the way of life, that it's the American thing to do, that it's the only way to provide for your family, and if you think differently, you must have lost your mind. There are people out there who don't understand this way of thinking, and yes, you will run into them, but keep your head held high! You will learn that tunnel vision is a good thing.

With each company I joined, I gained a little more knowledge that I have been able to carry throughout the years, so saying I failed isn't accurate because I have gained different skills and mindsets from each experience. They have allowed me to grow and get to where I need to be. A phrase that I have carried with me since college is "What do you need to do to get to where you want to be?" What's the next step? I personally believe that you can only answer that with a clear vision of where you see yourself and your goals and literally clinging to that on your journey. Without it, you will derail and not know how to get back on track. If you waiver in your vision, you will easily lose it and start chasing things that don't serve a purpose.

So what is my vision? To stay at home with my kids, provide for them while being WITH them, love what I do, and teach them that it's possible to love your job, have time and financial freedom, teach others to do the same, and unlock passive income to get away from the survival paycheck to paycheck rat race. I feel like in our culture, when you say you want to travel with your kids, go on a lot of vacations, or own a nice car/home, there are people out there who make you feel like it's an intangible dream. That you're being selfish, or that you're being scammed into thinking that could be your reality. Once I realized there was this group of people if you will, that thought I was wasting my time and money, it became my mission to mentally block them out and prove them wrong. I knew in my heart that this was my dream, this was my vision, and I wasn't going to let anything or anyone get in my way. If you are a visual person like myself, make your vision come to life. Get yourself a vision written out with clear, specific goals, and then live it out loud.

Fast forward a few years, now a single mom of two, that dream and vision was no longer something I was eagerly working toward but something that I had no choice but to achieve. Hoping to make money was no longer an option; it was the only option. I homeschool and have my kids full-time, so I knew that putting them in school so I could work was not something I was going to accept. My vision became extremely clear and hyper-focused. During the time of my divorce, I was working part-time from home as an office manager for a local music studio. Little did I know that would launch me into becoming a serious business owner and entrepreneur. Sometimes making that mental switch from employee to entrepreneur is hard. You no longer clock in and do what you are told. Now, it's all on you to grow your business, be wise with your money, and make the wisest decisions you can. I don't say that to scare you but to empower you that you can do it even with zero experience.

Let's chat about balance. As a mom, we wear many hats. Add on being a business owner and the hat collection grows! We sometimes have no choice but to be what feels like a circus balancing act on a daily basis. Even as I write this, I look around and realize that I have dishes to wash, laundry to do, and carpets to vacuum. I've had to get up and yell at the dog and help my kids for what feels like a zillion times already. Do we get it all right all the time? No! Will there be tears? Sometimes! Kudos to you if you have it all together, but for the rest of us and probably you who are reading this, we thrive in certain areas, lack in a few others, and it just rotates. It's a balancing act, and over time, you will learn how to balance most things at a time but don't worry if you don't. We are human, and there's only a certain amount of hours in a day to get things done. Stay focused, get yourself organized, and stay on task.

This past weekend both of my kids got very sick, and I literally had to drop everything to care for them. That's part of why I do what I do - the perks of owning your own business and calling the shots. You work hard to grow your passive income so on the days you have to tap out, you aren't worried about finances. We have enough to worry about, like *when can I get to the grocery store? Did I shut the garage door when I left? Did my child eat enough vegetables? Are they making friends? Have I failed as a mother? Did I even cook a healthy meal this week?* You know, the usual, daily anxiety of being a mom. Finances, however, should not be one of those worries, and in my opinion, that is something within your control. If you know you are lacking in a certain area, my advice to you is to take note of it. Realizing there is a need to change something is the biggest issue. Once that can be identified, take some time, even if it's just a few minutes a day, to figure out how to tackle the issue. For me right now, I need to focus on my health again. I can't put my nutrition on hold just to get by. That means not being lazy with meal planning, and when it comes down to it, just organizing myself is the real issue. Once you get that balanced out, all other entities in your life will start to flow better. When you are thriving in all areas of your life, it's a beautiful thing. If you find your business isn't doing well, that's a good indicator that something else in your life isn't quite right, and it's time to evaluate things.

I became the owner of the music studio I had managed for so long, and I won't lie, it was scary in the beginning! This was a real, physical business that now had my name on it. I paid the bills. I had employees counting on me to keep their jobs. All the fears flooded in, but the thing is, when you know beyond a shadow of a doubt that you are walking in God's Will, you can't fail. I have been successful in running the music studio, and it has taught me so much but in the back of my mind I know that the economy is wonky, and in a heartbeat that could all change. *What if I had to shut down? What if I couldn't afford the rent on my building? What if I lost students and revenue? What if my marketing skills are not up to par?* I'm not one to live in the "what ifs," but when owning a business, it's a legitimate fear, and being a single mom only enhances that. I could lose everything, and then what? That was my only source of income, and it did not sit well with me. I can honestly say that this path is what led me to my high-ticket sales business. Talk about changing lives. This is where it's at! If you want to learn how to earn passive income, listen up!

Going from low-ticket to high-ticket is drastic in a good way. I have a 20k monthly blueprint to prove it! If you put in the work, if you are dedicated, inspired, coachable, and willing to invest in yourself, then I encourage you to not ignore what is laid out before you. What would it mean to you and your family to make up to $7,000 per sale? Now imagine making four or five sales a month. That's just the tip of the iceberg. There's no starting over each month, you only progress from day one, and most people can come into this business with zero down and no interest, not to mention it's a tax right off! You gain organic leads, which means you don't have to cold message ANYONE! It's amazing, and this system works! If you have an entrepreneurial mind then this will make sense to you. It will be a no-brainer but some of you may think this is too good to be true.

To you, I say that is fear and disbelief in your mind, making an excuse not to do it. Push that all to the side and really focus on what your dreams are. Why would this mean so much to you? What could it do for you or your family? We are living in weird times, and I personally don't trust a 9-5. I've seen so many hardworking individuals get let go for no reason at all, and I'm not a fan of all the politics, nor do I have the energy to deal with them. It's just not a trustworthy system, and since I found a better (in my opinion) alternative, you better believe I'm shouting it from the rooftops!

If you could step outside yourself for just a moment, what would you see? Do you struggle with the daily routine? Do you struggle with all the commitments you have in a day? Do you wish you could spend more time with your kids? Are you a single mom who has no choice but to work to stay afloat? Are you setting your dreams aside just to survive?

What if you didn't have to? What if you could be present with your kids? Take those trips? Not having to deal with the 9-5 grind while trying to find childcare and pay for it! Could you just imagine that all of that is unnecessary? It truly is! We live in an age where you can make that choice. Gone are the days of having only one option to make money. Take the step, take the leap, and believe in yourself - that this is possible and that you can do it. The training is all there for you. All you need is a coachable attitude, wifi, and Facebook. Investing in your own business is the best decision you can make for yourself. Put in the work now to enjoy the life you want and desire.

Do you know the direction you want to head in with your business? Even in your life? Then what do you need to do to get there? It doesn't have to be every step planned out perfectly but you should be taking the next step. Just one, just a movement forward however slow or fast that step is. Take it. What's holding you back? We live in a world where fear and doubt are so present that it literally cripples us from doing anything. I'm the type of person who, if my to-do list is long, gets overwhelmed, and it stops me from doing anything! Fear is a liar, and if you choose to believe it, then how do you expect to receive the many blessings God has in store for you? How do you think your life will flourish? How do you think your business will grow?

I could use all the excuses to not move forward…my kids are so young and need me, I work full time and have no energy to put into my own business. I don't like putting myself out there, no one will buy from me, and my family will think I'm crazy. I'm a single mom and can't do this alone. Let's take those excuses and throw them out. They are not welcome to take up space in our minds. For my visual friends out there, take a moment and do this exercise. Hold your left out in front of you. Now, take your right hand and pretend to place each and every fear you have into your left hand. Name them one by one. Speak it out loud, and then, when you are all done, take your left hand, ball up all those fears and excuses, and let them go. Throw them as far as you can.

If you made it this far into the chapter I applaud you. It means you have a drive inside of you that isn't going to stop, that you will keep going and move forward no matter what. High-ticket is like nothing I've ever been a part of, and the reason is we aren't "selling" a product. We are simply offering time and financial freedom. Being your own CEO, calling the shots, choosing

when and how you spend the hours in your day, and not letting anyone else dictate that. The training is there, the leads come to you, and all you have to do is have an open mind to the possibility that this can happen to you. To know that you could make more than $7,000 on one sale, would you be ok with that? You wouldn't have anyone to answer to! Want to take that vacation paid in full? Go ahead, no need to request time off! Need new clothes or shoes for your kids? No problem! Need to put gas in your car or buy those groceries? Done! Want to buy that home? Now you can!

No starting over each month; continue to move forward at whatever pace you want because there's no going back to zero. You heard me correctly, you don't start over each month. You don't ever de-rank, so whether you make one sale a month or ten, you only ever keep moving forward and don't have to panic that a new month is about to start. You have it in you, now you just have to take that step. Remember, even when you think you can't, you can. The ones who win have all the reasons they can't, and do it anyway!

I mentioned earlier that you can become not only fully present in your family's lives but you can become a successful entrepreneur with zero experience while doing it. I give you the tools, you put in the work and dedication. That's the formula, and it's doable. Thousands of men and women wouldn't be doing it if it wasn't possible. The one thing that will get in your way is yourself, without fail, every time. The only requirement is that you have an inner desire to keep going, to believe you have what it takes no matter what obstacles come your way. Sometimes you'll have a bad day. I remember many days when I would have a migraine, the dishes were piling up, I had to feed the kids meals, laundry was on overload, and the dog was being exceptionally wild, and then I thought about how I didn't put one minute into my business that day. Or I would have a week where the kids had appointments and activities. I had to do school with my son, I had to help out at my daughter's preschool, the car needed work done, I had my church group, housework, grocery shopping, and the list went on. I thought about how I didn't put any time into my business that week. I could have easily beat myself up or given up, saying, "I had no time or energy to put into this." I stopped and reminded myself why I started.

See, the thing is, if you give up, you automatically fail, so do yourself a favor and find the grit deep inside and don't give up. You may have a bad day or even a bad week but that doesn't mean you can't do it. Reprioritize if you need to, reach out to a mentor if you need to, and make a daily to-do list. Get a cup of coffee if you need to, find what works for you, find what or who can pull you out of the funk, and keep going. Will it all happen on your own timeline? Probably not! It will happen in God's timing! He knows how badly you need that paycheck to come in, He knows that you need just one more sale that month to make ends meet, but He also knows your heart. He knows your goals, dreams, and desires, and that is not lost on Him.

The amazing thing is that when you join this high-ticket business you gain a whole tribe behind you so you are never doing this alone. I don't know about you but that gives me a sigh of relief. We are all in each other's corner, cheering and mentoring. I'm not talking about a Facebook group that welcomes you in and then forgets about you; I'm talking about a true tribe that wants to see you succeed, wants to help you reach your goals, and tells you the honest truth about how to change your mindset. You don't have to reinvent the wheel here, it's all mapped out for you! Can you take constructive criticism? That's a piece of what you get here, not to shame you or make you feel bad, but because we truly want you to learn the skill set to close the deals so that you are just one step closer to your goals.

It's like any other job - you have to learn, practice, and do things over and over again until it becomes natural. Think about riding a bike, it seems easy and effortless to you now but remember when you were learning? How did it feel when you thought you would never be able to take off? But you practiced, fell a few times, maybe scraped your knee or elbow, but you listened to what to do from those around you. One day you did it! It's the same concept. We are all our own worst enemies and get in the way of our own progress - don't let your ego take over. Listen to the mentors and coaches around you! I promise you, one day you will look back and remember where you came from and how you dug out of what felt like the bottomless pit. That's what life is about, my friend. You will go on a journey so that you can help others go through theirs, and that is such a sweet and rewarding thing.

Don't dream small. It's cute to think about the small things and the "oh maybe someday" fill-in-the-blank. I want to know what your dreams are! The ones that were created in the depths of your soul. If money and failure weren't an option, if time wasn't a factor, and if all the answers could be answered. What do you want in this life? For me, a few big dreams would be to open a coffee shop and sell cupcakes. I would also love to be able to open a facility to house women and kids who need to flee their homes from dangerous situations with nowhere to go and no possessions. I want to travel and experience new things with my kids. Can I do this all on my own right now? No! But I do believe those things were placed in my heart, and when you know things are from God, He will help make a way.

So I ask again, what are your dreams? Write them down, and use those as your driving force. When you feel the weight of the world, when you feel like giving up, when you feel too tired and don't really want to do anything, look at your list of dreams, remind yourself of your vision, find your inner motivation, and keep going. I will be your biggest cheerleader; I will go to war for you and would love to take you on this high-ticket journey with me. Be fearless, be bold. No one ever got anywhere by staying in their comfort zone. If I'm willing to fight for you, aren't you?

A special note. If you are reading this and you are specifically a single mom, I would like to give you these words of encouragement. If you are in the trenches at the start of your single motherhood journey, or if you have been one for many years, I see you but most importantly God sees you. He knew about this journey for you long before you did. You are not alone; you will get through this seemingly endless season. There are obstacles but I know beyond a shadow of a doubt that you are strong enough and wise enough to find your way. Hopefully, you have a tribe behind you to make this journey a little less stressful, but if you don't, know you are truly not alone. I'm available on social media if you need to reach out and need a listening ear.

It's hard talking to others about it when they haven't been through it, so I know the longing for someone to simply understand. It's ok that you don't have all the answers yet, it's ok if you feel like everything is falling apart. Take a deep breath, figure out what your first step is, prioritize, and move forward. As each day goes by, you will feel empowered, and know that you are doing your absolute best for your children. They will see you fighting for them and making life safe for them as best you can. In the end, all we can do is our best, and the rest we give to God. It is always hard for me to fathom the fact that God loves my kids more than I do. I mean, who could possibly love them and take care of them better than me, right? I promise you, He does, and sometimes, when you lay your head on the pillow at night, that has to be enough.

Cheryl T Campbell

Founder of 4 Winds of Change

www.linkedin.com/in/cheryltcampbell
https://www.facebook.com/cheryltcampbell
https://www.instagram.com/unlocking.cheryl
https://cheryltcampbell.com
https://empowerhertowin.com

Cheryl T Campbell is a guiding light for women seeking success and spiritual fulfillment. Beginning her entrepreneurial journey in 1983 as an international conference planner in hazardous materials and spill control, Cheryl has continuously reinvented herself, showcasing her diverse talents and creative spirit. As the founder of 4 Winds of Change, Cheryl has empowered women entrepreneurs since 2009, combining business acumen with spiritual insights. Her achievements as a best-selling author in 2011 and as publisher of Tribal Women Magazine (2011- 2014) further cement her status as a leading voice for women's empowerment. Cheryl inspires and guides women toward realizing their fullest potential through her signature program, EmpowerHer to WIN: Pathway to Business and Life Mastery, and as a mindset and spirituality expert for the Women's Impact Network. Her journey is not just a story of success; it's a testament to the power of resilience, creativity, and mentoring.

SOULFUL STRENGTH: THE PATH TO PERSONAL AND PROFESSIONAL EMPOWERMENT

By Cheryl T Campbell

"In the journey of self-discovery, every book we read is a step, every thought we ponder is a leap, and every limit we overcome is a triumph of the soul."
—Cheryl T Campbell

Imagine standing before a crowd of 600, the only woman in sight, heart pounding, each word a challenge fought and won. This isn't just a story about conquering fear; it's a journey that began in the harsh glare of ridicule and blossomed into a profound exploration of the soul. I am Cheryl T Campbell, and my path has been paved with trials and triumphs, a testament to the unyielding power of the human spirit.

"Soulful Strength: The Path to Personal and Professional Empowerment" isn't merely a title; it's the narrative of my life. A life that transformed from the depths of a challenging speech disorder and the piercing wounds of being labeled 'stupid' and 'dumb' by my second-grade teacher to a presence of quiet strength and perseverance in the realms of business and spirituality.

As a young girl, I was the target of relentless mockery not just from other children but from those entrusted to nurture my young mind. Yet, this very challenge sparked a flame within me—a flame that refused to be extinguished. Despite facing daunting odds, I set out to conquer my fear of speaking. With words weighed down by dysarthria, each syllable a struggle for clarity, my journey led me to a defining moment: addressing an audience at the International Liquid Terminal Association in the early 1980s. In a field dominated by men where I was one of just two women at the conference, this wasn't just intimidating; it was a bold defiance of established norms, marking a significant turning point in my life.

The tapestry of my life's journey began to weave its most colorful threads when I was just 11 years old. This chapter opened in the most unexpected place: aboard the flights and in the bleachers of the Providence College basketball team's games. The reason for this unique twist? The team welcomed the son of my dad's partner into their ranks, and with that, our lives became intertwined with the rhythm of basketball seasons.

There was a certain magic in following the team across the country, a sense of adventure in each tournament and game we attended. But amidst the cheers and excitement, a quieter, more profound transformation was happening within me. On those long flights, the players with their heads buried in books amidst the chaos of travel, unknowingly became the architects of my intellectual awakening. With the lightest of gestures, they would slide a book across the aisle into my eager hands, turning the hum of the airplane engine into the backdrop of my education.

In this way, the worn pages of Jean-Paul Sartre's philosophical teachings first landed on my lap. His existential musings on freedom, individuality, and the essence of being unfurled before me, opening doors to worlds and ideas that transcended the confines of that airplane. These moments, shared with athletes who balanced the rigors of sport and study, planted seeds of curiosity and a love for learning that would shape my path forever. This journey, born from the fusion of basketball and philosophy, was more than just a series of trips. It was the beginning of a lifelong adventure in understanding the limitless potential of the human spirit.

As I navigated the labyrinth of my teenage years, my thirst for wisdom and understanding only deepened. My companions on this journey were no longer just the basketball players but also the mystical writings of Carlos Castaneda. His words, echoing with themes of transcendence, nature's deep whispers, and a cosmic connection didn't just reside within the confines of ink and paper. They danced into my soul, sparking enlightenment and a spiritual awakening, guiding me toward a realm where the physical and metaphysical were embraced. These philosophies wove into the very fabric of my being, guiding me toward a path of empowerment and spiritual awakening.

My path went beyond a series of trips. It was the beginning of a lifelong adventure in understanding the limitless potential of the human spirit.

In "Soulful Strength," I invite you to walk with me. It's a journey that melds the tangible and intangible—intertwining knowledge, belief, and inner knowing with personal empowerment and spirituality. Through my story, I hope to ignite your own quest for self-discovery and remind you that the strength of the soul is the most potent force for transformation and empowerment. Let's embark on this path together, where each step is a leap towards our true potential.

EMBRACING THE SOUL'S JOURNEY IN THE BUSINESS WORLD

Carrying these lessons of resilience and empowerment, my path led me to a defining moment in the early 1980s that would test the very essence of these teachings – my presentation at the International Liquid Terminal Association conference.

As I stood before a sea of 600 faces in the vast conference hall of the ILTA, my journey of overcoming echoed within me. I was the solitary woman addressing an all-male audience, a daunting and exhilarating scenario. The weight of my past – a young girl grappling with a speech disorder, often derided as 'stupid' and 'dumb' – felt both heavy and distant as I took my place at the podium.

My hands, hidden from view, trembled uncontrollably, betraying the turmoil that churned beneath my composed exterior. Each heartbeat echoed the many moments of self-doubt and triumph that had paved my path here. My voice, initially hesitant, echoed through the room, carrying with it not just words but fragments of a hard-fought journey.

The audience listened, their expressions a mix of curiosity and skepticism. As I delved into the intricacies of spill control and hazardous waste management, I sensed the room's dynamic subtly shifting. Then, a profound silence fell. An unexpected pause hung heavy in the air. To this day, I am unsure if it occurred because the men in the room acknowledged my expertise in the field or if they were in shock that the presenter was female!

This silence was more than a mere absence of sound; it was a pivotal moment, a juncture where past and present intersected. As I resumed speaking, my words carried a newfound confidence. The trembling in my hands disappeared, replaced by a steadiness from an inner conviction. Once daunting, the audience's gaze now seemed to bolster my strength. Their nods, notes, and attentive postures spoke of a grudging respect slowly taking root. When I stepped off the podium, the applause that followed was for the content of my speech as well as the journey it represented.

Reflecting on that day, I see more than just a room filled with people. I see a pivotal chapter in my journey. I would love to tell you that the experience transformed me from a young girl burdened by a speech disorder and self-doubt to a young woman who stood tall and unafraid to speak her truth, but I can't do that.

I spent the next three decades of my life struggling to find my voice and realized that our challenges, much like the chapters of a book, build upon each other. Just as the basketball players and their books had opened my world to new ideas, this moment expanded my understanding of my potential. It was a reminder that our struggles can indeed become our strengths and that our deepest fears, once faced, can become our greatest triumphs.

SEASONS OF TRANSFORMATION: NURTURING GROWTH IN THE LATER YEARS

Recognizing the Path Not Taken

In my earliest memories, I recall an inherent sense of being different. The majority of my friends and family, wonderful as they were, seemed comfortably aligned with what society had deemed the 'normal' path. This path, worn smooth by countless feet before them, was laid out like a neatly drawn map—clear, predictable, and seemingly secure. Schools, careers, and societal roles were all pieces of a puzzle that everyone around me diligently assembled.

But within me, there was a different rhythm, an undercurrent of dissonance that I couldn't ignore. It wasn't born out of a singular, defining moment of epiphany or a dramatic life event that set me apart. Instead, it was a gradual dawning, a series of quiet, reflective realizations that their path – this well-lit, well-worn path – was not where my feet found their cadence.

This feeling wasn't a loud, rebellious shout. It was more akin to a persistent whisper, gently nudging me to acknowledge that I was not cut from the same cloth. The expectations and milestones that my peers pursued often felt alien to me. I found myself questioning the very ideals and benchmarks that were so universally accepted, wondering why what seemed to fit others like a glove felt like a misshapen garment to me.

In this sea of conformity, I began to understand an important truth: just because a route is well-trodden, heavily endorsed, and surrounded by nodding heads of approval doesn't necessarily make it right for everyone. There's a profound difference between a path that is right and a path that is right for you.

This understanding wasn't an overnight revelation but a slow and steady unfurling, like a flower blooming in its own time, indifferent to the blooms around it. It was the beginning of a journey to find my path and forge it, to understand that the 'normal' way is just one of many options and that sometimes the most fulfilling journeys are those that take us off the beaten track, into territories uncharted and uniquely our own.

The Courage to Question

Initially a subtle whisper, my inner unrest grew into a powerful driving force that propelled me on a journey of profound self-discovery. This restlessness arose not from a desire to rebel but from a deep-seated yearning for truth, an unquenchable thirst for understanding the world on my own terms. With each step I took along the well-trodden path of societal norms, my discordance grew more pronounced. The more I tried to fit into the mold that others had crafted for me, the more acutely I felt the mismatch between their expectations and my inner compass.

This journey wasn't about rejecting the beliefs and values I had been raised with but examining them with a critical eye and a questioning spirit. It was a quest not for rebellion's sake but for authenticity and genuine self-expression. The louder the voices around me proclaimed the virtues of the 'real world' — a world of pragmatic choices and unchallenged routines — the more determined I became to carve out a space for my own understanding of reality.

Each attempt by those close to me to draw me back into the fold of conventional wisdom only fueled my resolve. Their well-meaning advice, intended to steer me towards a path of security and predictability, instead reminded me of the unique path I felt compelled to tread. In their words I heard the echoes of a life that could have been — safe, perhaps, but unfulfilling in its lack of personal resonance.

So, I dug deeper, delving into the depths of my being in search of what truly moved me, what spoke to the core of my identity. This path was paved not with certainty but with questions about who I was, what I believed in, and how I wanted to shape my existence in a world teeming with diverse perspectives and possibilities. It was a journey into the heart of my own authenticity, a journey that promised no easy answers but an abundance of personal truth and self-discovery.

Embracing My Soul's Purpose

At a pivotal moment in my journey, a profound realization dawned upon me. The nudges and concerns expressed by my loved ones (which I initially perceived as hindrances) were in fact, catalysts propelling me towards a deeper understanding of my true self. It became clear that their attempts to steer me back towards conventional paths were not obstacles but rather signposts guiding me towards a more authentic expression of myself.

This epiphany was particularly evident in my approach to volunteering. Initially, what might have seemed like a noble pastime or a moral obligation, gradually revealed itself as a core element of my identity. Volunteering transformed into an extension of my very being, an activity that did not just fulfill a societal expectation but resonated deeply with who I am at my core. The joy I found in this endeavor was not rooted in recognition or measurable outcomes but in the simple act of giving and being a part of something larger than myself.

The beauty of my volunteer work lay in its uncertainty – the perhaps unknowable extent of the positive impact I was creating. Each act of service, no matter how small, carried with it the potential to ripple out into the world in ways I could never fully trace. This uncertainty was not a source of frustration but a wellspring of joy. It was a reminder that every action, guided by compassion and empathy, contributes to the vast tapestry of human experience.

Volunteering ceased to be just an act; it evolved into a fundamental expression of my existence. It became a channel through which I could express my values, engage with my community, and enact the change I wished to see in the world. This realization not only enriched my experiences of volunteering but also illuminated my understanding of myself. I found a profound sense of purpose and fulfillment in dedicating my time and energy to causes more significant than my own existence. Volunteering is not a separate aspect of my life; it is intrinsically woven into the very fabric of who I am.

The Entrepreneurial Journey

My entrepreneurial journey, often misinterpreted by those around me, appeared to them as a scattered path of jumping from one business model to another. It began with opening an upholstery and interior decorating business in 1999 and evolved into online marketing by 2009. This expansion encompassed various endeavors such as business coaching, affiliate marketing, e-commerce, and digital course creation. I also ventured into publishing a digital magazine for a few years. These varied pursuits seemed like a lack of focus to those close to me as if I were restlessly hopping from one project to the next. However, what was mistaken for indecision was, in truth, a purposeful journey of exploration and a quest to align with my authentic self. Throughout these diverse ventures, a singular constant remained: my dedication to serving women entrepreneurs.

Each business venture I embarked upon was not a random leap but a calculated step toward my destiny. These varied endeavors weren't just business interests; they were integral pieces of a larger puzzle, each contributing to developing my multifaceted identity as an entrepreneur. The transitions from one model to another weren't signs of a distracted mind but manifestations of a spirit driven by curiosity and a desire to learn and grow in every possible dimension of business.

I gathered knowledge and skills with every so-called failure or shift in focus. I forged resilience in the face of adversity, honed creativity in navigating new markets, and tested adaptability with each pivot. These experiences were far from setbacks; they were the building blocks of my professional wisdom.

To the outside world, and especially to those closest to me, my entrepreneurial route might have appeared unstable, even whimsical. They saw the surface - the changes, risks, and diverse ventures - but not the deeper consistency and purpose that tied them all together. Every move was a step in a dance guided by a higher calling that was as much about personal discovery as it was about business success.

This dance with divine guidance was not random; it was an active, passionate search for where my skills and interests could make the most significant impact. The journey was exhilarating, punctuated by profound clarity and inevitable uncertainties. Yet, my belief never wavered. Through it all, I was moving toward something meaningful.

The myriad experiences from each business model sculpted me into a well-rounded businessperson. I evolved not only in understanding different markets but also in realizing my potential and strengths. The journey taught me to trust my instincts, value my vision, and see leadership as a role that extends beyond business into community influence. My path, diverse as it was, stood as a testament to the idea that success is not a straight line but a tapestry woven from varied threads of experiences, insights, and discoveries.

Rediscovering Ancient Wisdom

What many in my circle, and indeed in society, brushed off as 'new age' or 'woo-woo' was, for me, a profound dive into ancient, timeless wisdom. This exploration was a rediscovery of age-old philosophies and spiritual practices guiding humans for centuries rather than a mere curiosity or trend. I delved into texts and teachings that spoke of the interconnectedness of all beings, the power of mindfulness, and the deep-seated truths that lie within us all. This was not about logic or science but about complementing them with a deeper, more holistic understanding of existence.

As I journeyed deeper, I saw the cracks and limitations in our established systems – be it in education, corporate structures, or even traditional healthcare. Often rigid and dogmatic, these systems overlooked the human spirit's need for meaning, connection, and introspection. It became clear that true wisdom and understanding couldn't be confined within the walls of conventional thinking.

This path of exploration reaffirmed my belief in the indispensability of spiritual understanding and personal truth. I learned that each individual's journey is unique, and the wisdom one gathers along the way is deeply personal yet universally applicable. It taught me that a conscious life is not led by following the footsteps of others blindly but by listening to the inner voice that echoes the timeless wisdom of our ancestors.

This journey was about transformation. It challenged me to rethink my values, reassess my priorities, and realign my life in a way that resonated with my deepest understanding of truth. It taught me to embrace my intuition and trust in the unseen, the unmeasurable—the very essence of what makes us human.

In embracing these so-called 'new age' ideas, I found a path that led me to a more conscious, fulfilled, and spiritually enriched life. It was a path that intertwined ancient wisdom with modern living, revealing that the secrets to a rich and meaningful existence have always been within our grasp, waiting to be rediscovered and lived.

Making Health-Conscious Choices

Informed by my background in hazardous waste, my decision to scrutinize labels, avoid harmful chemicals, and create my own products was a deeply considered one. This choice wasn't merely a matter of personal health; it was a stance against the harmful corporate practices I had become acutely aware of in my professional life. Witnessing first-hand the impacts of hazardous materials on the environment and human health, I could no longer remain a passive consumer in a system that often prioritized profit over well-being.

My journey, rooted in this unique expertise, was a form of activism. Every label I read, and every chemical I avoided was a personal rebellion against a culture of irresponsible consumption and production that I knew all too well. Making my own products was more than a return to self-sufficiency; it was a reclaiming of control, an assertion that I wouldn't compromise health for convenience (something I'd seen too often in my work).

Despite criticism and skepticism, my actions were a conscious advocacy for balancing consumer well-being and corporate responsibility. This wasn't a choice made in a vacuum. It was fueled by a deep understanding of the consequences of neglecting this balance. My background in hazardous waste didn't just inform my choices; it propelled them. It was a call to others to recognize the impact of their consumption choices, not just on their health but the larger environment.

By aligning my personal practices with the knowledge gleaned from my career, I wasn't just taking care of my own health. I was championing a movement towards a future where corporations are held accountable and where the safety and well-being of people are prioritized.

Aligning Life with Truth

Integrating these profound realizations into my life marked a metamorphosis, a complete reformation of how I viewed myself and my place in the world. Each realization was like a step up a steep, enlightening path. Some steps were small, others were leaps – but each one was crucially important, leading me to a deeper understanding of my true essence.

This journey was not a mere collection of self-improvement tactics. It went far beyond, aligning every fiber of my being with my deepest values, beliefs, and purposes. It was as if every experience and every bit of knowledge I had accumulated over the years started to click into place, forming a clear picture of who I am and what I stand for.

With each revelation, I felt more in tune with my inner self. It was as if I was peeling back layers, uncovering the core of my existence. The values I had long held but perhaps not honored fully now became the guiding principles of my life. This alignment wasn't always easy; it required letting go of old patterns, beliefs, and sometimes relationships that no longer served this true version of myself.

But as challenging as it was, this process brought unparalleled peace and fulfillment. I began to live more authentically, making choices that were in harmony with my inner truth. This process affected every aspect of my life—from the way I conducted myself in personal and professional relationships to the causes I dedicated my time to the daily rituals I practiced for my physical and spiritual well-being.

Most significantly, this transformation led me to understand the power of my voice. I recognized that my thoughts, actions, and intentions profoundly affected my life and the world around me. My journey of self-discovery became a journey of impact, where living true to myself meant contributing positively to the lives of others.

I found a sense of completeness in this holistic alignment of my being. It was as if all the different parts of my life were finally working in concert, creating a symphony of purpose, passion, and peace. This wasn't just a phase or a momentary realization; it was the beginning of a new way of living – fully, deeply, authentically.

Understanding Our Interconnectedness

As I ventured further along my unique path, a profound realization dawned on me: the world is not a collection of isolated entities but rather an intricate and interconnected web where every strand is linked. This epiphany was both humbling and empowering. Each choice I made, every step I took, no longer seemed like solitary drops in the vast ocean of existence but rather like integral parts of a much larger, dynamic tapestry.

The small, seemingly insignificant actions I took in my daily life – a kind word to a stranger, a conscious decision to reduce waste, and nurturing a plant or a relationship – began to take on new meaning. I saw these acts not as mere personal achievements or responsibilities but as contributions to a greater equilibrium, an investment in the world's well-being. Every positive action, no matter its size, had the potential to send ripples of change across this web, touching lives in ways I could never fully comprehend.

Similarly, my business and volunteer ventures were no longer just about fulfilling personal goals or ambitions. They became platforms for broader impact, ways to enact change, and catalysts for collective empowerment. I realized that by elevating myself and discovering my potential, I was naturally helping others rise as well.

This understanding brought with it a sense of unity and responsibility. The realization that we are all interconnected meant that my actions had a direct impact on the world around me. The health of the environment, the well-being of my community, and the state of global affairs were not just external issues; they were personal. I became more mindful and compassionate, realizing that by contributing to the collective good, I was nurturing myself.

This new perspective also fostered a deep sense of solidarity and empathy. I began to see others not as strangers, competitors, or mere acquaintances but as fellow travelers on this shared journey of life, each with their own unique contributions to the web of existence. It made me more aware of the struggles and triumphs of others, driving me to extend support, understanding, and collaboration.

By accepting our interconnectedness, I discovered a deeper sense of purpose. The belief that our actions, when united, can uplift everyone guided my life. This principle highlighted the strength of working together for shared objectives. It went beyond mere theory, becoming a real-life example of how aligning our efforts with collective well-being can create remarkable change.

Choosing to walk my path has connected me deeper with myself and the world around me. I hope my story will inspire others to embark on their own journey of self-awareness, awakening consciousness, and embracing our shared human experience.

Conclusion

As I look back on the pages of my life, I see not just a journey of self discovery and resilience but a vibrant tapestry of experiences, each thread woven with the strength and knowledge I've gained along the way.

I have found my voice walking the winding road that has taken me from the depths of self-doubt to the heights of spiritual and business growth. I look forward to discovering where the rest of my journey will take me, embracing each new chapter with anticipation and an open heart.

In "Soulful Strength," I've shared my story, now I encourage you to write your own. Embrace your soul's journey and discover how your unique strengths and wisdom can light up your path and the paths of those around you.

Let's walk together, guided by the lessons of our past and the dreams of our future. A future where our potential is limitless and our impact is profound. Together, let's create a world where every woman's voice is heard and her power is celebrated.

Cheyenne Burnett

Founder of Women's Health Warrior

https://www.linkedin.com/in/explantsecretswithcheyenneburnett/
https://www.facebook.com/iamcheyenneburnett
https://www.instagram.com/iamcheyenneb/
https://www.explantsecrets.com/
https://www.explantsecrets.com/podcast

Cheyenne is an accomplished and charismatic women's health advocate, author, and speaker with a passion for helping women regain their health and self-confidence. As founder of ExplantSecrets.com, she has become a leading authority on breast implant illness education, offering effective and affordable solutions to those in need. Cheyenne has been featured on FOX News, CNC, The Times, Women On Topp, and recently made her red dot debut at TEDxWoodinville. When she's not empowering women to put their health first and embrace their natural beauty she can be found exploring the great outdoors with the love of her life Brad, and their three awesome kids.

YOU ARE NOT THE PROBLEM

By Cheyenne Burnett

My name is Cheyenne Burnett, and I am a Breast Implant Illness Survivor, Self-Worth Advocate, a beauty culture dropout, and perhaps most importantly, a woman who is fed up with unrealistic beauty standards aimed at cashing in on our insecurities.

I grew up in Utah County where the ideal standard of beauty is super skinny, big boobs, tan (but not too tan), blonde hair, and those nails - GIRL, well, they better be done.

As a teenager, I had the skinny part down because I vividly remember being praised for how little I was. How petite I was, how cute. So at 12 when the scale hit 100 and then 105, that's when my journey of disregarding my health for the sake of "being beautiful" really began. At 12, I hadn't even started my period, and yet I found myself consciously deciding that throwing up was not going to work for me, so I'd just have to stop eating instead.

Then, when I turned 18, I chopped my hair short. Not the typical version of beautiful, sure, but I felt edgy and cute. Well, that is until I was wearing a boyfriend's t-shirt and basketball shorts in the grocery store one day and got mistaken for my little brother from behind.

I will never forget the moment I realized it was my brother's friend, yelling his name at me down the grocery store aisle. My heart sank, and though I brushed it off at that moment like it was no big deal, I went home and destroyed myself in the mirror. Picking apart every little thing, I felt wasn't pretty or feminine enough.

Less than a year later, I was in a plastic surgeon's office, discussing breast implants with my mom because I was still a child.

I often joke that choosing therapy over breast implants would have been a much smarter investment. And though I say it jokingly, there's a lot of truth to it. I've learned the hard way that plastic surgery doesn't give us more self-confidence; it simply offers another layer to conceal our lack of it.

So, let me be the first to admit that I've been both over- and underweight in my life. I've had long, flowing hair, I've been dressed to the nines, I've had full glam makeup, eyelash extensions, and nails done. Even with all of that, I was still scared to death to put a swimsuit on because someone was going to judge the cellulite on my legs, I was sure of it.

I've done just about all of it. I've had the boobs, I've done the fake tans, the spray tans, and the chemical peels. I've worn shoes that made my back hurt for two days, and I've had neurotoxins in the form of Botox pumped into my face, and none of it changed the fact that I was wildly insecure.

Why is that?

Why is it that I could have, done, and been all the things society told me *I needed* to be beautiful and still destroyed myself every time I walked past a storefront window?

Why didn't it ever occur to me to even ask if the steps I was taking to *"become"* more beautiful and *"gain"* confidence could carry significant health risks?

Well, it's because the standards of beauty I was so desperately striving to reach weren't ever my own.

Of course, I could never quite get it right; it was always someone else's opinion of beauty that I was trying so hard to be, and the reality is, that "someone else" is a beauty industry that thrives on insecurity and profits every time we buy "the thing."

If we believe our faces aren't as worthy as they are, then we will buy products that promise us the acceptance and attention we believe we need.

If we believe our upper lip disappearing when we smile is a problem, then lip filler quickly becomes a solution.

If we believe feminine and sexy only come in one form, then plastic surgery is the only option.

I was just having this exact conversation with a friend recently, and her response took me completely by surprise. She said, "Yeah okay, Cheyenne, but I don't do these things for other people. I do them for myself. I do them because they help me feel more confident in my own skin."

So I sat with that for a minute and then I said, "Listen, I do not claim to have all the answers, and don't think for one second that I believe I have fully escaped the grip of social pressure. I still dye my hair because God forbid I have grey ones in my 30s, and trust me, my shoe collection isn't going anywhere. So I hear you, I am with you, which is why I have to ask: Is it really our own skin we feel confident in if we have to douse ourselves in chemicals to feel beautiful? Are we really confident in 'our own skin' if we're unwilling to leave the house without a full face of makeup on?"

Now, I am not saying wearing makeup is bad. What I am saying is the reason we wear makeup might be.

The reason we spend thousands of dollars on eyelashes, hair products, and plastic surgery, that's the problem. **Not us!**

We are not the problem. Profit-driven, unhealthy, and frankly, unobtainable beauty standards are.

Did you know that 83% of women today don't believe they are good enough in their current form? 83%! And 89% of us will actually opt out of meaningful connections like being with friends or loved ones when we don't like how we look.

And 1 out of 3 women today are choosing to alter their appearance based NOT on real people, or real bodies, but instead on computer-created images.

AI-generated photos, filters, and enormous marketing budgets have us believing we are not good enough, and if that belief is what drives your decisions, then both your mental and physical health are at risk. And that is unacceptable.

Or, at least it should be.

But that is what our culture is pushing. Because our culture, steady as it may be, was built on and benefits from the control of women. And a woman focused on fitting in will not consider standing out.

A woman preoccupied with conforming to social pressure is very, very unlikely to speak up against that pressure's source.

So the less we like ourselves, the easier we are to be controlled. The less we trust ourselves, the easier it is to convince us that we are the problem. And if we believe that, then we are perfectly primed to buy all of their solutions.

And, if you're a mother, then times that by two! Ladies, as mothers we are the first example of both beauty and love our children ever see. So, if we can't see beauty in who we truly are, our children won't be able to see it in themselves either. And a child who grows up valuing only what they see in the mirror becomes a consumer of things like weight-loss fads and plastic surgery.

Many of us are those children, and now we have our own children following in our footsteps.

So what do we do?

How do we lead a better example?

How do we start feeling good about making decisions based on what is truly in the best interest of our health and our hearts rather than what's going to get us the most external approval?

WE TAKE THEM BACK!

We reclaim and relight OUR standards of beauty.

We have to stop believing our self-worth is tied directly to what we see in the mirror and start learning that beauty has as much to do with how we feel physically and emotionally as it does with how we look.

And trust me, as someone who knows the kind of mental gymnastics it takes to finally believe I'm beautiful *(more often than not)* regardless of my weight or breast size, I know to do that we have to start with self-acceptance.

Not self-confidence.

Not self-love.

Self-acceptance. Which is actually a very different thing.

But the cool part about true self-acceptance is that it is less about learning new things and more about unlearning the beliefs that have us convinced we are not already enough. It can look in a few different ways.

If you find that judging or comparing is easy when you're on social media, then maybe it's time to give that one a break.

Or maybe it's putting your "skinny pants" on and wearing them because "they fit" but you feel terrible in them…

If that's you, then girl, throw those things away and buy some pants that fit your current season of beautiful.

Or maybe it's someone. Maybe your mom, sister, or cousin always seems to have something to say about how you look. One of my closest friends can not be in a room with her mother for more than five minutes without that lady praising her for how skinny she is and telling her how good she looks. That friend has struggled with an eating disorder off and on her entire adult life.

And can we just talk about the fact that grandmas are notorious for bringing up how much weight we've gained since we saw them last… Girl, if granny can't keep her judge-y thoughts to herself, then granny isn't invited to brunch!

My point is, don't be afraid to start putting some space between you and whatever or whoever it is that triggers the belief that you need to change or fix something about how you look because you don't. That belief was planted for the sole purpose of profiting off us. So let's not give them the satisfaction.

Instead, let's relight OUR standards of beauty with what is healthy and with real bodies! Better yet, let's realign our standards of beauty with OUR bodies, as different from each other as they may be. Because when we do that, we can stop searching for ways to *become* more beautiful and start seeing what we already are.

So today, I am going to challenge you to give yourself the gift of self-acceptance and start focusing more on how you FEEL than how you look.

Now, ask yourself is it possible, not is it probable, not is it likely, just is it possible that you are so much more than what you see in the mirror?

Is it possible?

It is.

Now give yourself permission to see it.

Give yourself permission to start believing who you are right now is more than enough, and please know, you don't have to prove that to anyone. All you have to do is believe for yourself that it's possible because if you can believe it's possible; you can see that it's true.

Claudia Brown

Founder of Strategic Business Coach

https://www.linkedin.com/in/claudiacbrown/
https://www.facebook.com/claudia.brown.5249/
https://www.instagram.com/haniel.consulting
www.hanielconsulting.com

Claudia Brown works with Owners, CEO's, and Executives who want to take their business to the next levels of efficiencies, productivity, revenues, and profits. She has an MBA in Marketing and Finance from the University of Rochester Simon School of Business. Using her expertise in marketing, sales, and business, she served for many years as a strategic acceleration business coach and trainer for Chet Holmes and Anthony Robbins, advising, training, and coaching hundreds of companies from start-up to multi-million dollars to take their businesses to higher levels. She currently owns a business coaching company, Haniel Consulting, where she helps clients in marketing, sales, and strategic business growth. She specializes in helping companies to acquire, convert, and lock in clients for life. Claudia has trained with self-development and high level energy healers over the past several years and may incorporate some of this training into her coaching sessions.

CHANGING YOUR BELIEFS SYSTEM

By Claudia Brown

Our lives are built out of our beliefs. Core beliefs bring us together or tear us apart. Why do we have these beliefs? Can we change them? Who are we changing them for?

When I was about four years old, we moved into a new home. I grew up in a family of seven kids, and there were five at that time. So, with another one on the way, my parents decided to move all of us to a bigger house. I had four brothers at the time, and I was the second oldest child. We would all sit together for dinner at night, and my mother would cook and clean. At some point soon after we moved in, my parents told me that I needed to help my mother cook the dinner and that I needed to do the dishes afterward the dinner was over every night. I wasn't quite sure what that meant. I did help my mother cook dinner every night, but when it came to washing the dishes every night, I started to feel resentful. Why was I doing all the work during dinner and my brothers weren't helping at all? This didn't seem fair to me, so I brought it up to my parents that it didn't seem fair.

Now, this was not something that I normally would do. But I felt so strongly about it that I got over my fear of talking back to my parents and told them that I didn't think it was fair that I had to do all the work around the house, and that my brothers didn't have to do any of that work. They said, "Oh, well, that's because you're a girl, and girls help out in the kitchen."

And I said, "Well, I help out outside, so why do the boys not help around the kitchen while I have to help outside?" They thought about it and they agreed with me and said, "Great. Here's what we do: all the boys and you will take turns washing the dishes, and we still would like you to help make the dinners." That turned out to work out beautifully because I didn't mind helping my mother cook, and there were five of us who could wash dishes at the time so that took up five days or most of the week.

That was my first foray into dealing with how boys and girls weren't treated fairly in the household. We as girls were expected to do things that didn't seem to make sense to me. If boys could cook and do dishes, that seemed to me like a really good thing for them to learn to do. And it also seemed like a really good thing that I helped out in the yard with my brothers. With the new expectations agreed upon by my parents, my brothers and I all learned to work as a team. The core beliefs of my parents had shifted.

Years later, I learned that a couple of my brothers said they were really happy that they did dishes and learned to cook as well because it helped them in their lives going forward and gave them an appreciation of cooking. So I'm happy to say that it all turned out well in the end.

I loved sports when I was young and loved to play and run around. Of course, I had all my brothers to play with so that helped. We ended up as a family of five boys and two girls, my sister being the youngest and nine years younger than me. I would play sports in the yard with my brothers and their friends and neighbors. and we had a lot of fun. We all had to play outside a lot even in the winter so I got plenty of exercise as a child. In the winter we'd go sledding, have some snowball fights, and play in the snow. In the summer, we would play football, soccer, baseball, and other sports in the backyard. I loved playing sports! In school, though, there was very little opportunity for girls to play sports. I went to a Catholic school, and sometimes we got to play kickball and a little baseball, but we had few other opportunities for girls to play sports. That's all I really remember playing. Most of the time we just had recess and would play around outside for half an hour or an hour.

In the summers, as we got a little bit older, say 11 or 12, my mother would send us down to the elementary school that was at the bottom of the hill and go to summer camp. My brothers and I would walk from the house down to the school as it was a bit more than a mile away. When we initially attended, I found out that the girls were supposed to do crafts most of the day and then a little bit of kickball. The boys would play baseball and other sports out on the field, and they would play kickball too. The girls stayed on the concrete to do the crafts and kickball. I was not happy about that. I wanted to play baseball with the boys since I had already been playing with my brothers for a long time, and I got pretty good at it. So, I spoke to the woman leader and proposed that I could go play with the boys. I really wanted to play baseball and run around and do other sports. I didn't want to sit around doing crafts all day because that just wasn't something I enjoyed at the time. It took a bit of convincing, but I finally convinced both the woman leader and the boys' coach to let me play with the boys' team. Of course, I did pretty well, but I was put in the outfield, and the boys heckled me a lot because I was a girl playing with the boys. I stood on my own and played as best I could, and after a while, they stopped heckling me as much. But they still resented that a girl would be playing on a boys' team. Now, these days, girls playing on a boys' team is quite common, but when I was growing up, it was pretty rare.

As I mentioned, I grew up in a Catholic family. When I was very young, we used to have only Sunday mass and were told that mass could only happen on Sunday. Years later, the Catholic Church changed its rules to allow us to go to mass on Saturday night. It took a lot of people many years to accept that they could go on Saturday night because the rule was for Sundays.

The above examples illustrate how some belief systems that were in place when I was growing up and how they have slowly changed. During that time, girls had to do what girls "should do" and boys had to do what boys "should do". There was little crossover.

The belief system was then that girls should be girls and boys should be boys. Each group was expected to do certain things, be treated a certain way, was expected to do things a certain way, and say things a certain way. I realized pretty early on that that was pretty silly, given that I had five brothers and we all worked around the house equally. But even then, it was only owing to my making my parents aware of the inequality, and, to their credit, their realizing that those rules were pretty silly. So, they changed their beliefs and expectations, which was great.

Today, many such belief systems have changed. Yet, even though they appear to be changed by society, many people hang on to some or even all of their old beliefs, many of which are serving and many which are not.

Our beliefs can be changed at any point in our lives. It is harder to change beliefs as a child while we are in the learning process and are creating beliefs based on our lived experiences. As we get older and more discerning, we can better examine ourselves and see what beliefs we want to keep and which to let go of and/or change.

I'm the kind of person who likes to see different sides to things and can understand different perspectives. I found over the years that many people can only see their own perspectives and aren't open to seeing other people's perspectives if they don't align with their perspective. This is where interpersonal clashes can happen.

That brings up a point about who you are changing your beliefs for. If you are changing them for yourself, and you want your beliefs to change, that is done out of self-love and self-awareness. If you are changing them because someone else wants you to change them, then you must decide if that change in belief is authentic for you and good for you and not just a change out of obligation. If you are making belief changes just for someone else, that likely is not authentic to you or your well-being.

Our personal belief systems can be changed at any time, and often quickly once we have self-awareness and discernment. We can change a belief that we have had for years if we want to change it. The first part is to be academically aware of the belief. The next part is figuring out why we believe what we believe. Is it something our parents told us? Is it something that our teachers or church or others in our lives convinced us of? Where did that come from? Was it an experience that we had in our lives that formed a belief? Was it from a trauma that occurred in our lives, where we had to protect ourselves in some way or another, and we created a belief system in ourselves?

Awareness of the belief is the first part of the process of potential change. Figuring out where the belief stemmed from is the second part of changing beliefs. The third part is wanting to change that belief for our own purpose, not because of someone else's demands, and accepting that we can have a new belief. Many times, our beliefs are attached to our emotions, our internal resistance to what others have told us, or other influences. The fourth part is creating a new belief. What is that new belief? Do we really believe it? Is there some other emotion or reasoning around that new belief, and can we be open to changing even that belief at some point in time if it doesn't continue to serve us? What if we saw a different, more positive perspective on a negative belief?

Older belief systems continue to be pervasive even today. We see that on the news every single day. We see it in advertisements. We see it in the movies. We see it in the workplace. We see it in our homes with our loved ones. At the same time, we are also being presented with new belief systems, such as becoming open to homosexuality as being part of the norm, girls being able to play sports on boys' teams, women having their own professional sports teams (hockey, soccer, and basketball), women being paid equally to men for the same level of work, and many more. Women, for instance, are still fighting for equal compensation at work where there is an unwritten rule that men get paid more for the same work.

Let's review some examples of current belief systems in advertising. In advertising, the people in the advertisement are almost always smiling and laughing even if the commercial is about something negative. The appeal of a smile works because of a phenomenon known as "emotional contagion". In most people, our mirror neurons work when we're exposed to a recognizable facial expression. If that facial expression is happy, our "mirror neurons" make us brighten up automatically. So, when you look at a smiling face, however subtle, something in you automatically brightens up as well. It works because we simply feel better when we see other people happy. That's how we're wired. Therefore, a smile on a model's face can ignite consumer joy and improve our attitude. So, commercials conspire to shift or change our belief systems and encourage us to buy their products by using smiling people in their ads.

That same thing happens in the news. Over the last several years, "fake news" has become a common term. We have become aware that every news station offers us the same, negative news in virtually the same words. This is because most of the major news stations are owned by the same owners, and they want the news to be consistent. They also dictate what to add to the news and what to keep out or suppress. They determine how the news is presented, what is said, and how it is said. This may seem conspiratorial, but many people are aware that this is happening.

The movies are a great place to solidify old belief patterns or create new beliefs. The power of audiovisuals has been manifested and exploited politically, socially, and economically throughout recent history. Besides mirroring our diverse cultures, films have, for a long time, been shaping our beliefs and values. A good example is when people copy fashion trends from movie stars and musicians. It is also common these days to find societies using figures of speech that are inspired by the film industry. At the very least, film solidifies selected cultural beliefs. and renders some redundant. For instance, romantic movies make sex look "cool". Crime movies make lying seem calculative. There are also genres that normalize stealing and dishonesty. Teenagers are now able to access pornographic content online and watch music videos where the words advocate for drug and substance abuse. All this content is misleading to young boys and girls, but parents can't seem to find reliable, foolproof strategies to stop their kids from accessing it. Even adults are exposed to movies where there is almost always a homosexual couple for the media to use to influence our attitudes towards them (not a bad thing but noticeable).

For every visual medium, our awareness of the messages being communicated is important. Watching a movie and observing the subtleties of the perception that the movie is projecting is essential for us as individuals. You can ask yourself what you want to believe by having this awareness. How are your beliefs compromised, or influenced, or solidified by the media? Only by becoming aware of that influence can you really determine what you want to believe or can believe (even if you didn't before). Again, changing belief systems, even those that are subtly reinforced over time by society can be done if you are aware and challenge them and your own beliefs and decide to change your thinking or not.

Belief systems in the workplace are pervasive. It does depend on where you work, how many people you work with, and the internal, collective beliefs of the workplace. Many people must "go along with" the collective beliefs of those in the workplace to fit in and continue to be paid.

Workplace culture refers to the collective values, beliefs, attitudes, and behaviors that shape the environment and interactions within an organization. Workplace culture influences how employees feel, communicate, and collaborate. Company culture is the collection of unwritten norms, beliefs, and collective attitudes that shape how things get done within your organization. This means it can contain any combination of elements. Creating an environment where personal beliefs do not affect the overall work expectations is critical. Certain beliefs may still be in place, even if the culture is positive.

In 2020, Covid produced a massive work-from-home shift. Belief systems on all levels shifted dramatically because there was no other alternative. Even the health system learned to do health checks via phone and Zoom calls. That was an unprecedented move from the past demands of the patient having to physically go into the health office. Covid brought about massive shifts in belief systems worldwide in all areas of our lives. Telehealth, as it was called, opened up where doctors and nurses could talk to patients on the phone or via Zoom. Working from home was mandatory so people didn't need to drive to work. Zoom became a common household word. Opinions about the Covid shots became polarized. Life appeared to move slower because people weren't rushing to and from work or school or church. There were little to no social activities, isolation from family became good or bad, and there was more freedom to relax because people were stuck in their homes. Additionally, there was a renewed appreciation for the things that mattered to people. Teachers were now teaching remotely. More homeschooling came about because teachers sometimes couldn't attend to the students. Less money was being spent because there was nowhere to go, church attendance from home by remote viewing became commonplace, and many businesses went out of business due to a lack of sales. Many business owners created new and different businesses by "pivoting" in business. There were no sports activities for kids, so parents weren't rushing around driving their kids to activities. Close family and friends many times got closer while many family and friends relationships dissolved. More time was spent outside. Toll booths were shut down at curfew, curfews were instated, highways were almost empty or empty at times during the day or night, and so much more.

We have had proof that we can change our beliefs through many external influences. What about challenging and changing your own internal beliefs? How many of your beliefs can you list?

These days, because of the shift in where we can work and prices going up at an increasing rate, people are looking to create their own business, work part-time at a remote job, or join a direct marketing company or similar.

Changing our belief systems of today can be more magnified than in past years and many are being changed using our current technologies, where information on almost any subject can be found. The internet is a powerful communication medium, and we see so much every day that can impact us in subtle or overt ways.

The beliefs of our parents remain incredibly strong. We have been influenced by them all our lives. If we disagreed with them when we were younger, and they didn't see or respect our point of view, we most likely had to tolerate them until we got older and moved out and away from their influence. Even when we are older, if we do or do not agree with members of our family, it brings heavy emotional disturbance to the family members.

We also tend to gravitate towards people who share our points of view. Many can become good friends for a time or a lifetime. True, long-term relationships are based on shared beliefs and respect for different beliefs.

Beliefs are created by people. Shared beliefs by a large enough collective can influence others' beliefs. A strong speaker with strong passions can shift the collective's beliefs. The key is remembering that we are all individuals and are unique. Respecting people's basic rights is important. Listening is essential.

Many times, beliefs are negative in nature. You can challenge yourself to figure out if they are and what a positive new belief might be. Imagine if you had more positivity in your life. If you focus on the positives, more positives come into your life.

Here are some examples of beliefs that are still strongly held but have shifted over time:

- Don't wear white after Labor Day.
- Wear high-heeled shoes to work.
- Wear a suit and tie to work.
- You're not feminine enough if you're a girl who plays sports.
- Sexual harassment.
- Race discrimination.
- Don't wear a white wedding dress if you are remarrying after divorce.
- Boys shouldn't cry.
- You're weak if you cry.
- Only men can wear men's clothes.
- Boys shouldn't show any signs of weakness.
- Girls should not be aggressive.
- Aggressive boys and men are strong and leaders.
- Boys/men should be physically strong.
- Real men don't do yoga.
- Don't talk to anyone about negative things going on in the household.
- The adult/parent is always right.
- Same-sex parents harm the children in their emotional development.
- Don't talk about your real feelings.

Here's an exercise you can do. Make a list of as many of your beliefs as you can. Then, go through and list where that belief came from. In the next two columns, write down the pros (how are you feeling that is positively impacting you) and cons (how are you feeling that is negatively impacting you) of each belief. In the last column, add what new positive belief you can create for each and why you want to change it. Some you may want to keep, but what about the ones that are not serving you in some way in your life? Even everyday beliefs that you assign "always" or "never" to can be listed, and you can decide if those are really true or not.

Current Belief	Pro's	Con's	New Positive Belief

What would your life be like if you changed your beliefs to be more positive? I have changed so many of my beliefs over my lifetime. Many of my beliefs were not serving me and I have had to unravel and heal and shift or change those beliefs. My spiritual and self-development training, particularly over the past five years, was instrumental in making me aware of how our beliefs are just thoughts that we have attached meanings to and we can change those meanings to something more positive, which in turn helps us change the beliefs to be more positive. This understanding has helped me to realize where I was in victim mode and how I could shift the meanings and create more self-love and self-empowerment. This has helped me to continue to pay attention to my beliefs and be more positive and aligned.

We are all unique individuals and yet also part of a larger collective. Many beliefs are created to shift our collective minds. Paying attention to rules, regulations, media influences, people's opinions, our parents' influences, politicians' influences, etc., have shaped how we think. If we start to pay attention to those beliefs and see where we can change negative beliefs to positive beliefs, we can start to love ourselves more. If we all learn to start thinking more positively, seeing people for the good they bring, becoming kinder and more tolerant to others, and seeing people for their inside beings, then our world could shift dramatically, and we can all be happier.

Clodagh Meiklejohn

Transformational Coach, International Speaker & Energy Healer

https://www.linkedin.com/in/clodaghmeiklejohn
https://www.facebook.com/clodaghmeiklejohnco
https://www.instragram.com/clodaghmeiklejohn
https://www.clodaghmeiklejohn.com

Clodagh Meiklejohn is a visionary coach, international speaker, and energy healer from Scotland. Passionate about empowering women, Clodagh has dedicated over a decade to studying human potential, and applied her knowledge to help individuals achieve true fulfillment. Drawing on extensive experience in overcoming personal and professional challenges, she guides clients through transformative journeys to overcome barriers to growth and success, both in life and work. Blending holistic healing with practical coaching techniques, Clodagh has developed her proprietary Intuitive Alignment Method™ to facilitate living authentically and achieving one's full potential. Her work as an energy healer adds depth to her coaching, facilitating not just change but lasting transformation. A sought-after speaker, she shares her insights and strategies worldwide, inspiring action and deepening the understanding of personal and collective power. Her book 'Your Limitless Life' is due for release in 2024.

UNLOCKING POTENTIAL: A NEW LIFE

By Clodagh Meiklejohn

I felt the energy resonate all the way from the other side of the Atlantic.

Seeing the smiling faces of women on the livestream — women who had shown up for themselves and experienced profound inner shifts — was deeply moving.

I loved my work, and the sense of living with purpose was far more fulfilling than any achievement could ever be.

As the livestream concluded, I thanked the host and all the participants with a full and open heart. I turned off my camera and allowed myself to revel in the moment, letting the heartfelt connection with hundreds around the world fully sink in.

I exhaled slowly and looked out the window, watching the sunlight as it danced on the sea, its rays splintering into countless, shimmering shards. It dawned on me that in just a few years, my life had become unrecognizable. I now lived in a different country, had shifted careers, and found happiness in myself and my mission. Most importantly, I was a happy, present mum. Gone were the days of rushing up the windswept hill to the school gate; now my school run and commute were done with a smile, against the brilliant backdrop of the ocean. The beach was the view from my office, and the sea was our playground.

And it struck me just how far I had come from not so very long ago…

* * *

A few years earlier, I rolled over in my bed with a heavy sigh and reluctantly opened my eyes.

The clock blinked 03:00 AM… Again.

I marvelled grimly at my body clock. This used to be the hour for my baby's night feed. Now, years later, it was time for... insomnia!

It wasn't just the sleep deprivation that worried me. I was scared my panic attacks would come back.

If you've ever experienced a panic attack at night, you will know they are terrifying. You wake up gasping for breath, thinking you only have seconds to live. Your body is in hyper-drive; your heart races and adrenaline surges in a way you've never felt before. It's a nervous system overload. At least, that's what I have experienced countless times.

Unfortunately, they don't get any less terrifying with experience.

This December morning was panic-attack-free. Yet, there I was again, lying in the darkness, yearning to fall back asleep and watching the hours tick by until it was time to get up.

And this December day, it was particularly hard to keep going. Sometime in the early afternoon, exhausted, I crumbled to the floor and began to cry. At first, my sobs were gentle, so as not to wake my little boy sleeping blissfully upstairs.

But then it seemed like a well was opening within me. Pain arose with a vengeance. Over time, the sharp stab of betrayal had given way to the agony of grieving what was gone. Now, everything seemed to well up at once, accompanied by anger and confusion.

I had been trying to keep everything going. EV-RY-THING.

But at that moment, it felt like nothing had improved.

After the birth of my son, for a short time, I felt utterly blessed. I was taking some maternity time off from a great job as a TV director. My husband and I had bought a house, and we'd just had a beautiful, healthy baby boy.

But within a very short time, everything seemed to fall apart. My husband was in crisis and decided to leave us. While I was fortunate enough to dive straight back into work, as any new mom knows, it's an exhausting time. Sleep deprivation is a given, and the physical demands of long filming hours didn't help one bit. I also felt tremendous guilt leaving my baby in the nursery when he was so tiny.

What was worse was that, despite working full-time, my single paycheck didn't cover the mortgage, childcare, and the high cost of living in London. In order to boost my income, I turned my painting hobby into a professional side hustle. But the only time for this was in the evenings, which was far from ideal.

I was heartbroken, grieving, and I felt desperately alone. At the same time, I was exhausted and constantly stressed; despite my best efforts, I was spiralling into debt. The worst part of it all was that I wasn't being the mother I wanted to be for my son. I felt like a failure.

As I lay on the floor that December day, I no longer recognized who I was.

I wondered if my insomnia was due to stress or depression and if my panic attacks stemmed from feeling trapped in a relentless cycle.

Why couldn't I work my way out of this when I was fortunate enough to have a job, and I was trying everything I could think of? How could I still be feeling so shattered and so stuck? In despair, I cried out into the void: "What do you want me to DO?"

Then, I lay on the floor and gave up. I let go and allowed everything to relax. Even my sobs petered out. The silence that followed was a relief; the stillness a blissful contrast to the relentless effort of overthinking, doing, and trying. As I surrendered to the moment, my body softened and my mind stopped spinning.

And from the stillness, I heard, "Live Your Life. Be Free!"

Live my life, be free?

* * *

There is power in stillness and silence, and there is strength in surrender.

Unwittingly, I had created space for guidance that comes from beyond the problem-solving mind.

Later, as I pondered what it meant to 'Live Your Life. Be Free!' I found myself confronted with some thought-provoking truths.

I was nowhere near living as fully as I wished.

And I certainly wasn't free.

In fact, it dawned on me that it was my own choices that were keeping me trapped in some kind of nightmare.

In a moment of clarity, I realized that instead of doggedly trying to fix what was broken, I had the opportunity to create something new — possibly something very different.

But what did that look like for me? With a full-time job, a house and a mortgage, a mountain of monthly payments, and, most importantly, a young child to care for, what were my options?

* * *

That day marked the beginning of a fresh chapter, one born from the depths of despair.

Within a few short months, I had packed up our house and rented it out, and we set off in my trusty Audi A3, packed to the brim with essentials and a large painting easel. Our destination: Sitges, a pretty seaside town just south of Barcelona, Spain.

The sense of adventure was exhilarating.

Upon arrival, we didn't know a soul. Starting from scratch in a small town in Catalunya wasn't all plain sailing. However, my experience from filming trips in various countries honed my ability to quickly sense the energy and nature of a place. The international, fun-loving spirit of this charming town had drawn us there, and we were met with refreshing kindness and generosity.

As we consciously built a new life from next to nothing, I had the space and time to question all my decisions. I realized that in every moment, we have some kind of choice — and freedom lies in those choices.

With some distance from my London life, I could see how much I had conformed to societal norms. I recognized the expectations placed on me as a mother and the pressure to balance my career with motherhood.

I could also see the conditioning that had invisibly influenced me. I slowly began to replenish my energy and to heal. As I did so, I also began to take complete responsibility for my life, peeling the layers that were holding me back from doing what I truly wanted and creating what I yearned to create.

My intention had been to follow my intuition and spend a few months away from obligation and relentless financial pressure. Even though it had seemed extreme and illogical to uproot my life with a young child, I realized that nothing would change while I remained trapped in a routine. I also sensed I was alarmingly close to breakdown, and that was the last thing we both needed. Deep down, I knew a break was essential; it would be rejuvenating to immerse myself in a fresh culture and savour the simple, natural pleasures of seaside living while working on paintings for an upcoming exhibition. Most importantly, I wanted to cherish quality time with my son.

But the entire experience ignited something within me: the joy of new possibilities.

As our new life took shape, I quickly recognized that a few months would merely scratch the surface. Seeing everything from a fresh perspective, I was drawn to the boundless possibilities life offered rather than its constraints. It sparked a desire within me. I wanted to help others feel more empowered to make choices and to live a life they loved. I rewrote my story and turned my pain into purpose.

I became fascinated by who we are and what we're truly capable of and dived eagerly into the study of human potential.

I explored various fields of cutting-edge science which now allow us to understand ourselves in unprecedented ways. Quantum physics, for example, is the study of particles at the subatomic level — a realm previously beyond our reach. It reveals that everything is energy: you, me, the chair you're sitting on, and even the book you're reading. Everything is energy, and everything is connected.

Grasping this concept of energy is the first step towards living a more intentional, purpose-driven life. Every thought, emotion, and action contributes to your energy field. By changing habitual patterns, you can liberate yourself from feelings of being stuck and unfulfilled.

Choosing new thoughts can forge new neural pathways. With repetition, you can 'rewire' your brain and change your thinking. Your thoughts trigger emotions in your body, giving you the power to transform how you feel. New thoughts and feelings can lead to new behaviours and fresh outcomes. And since everything is connected energetically, these changes can profoundly affect how you experience life and therefore alter your reality.

This understanding opens the door to experiencing life in an entirely new way.

So, wherever you find yourself now, I invite you to pause, as I once did, and ask yourself, "How do I want to experience life?"

Is it through a lens of scarcity and blame, feeling the need to compete, living in a state of reactivity, fearful of what may or may not happen?

Or is it through a lens of abundance, acceptance, and love, living in a state of joyful creativity?

If you question whether this choice will make a difference, consider this. Have you noticed how some people focus on the negative and attract continual drama, while others seem happy and blessed, and even when they are navigating life's challenges, they remain philosophical?

Your experience changes when you change your perspective.

My work in the world today and my invitation to you now is this. I invite you to awaken to the truth of who you are — a powerful creator, a source of creative energy. I urge you to create the things you love in your life, and to live life on your terms, free from self-imposed limitations. I encourage you to transition from feeling uncertain about your path to living purposefully; from feeling incomplete in some way to experiencing the wholeness of your true nature.

This is how to feel fully alive and fulfilled. For me, this is the essence of really living — embracing the fullness of who you truly are. Reaching your full potential.

The Journey to Limitless Living

We're all on a similar human journey. We all feel the pull of our innate creative power and potential yet find ourselves hindered by our limited perspectives, identities, or circumstances. So many of us are doing and being from a place of reaction and fear. We hold on to things that no longer serve our highest good, and we don't make space to tune in to our desires and callings because we fear the unknown.

This experience mirrors the journey of the mythical 'hero' — central to all our most-loved stories and films — who hears the "call to adventure." The hero must not only step into the unknown but also undergo trials and tribulations to become more empowered and aligned with their true purpose. This monomyth resonates deeply with us because it reflects our own struggles and aspirations.

The calling to live to our full potential can manifest in various ways. You might feel a general dissatisfaction with life — a sense that you're destined for something greater. Or, as in my case, it might take an unexpected or painful experience for the structures around you to be shaken or stripped away. An event might shatter your world, forcing you to question all that is familiar and known.

But it doesn't have to reach that point. The fact that you are reading this book suggests you already sense you are destined for something more.

I have come to understand that sense comes from your most expansive, energetic self, your highest consciousness. Some call this your higher self.

You'll be all too familiar with the thoughts that fill your conscious mind. However, 95% of your behaviour is not driven by these thoughts but by programming acquired throughout your life, much of which operates subconsciously. Beyond the conscious and subconscious, you have a superconscious awareness — your most expansive level of consciousness which is connected to all that is. It is from this plane that you receive intuitive nudges and callings. But these can only be sensed when you quieten the noise of the conscious mind and pause your unconscious behaviour.

How can you recognize these intuitive nudges? They are consistently expansive rather than contractive, emerging from a place of possibility and openness rather than fear. With practice, you can learn to attune to the sensations of inner-knowing within your body.

The reason you may hesitate and doubt this information — the reason you feel held back — is that your conscious, analytical mind prefers the safety of what is familiar, logical, and known.

Yet, much like the message I received —"Live Your Life. Be Free"— intuitive information doesn't always make sense to your logical mind.

Change begins when you step out of your comfort zone and do something different. Like our mythical 'hero,' you will face challenges; perhaps a metaphorical death and rebirth or a life-changing shift in awareness.

True transformation occurs when you BECOME different. Your energy and your entire vibration shift. If you embark on this journey and commit to it, your life will never be the same again. It's not just a path of personal transformation but a journey of freedom and liberation to becoming the best, most expansive version of yourself.

This is why I have created a way of navigating this journey for those who feel called to live life in a more expansive way, but don't know how to start or don't know how to overcome the resistance, trepidation, or fear that will absolutely and inevitably arise.

All of us arrive at a crossroads in life. What I've learned is that the power lies in embracing these moments and all the possibilities that exist, in opening ourselves up to the infinite number of ways that life can take shape with each moment of choice.

It all starts with a choice.

Step 1: Recognize Your True Nature & Power

We are all co-creating our lives. Embracing this truth involves making a choice about how you want to experience life. It means becoming more conscious about where you focus your energy and recognizing that your thoughts, feelings, and actions impact every aspect of your existence. What you focus on, you will experience more of — this is your creative power.

Activate your full potential by expanding your awareness and honing your intuitive senses. Learn to distinguish between the chatter of the protective ego and the calm wisdom of your superconscious. Like a muscle, your intuitive capacity strengthens with use. Carve out moments for stillness and quiet in your daily routine; dedicate regular time to practices that quieten your overactive, analytical mind.

Raise your vibration by tuning into the energy of gratitude and love which resonate at high frequencies. Open your heart and tap into the wisdom you find there.

Affirm to yourself:

"I accept that my inner voice will always guide me correctly."

When seeking guidance, pose powerful, open-ended questions that inspire creativity and evoke possibilities rather than asking from a place of fear or scarcity.

Start where you are. Just a few minutes each day can open you up to living more intuitively and expansively.

Step 2: Make Authentic Choices

To make authentic choices, you need to get really honest about what you truly desire for your life, free from external expectations or ingrained conditioning.

It can be tricky to dismantle what you cannot see. Your conditioning is an integral part of you, shaping your thoughts, beliefs, and your whole identity.

The way to begin this process is to question every assumption you hold and be open-minded. Tune inward, not just to your rational mind but also to your heart's deepest desires.

Interestingly, the word 'desire' originates from the Latin phrase "de sidere" meaning "from the stars." True desires — the ones that inspire us to pursue our dreams and achieve true fulfillment — arise from our higher awareness, which is intricately connected to the cosmos.

To access these desires:

- Get into an expansive state where your heart feels open by focusing on feelings of love or gratitude.

- Notice the feeling of expansion versus contraction.

- Ask yourself, "What do I truly desire?"

- Listen to the answer without imposing limits.

Many of us hesitate to explore our desires fully. We've been conditioned by a predominantly masculine, linear approach to creation where each step is logically laid out. Because of this, if we don't immediately know how to do something, we assume we lack the power to create it.

This is a falsehood. A lack of know-how is not the same as a lack of ability. We do well to remember that all of life is inherently creative and is constantly evolving, including ourselves. Realizing your desires often means courageously taking a first step, embracing change, learning new things, and adapting — this is a natural part of life.

I believe that our desires are not only achievable but are also important and unique expressions of the energy that connects us all.

So, take some quiet time to deeply consider:

"What do I want to create or change in my life?"
"What does my heart yearn for?"
"What am I feeling called to do?"

Close your eyes, open your heart, and smile! As you breathe in, feel life-giving energy filling you up. Open yourself up to embrace new possibilities. Allow yourself to dream and visualize what you would love. Every moment is an opportunity to acknowledge your truth and embrace transformation; to break barriers and ultimately realize your true potential.

Step 3: Break Through Your Limitations

It's likely that once you've acknowledged your true desires, as soon as you step out of your expanded vision and your energy begins to contract, you will immediately feel doubt.

Your logic will intervene and attempt to make sense of it all. Despite its remarkable problem-solving abilities, your conscious mind is limited compared with your expansive superconscious awareness. It tends to fear what it cannot understand.

Remember, energy is malleable and can change instantly. It's essential to accept that this inner conflict is normal. Just take a moment to note what you're feeling. Is it self-doubt, or perhaps fear of others' opinions?

These reactions are your body's way of keeping you safe and preventing you from taking risks. They are natural responses to change. Becoming aware of these reactions is crucial for breaking through internal barriers, like fear and self-doubt, and external ones, such as societal expectations or professional obstacles.

A simple yet powerful method to uncover some of your inner-conflict involves a quick reflective exercise:

Bring one of your potent desires to mind, and then complete the following sentence out loud, responding immediately with whatever comes to you:

"I'd love (insert your desire), but —————————————"

Finish the sentence quickly without overthinking. Your response might be something like "It's silly," "It's too difficult," or "I don't know how."

Maybe you'll find yourself saying, "I don't know why, but I just keep putting it off."

All these responses provide valuable insights, and this inner conflict is perfectly natural.

You might also recognize behavioural patterns such as never quite finding the time for a project you're passionate about because you're always too busy.

Many of my clients are remarkable women — creatives, coaches, and leaders — who are blazing new trails in their businesses and personal projects.

They are the change-makers our world needs in these times of profound transformation. Yet, their path isn't a familiar one; it demands doing and showing up differently, free from the conditioning of the past. We've been fed narratives about what's possible and what success should look like, molded, "fit for purpose" for traditional roles, and steeped in the deep-rooted norms of patriarchy.

Because of this, I notice ingrained patterns that show up. We frequently grapple with self-doubt, so we need to instil confidence and reinforce our sense of self-worth and value. Often, we need to overcome a fear of visibility so we can express ourselves and get our work out in a way that feels authentic and safe. Additionally, many of us are conditioned by a scarcity mindset, leading to blocks related to abundance and money. So, we need to expand our capacity to receive as well as hold wealth.

Internal resistance can stem from unconscious beliefs, stored emotions, deeply buried memories, and ancestral imprints. Without deeper exploration, pinpointing its exact cause can be challenging. But overcoming these barriers is crucial to creating what you want with ease, joy, and flow.

There are numerous ways to do this including consciously creating new thoughts and emotional patterns by reprogramming subconscious behaviours. One of the most effective methods I've developed is my Intuitive Alignment Method™. This proprietary process aligns your thoughts, feelings, and actions with the help of your superconscious awareness. By synchronizing every aspect of your consciousness—conscious, unconscious, and superconscious — you can eliminate internal conflicts and resistance. Many clients report that when they use this method the resistance they once experienced seems to dissolve.

This alignment opens the path for unhindered and inspired action. When you're aligned, you're not merely functioning; you're thriving as a powerful creator, fully activated and optimized to manifest your desires and visions.

Step 4: Take Aligned Action

Every creation in the physical world begins as an idea — an invisible form of energy that transforms into physical reality. To manifest your desires in this three-dimensional world requires both intention and action.

The final step in the journey to limitless living is to take decisive, aligned action toward your desires so you're actively creating a life you love.

Take small steps every day. Small shifts lead to big changes over time. And because everything is energy, when you're aligned and in flow, things can change very quickly.

Step 5: Create an Energetic Impact

Unlocking your limitless potential as a creative being and living a life filled with purpose not only brings a sense of fulfilment but also empowers you to make a profound impact, to break through barriers, and make a difference.

I'm sure you can recall a joyful moment when you created something meaningful. Perhaps there was a time when you felt as if you were "on a roll," immersed in a flow that seemed almost magical. You might have also sensed the vibrant energy of those who are living wholeheartedly with power and purpose. This isn't just your imagination; the energy is real. Research in neuro-cardiology has shown just how powerful a state of coherence between the heart and brain can be, as well as how profoundly our energetic field (especially the electromagnetic field of the heart) can influence those around us.

Energetic alignment is potent. Its effects extend far beyond the individual, rippling out to influence the world in unexpected ways. When you live in such a flow, synchronicities begin to appear almost like magic.

This is how you can experience life in a whole new way — a way that is filled with new possibilities and boundless creativity.

* * *

So, if you feel the call to more in your life; if you're ready to shatter the barriers holding you back, and if you're feeling the pull to make an impact in your own way, don't hesitate any longer.

I invite you to nurture your deepest, heartfelt desires and allow your imagination to run wild. Listen to your intuitive callings because you are equipped with everything you need to break through your limitations and achieve your desires.

Each of us is alive during these transformative times for a reason and we have a unique contribution to make. This journey of empowerment doesn't just help us realize our own potential; it also sets the stage for a transformative impact on the world around us. Right now, the world needs feminine qualities, healing gifts, and leadership more than ever — a sentiment shared by the Dalai Lama during the 2010 Vancouver

Peace Summit when he said, "The world will be saved by the Western woman."

As we channel our collective strengths and shed our limitations, we undergo our own evolution and pave the way for a world full of creativity, love, and collaboration.

This is the path I envision for you. Together, let us move forward as women who do more than dream of change — we create it every day, leaving lasting legacies with our voices, visions, and contributions.

Donna Palamar

4 Winds of Change LLC
Pause/Retreat Specialist

https://www.facebook.com/search/top?q=therunawayretreat
https://therunawayretreat.com/

As an international educator, author, speaker and empowerment coach, Donna Palamar helps woman discover their power, honor themselves and recreate who they are so they can live fully. She believes in transformative experiences such as Runaway Retreats, Pause Events and Experiential Subscription Boxes. These allow opportunities to restore & rejuvenate and surpass all that life brings your way. Donna holds a Masters Degree in Educational Leadership from Seton Hall University. She cherishes the journey of life, learning and the pursuit of dark chocolate with women all over the world. She is a modern-day Change Agent who celebrates the magic, mystery and mayhem of life. Donna takes bold action to educate, celebrate and collaborate with women in all phases of life around the globe to heal, grow and "BE the best versions of Yourself possible!"

PAUSE, PAMPER & PROSPER

By Donna Palamar

Do you ever wish that you could just run away from all the chaotic pressures and responsibilities of daily life?

Just for a few days at least?

The tension keeps building up. It seems unbearable and you wonder which end is up. Yet, you keep thinking, "If I could just push through, things will calm down, and I'll get a break."

You multitask like a pro and keep all those plates spinning. You think, "I'll finish this project and then things will be easier for a while, and I'll catch my breath." Surely, sooner or later, it will all even out.

You rush around to meet deadlines, being pushed and pulled in all different directions, thinking you're making everyone happy, keeping them on track, making them look good, keeping everything looking like it's running smoothly.

What about YOU? What do YOU need? What price are your life and health paying as day after day goes by and you're STILL on that hamster wheel? What is your tired, overworked self telling YOU that you need? When do YOU get time for YOU? Do you dare be so selfish as to feel or think that you could take the time to regroup and hit the reset button on everything?

It seems reasonable to be all caught up in the minutia and more than necessary as you rationalize it because you know how important it is to you and others. You justify it by saying that someday, one day, you'll have time for yourself, especially since you put so much time and effort into all these areas of your life. You'll get that much-needed and deserved break.

I thought so too but never made the time for myself, and because of that, I found myself exhausted, empty, and bankrupt in every sense of the word. At that point, no amount of tears could resolve my situation, no amount of wishing could take me back in time to make better decisions, and no amount of yearning could fix all the broken pieces. If only I just took a break, this could have all been avoided. I didn't listen to the warning signs, thinking I could do it all. It was draining the very life out of me. I pretended not to see the red flags when my sleep was affected, and no amount of it ever seemed enough. I was waking up tired and wasn't feeling rested. I went from task to task with urgency, and the days blurred into months. I had nothing to show for it except bags under my eyes and a flabby middle from all the snacking and eating on the go. Stress was causing my health and productivity to decline.

By this time, I needed to find a way to put myself back into the equation of a busy life and be able to not only survive it but also enjoy it and have it be manageable. But how? I was burnt out, resentful, and overwhelmed. How do I get out of this tangle? Is there a way to escape all of this? What kind of legacy can I possibly leave behind?

When you're down, there's only one way to go, and that's back up. By being honest with myself, assessing my situation, taking a good look at reality, and realizing that I needed to reach out for help, I allowed myself the experience of getting what I really needed. A time-out! Here's what I've found that has made all the difference.

1) **CHANGE YOUR ENVIRONMENT**. Get out of Dodge for a while and away from all the who's and what's that are tiring you out. You'll find a new perspective on life once you're away from the everyday routine. You won't be running away forever, just a few days. You'll be back before you know it! Being in the space of other women allows us to learn and grow in ways that we can't or won't do on our

own. We build trust and allow ourselves to receive guidance, friendship, and hope. We create bonds and are open to the possibility of keeping in touch and finding camaraderie in our quests to get the most out of life. Gather some girlfriends or join us on our next adventure and create some new memories as you use or rack up those frequent flyer miles. Linktr.ee/donnapalamar

2) **DON'T GO AT IT ALONE**. It's great to take a time-out, but you don't need to be isolated or excluded from others. There are plenty of like-minded women who understand your plight and appreciate sharing enriching experiences while knowing that they are not alone in their feelings and situations either. Women are nurturers by nature. It's one of our greatest gifts. We can hold space for one another to speak our truth and not be judged as we find the acknowledgment that we so desperately need. We hear and see ourselves in others, and this gives us a chance to look in that mirror and honor ourselves for what we have done. We are also able to look at the parts of us that could use some love, kindness, forgiveness, slack, encouragement, grace, and perhaps tweaking. Be seen. Be heard. Be understood. Don't have time or the budget right now to get away completely? Join us online for one of our Pajama Parties for a few hours. Women from all over the globe connect and enjoy some pampering, fun, conversations, and activities. Linktr.ee/donnapalamar

3) **TRY SOMETHING DIFFERENT**. Different perspectives and experiences can be beneficial and allow you the nurturing and revitalization that you so crave and need. Taking time for yourself is worthwhile and crucial in this day and age of uncertainty and tension. Are you open to treating yourself to a monthly Pause, Pamper & Prosper subscription box to enjoy in the comfort of your own home? Each month we have a different pamper box available to enjoy. Check it out Linktr.ee/donnapalamar

What I found is that it IS possible to take some time away, to replenish myself, whether it's online in the comfort of my own home for a few hours or some time away for a few days. There's always a way. We have to fill our own cups first before we can pour into others.

What I felt was deep gratitude for saying yes to this radical self-care that saved my life. I stopped the hamster wheel if only for a while to be able to take care of my own needs and sanity in this crazy, busy world. What I learned is that it's necessary to use my own "oxygen mask" first. Once I reset myself, I feel rejuvenated and am ready to take on the world again in a healthier, happier way.

What I know is that what I need is important and essential. My needs matter. I don't need anyone's permission, and I don't have to apologize for wanting to enjoy life.

What I share is an invitation. An invitation to help yourself before you lose yourself. Before it's too late. Before you burn out, again.

Just in case you're still thinking that you can't take time off because you think that you need someone's permission, let me ask you why you don't have your own (permission, that is).

Who said you couldn't have it? Shouldn't have it? Can't have it? Why? Do you really need it from someone else?

In case you don't know where to find it, I'm here to give it to you. Right here, right now. Are you ready? Here it comes....

_____ IS HEREBY GRANTED FULL PERMISSION TO TAKE A MUCH-NEEDED BREAK, REST, TIME AWAY, AND/OR TIME TO BE THE FULL AND COMPLETE WOMAN THAT SHE IS.

I put it in writing. In case you missed any of that, doubt any of that, or think you can't remember any of that, you can get your very own copy of the full permission slip and statement at www.Linktr.ee/

donnapalamar You can print it, frame it, laminate it, fold it and keep it in your purse, tape it to the bathroom mirror...whatever you'd like. It's yours. Your very own permission slip. Just for you.

The one thing I do suggest is that you use and enjoy it! In the meantime, try these permission activities on for size...

- Find a few minutes to get still and take a few deep breaths, a quick five-minute time-out. If you need more...
- Listen to a 10-minute meditation and relax your body and mind. You'll feel more able to get on with your day. If you need even more...
- Go take a walk to clear your head and get some fresh air. The movement can be invigorating, and you can come back and complete your tasks. If you still need more...
- Have a pajama day and chill out. No drama, no deadlines, nothing but taking time to regroup and reenergize. You can do this on your own, with some guidance from my specialized kits, or even by joining one of my online international pajama parties. Linktr.ee/donnapalamar And if you need even more than that.....
- Find out what awesome retreat I have coming up. Book your spot, whether it's for a week or a weekend, online or in-person, and come join me for some much-needed connection to rejuvenate yourself so you can return home and enjoy life like never before. Linktr.ee/donnapalamar

The choice is yours. You can take the chance of keeping the pace at which you're going and risking total frustration, depletion, and staying worn out, or say yes to your health, sanity, and self-care to take a break for a while and exhale. You'll be so glad you did. I look forward to seeing you soon. It's time to pause and pamper yourself so you can prosper!

Dr. Shellie Hipsky

Inspiring Lives International & The Global Sisterhood
CEO & Exec. Director

https://www.linkedin.com/in/shelliehipsky/
https://www.facebook.com/shellie.hipsky
https://www.instagram.com/dr.shellie/
https://www.globalsisterhoodonline.org/
https://inspiringlivesinternational.com/

Dr. Shellie Hipsky is a notable figure, holding leadership positions in various organizations such as CEO of Inspiring Lives International and Executive Director of Global Sisterhood. As editor-in-chief of Inspiring Lives Magazine, she showcases her expertise in education, holding an Ed.D in Educational Leadership from Duquesne University. Her achievements include the Presidential Lifetime Achievement Award and titles like "Empowered Woman". Dr. Hipsky's literary works, including the Common Threads trilogy and bestsellers like "Ball Gowns to Yoga Pants" and "Mom Magic Mompreneur," reflect her profound impact. With a background in academia and special education, she has excelled as a professor, special education teacher, and Assistant Principal. Dr. Hipsky's influence extends to media, where she hosts radio and TV shows and graces numerous magazine covers. Through her Global

Sisterhood initiative, she supports women globally, addressing critical issues. Currently, she empowers women through her EmpowerU Master Class and VIP coaching, solidifying her position as the world's leading global empowerment coach.

WHATEVER IT TAKES WITH THE GLOBAL SISTERHOOD!

By Dr. Shellie Hipsky

As I had too many times before, in one smooth motion my 13-year-old self made a smacking sound on the roof of my mouth, rolled my eyes, shrugged my shoulders in a way that would tick off any parent, and sighed a word that I knew would make my father cringe … "Whatever!"

My frustrated father stopped everything and exasperatedly bellowed, "You are never to say that word again! You are grounded, young lady!" My teenage angst and rebellious attitude had reached a boiling point with my father. This great man had reached his limit after working as a medical doctor all day and hearing about my low grades. He found out I had been getting into some trouble with my social group of girls at middle school. I was putting my social connections above my education as I made the girl's bathroom a place where I'd meet with my friends to conduct what I called "therapy sessions," and I had a permanent seat in Saturday detention as if I was in the 80s movie The Breakfast Club. Dubbed the "social butterfly" by my teachers, I acted like it was my duty to support those in need, even though back then it was mostly just teenage drama.

Fast forwarding to the last decade, I now use the word "Whatever" quite often when referring to my Global Sisters and our 501(c)(3) nonprofit that helps women and children in need around the world. Nowadays, saying the word doesn't include an eye roll or an obnoxious vibe. "Whatever…" is almost always my initial response to the inquiry. "What does the Global Sisterhood do to help women and children around the world?" The answer is now stated with a smile as I exclaim, "Whatever it takes!"

After I volunteered extensively, grew up, and learned that I have a servant-leader heart, I knew I wanted to help people through my natural abilities to connect and teach, and my career in educational leadership blossomed. I was a special education teacher, helping those who learned differently, and went on to be an assistant principal at a school for emotional and behavioral needs. Then, I had a tenured teaching position at the undergraduate to PhD level with future teachers and leaders. I went from writing books to having the television show on NBC, Inspiring Lives with Dr. Shellie. When I went through a divorce with three and five-year-old children, the format switched to the Empowering Women Radio show that was listened to on 120+ stations around the world.

Through the power of technology, in a male-dominated society in rural Pakistan, a woman with a master's degree who was doing work with women in need, Hena Gul listened to my Empowering Women Radio program. She was inspired by my interview with Haseena Patel from South Africa and the story about how I had been Skyping in to work with the teenage girls outside of Johannesburg in their Empowerment Circles. Hena approached me with her needs for her own nonprofit and for her story to be told on my platform. It was Hena who named our organization the "Global Sisterhood" after she witnessed the bonds, connections, and shared resources with like-minded women globally. Hena stated, "Because of the Global Sisterhood, I do not feel alone anymore. Through Dr. Shellie Hipsky and Empowering Women Radio, I have met some of the greatest women in the world."

For over a decade, we have served the needs of countless women through our charity partnerships. Collaboration with these impactful nonprofit charitable organizations serves as vehicles for creating positive change and supporting women and girls around the world. We also take requests for #PopUpGiving projects when women are in desperate need of immediate resources. Women through our local, national, and international reach have been served and supported through trying times such as domestic violence, homelessness, addiction/recovery, human trafficking, disabilities and disease, water and food insecurity, trauma/grief/mental health needs, and many more life obstacles and traumas that can seem insurmountable. Yet, with a Global Sisterhood, you aren't alone. How do we do it? We support, advocate, mentor, educate, fundraise, network, and uplift with respect. We create positive change by doing "Whatever it takes!"

The Power of Sisterhood

"When you are kind to others - It not only changes you – it changes the entire community, country, and through the Global Sisterhood it transforms the World."
—Dr. Meena "Didi" Singh Khadka,
Women's Education and Skills Village-to-Village in Nepal

The Global Sisterhood is a supportive network of women united in the pursuit of common goals and aspirations. We empower women to amplify their voices, advocate for their rights, and uplift one another. By working together through solidarity, empathy, and mutual support, we foster a sense of belonging and empowerment among women from diverse backgrounds and cultures. One of these empowering examples of the power of sisterhood can be found in a former Harvard Researcher Dr. Meena Didi who is teaching in the foothills of Mount Everest in Nepal.

The Meena Didi Women's Literacy Class goes village-to-village providing training opportunities, income generation, and promoting a spirit of volunteerism so that women are encouraged to support each other to fulfill their potential. I have been mentoring Dr. Meena in multiple ways prior to funding such as when I provided a scholarship for Dr. Meena to learn through my EmpowerU Master Class curriculum. Through this connection, I was able to identify a very real need for funding to support Dr. Meena's valiant efforts to change the illiteracy rates in Nepal so that women could thrive. When the Global Sisterhood obtained its first foundation grant, it sent funds directly to Dr. Meena in Nepal to help meet these three specific needs:

1. A computer was purchased for teaching, learning, and creating marketing materials so that the school could acquire other funding in the future to remain sustainable.

2. Teacher training was updated with current education systems that encourage individuals to respect each other, share each other's experiences, and provide a quality education. They conduct leadership workshops, skills training, and literacy courses while providing a platform for all to share their own experiences. Dr. Meena Didi continues to teach women how to read and write by the tens of thousands.

3. The Global Sisterhood Tea House is a gathering place for women to learn to read, have a cup of tea, and have children read to by their parents or grandparents. In the evenings, they host classes on Literacy and Awareness. Also, it is an entrepreneurial venture for a single mom to start her own business independently.

With the support of The Global Sisterhood, lives are being transformed. The Global Sisterhood even heeded the call of desperation and raised the money for a well system in Nepal when they needed clean water because the women's and girls' lives were endangered, walking up to five hours to fetch the water.

As Dr. Meena Didi explained, "I came into contact with Dr. Shellie Hipsky who was very kind. Through her and The Global Sisterhood,

I learned many new tips for running my 'Meena Didi: Women's Literacy Class' Village-to-Village. Plus, it was a Godsend when we received the funding from The Global Sisterhood to be able to support our literacy Global Sisterhood and empowering education."

Supporting Charity Partnerships for Incredible Impact

"I've been part of the Global Sisterhood since its beginning and the richest lessons I've learned are the common threads we women share throughout the world. We all long for a better life… for ourselves, for our families, for our neighbors, and we are passionate about helping those whom we serve!"
—Sally Power, Founder/Executive Director of
Treasure House Fashions

Our charity partnerships in the states and abroad mobilize resources, expertise, and networks to address pressing social issues affecting women and girls. There are numerous benefits of collaborative approaches to philanthropy including increased efficiency, scalability, and sustainability of interventions. We have showcased many successful examples of charity partnerships that have made a tangible difference in the lives of women and communities both locally and globally. One prime example of a charity partnership and woman leadership in the Global Sisterhood is Sally Power of Treasure House Fashion.

In 2000, Sally Power was navigating a divorce and "inherited" over $200,000 worth of debt. In an attempt to stabilize her personal finances and provide for her three children, Power secured a small women's resale shop to augment her teaching income. The women who frequented this new venture were in similar or worse financial situations, and Power began to literally "give away the store." An astute business friend encouraged Power to become a nonprofit and walked her through the process. Since then, the organization has grown tremendously. Clothing, however, is the means, not the mission. The heart of the Treasure House Fashions (THF) nonprofit is to affirm the worth of women on challenging journeys - clothing is simply the convenient medium! THF has given away millions of dollars' worth of clothing.

I was introduced to Sally Power by the now Director of Governance for the Executive Board of The Global Sisterhood Alice Beckett-Rumberger. I hosted Sally on the TV show Inspiring Lives with Dr. Shellie and I was blown away by Sally's story and her incredible heart for helping women in need. We became dear friends following that show. Sally was then featured on my Empowering Women Radio, and her story was in my international bestselling trilogy *Common Threads*.

I love joining Sally as a "shopper" with the ladies in need of some pampering. Many of The Global Sisterhood have done this over the years, and we like to help the ladies who don't have the funds to get a new outfit to pick out the perfect one so that they feel amazing.

One of the most awesome Global Sisterhood memories was when we organized a Mommy Makeover at the local home for homeless single moms. Haircuts were provided, and Sally Power's Treasure House Fashions dressed the ladies from head to toe. The women were so appreciative, especially when they had professional photographs taken with their children. It was such a blessing for them to see themselves in a positive light. That's what Treasure House Fashions does: it shows women that they are indeed treasures.

During the Covid-19 Global Pandemic, Sally Power was awarded the 2020 Empowering Women in Philanthropy Award at a virtual awards show. She is a true winner for the incredible grace she has shown to the women in need for many years. Sally Powers has been an active part of the Global Sisterhood in multiple ways. Sally spoke passionately during the Survivors to Thrivers Fashions Show as the domestic violence survivors walked the runway in gowns procured from Treasure House Fashions and designers such as Eva Dixon who has spearheaded the Global Sisterhood Sewing S.E.E.D.S. Sisters in Extraordinary Entrepreneurship Development Services which has leaders and programs in India to Africa. Treasure House Fashions is one of many examples of a charity partnership that has stood the test of time. This benefits over 60 charities ranging from women coming out of domestic violence shelters to women with mental health needs to regain their self-esteem.

Promoting Women's Health, Safety, and Well-being

"The Global Sisterhood has connected my organization to hundreds of international resources. We were honored to have been the very first recipient of The Global Sisterhood's Charity Partnership contribution funds, which helped send multiple survivors of domestic violence to our life-changing Bootcamp Retreat!"
—Dawn Diaz, Founder and CEO of Milagros Day Worldwide

In the Global Sisterhood, women's empowerment includes access to healthcare, support for those experiencing disabilities and disease, and mental health support. Some of our charity partnerships and women leaders support funding and delivering essential health services, education, and resources to improve women's health outcomes. There are important initiatives that address gender-based violence, maternal mortality, and other health disparities through collaborative efforts between NGOs and community-based organizations. One organization that should be noted is an important part of the Global Sisterhood, and that is Milagros Day Worldwide.

The mission of Milagros Day Worldwide is to empower survivors of domestic violence and childhood trauma with healing leadership coaching, mentorship, and a commitment to turning abuse into success. Dawn Diaz's Milagros Day Worldwide has been a focus of support and advocacy for years from the Global Sisterhood and our publication *Inspiring Lives Magazine*. It all began when Dawn Diaz was a featured guest on my TV show, Inspiring Lives with Dr. Shellie. She told the story of two generations of domestic violence and how she created this international organization to help women be more than survivors but to live their life purpose and dreams as well.

Dawn was able to tell her amazing story at The Global Gala and Mastermind (where women come from around the world to help inspire and empower each other) during the Inspiring Lives Talks. Dawn and I joined missions and supported each other through the Global Sisterhood. I had the opportunity to keynote at the Milagros Day Worldwide Mother's Day Walk across the Brooklyn Bridge, and the Global Sisterhood donated funds directly to support 25 women being able to attend the MDW Boot Camp Retreat to recover and heal their hearts after abuse.

Milagros Day Worldwide was featured in *Inspiring Lives Magazine,* and it focused on making women survivors feel beautiful and shine. Also, the striking images of the survivors were featured in a gallery at the Inspiring Lives Magazine Launch Party.

While I keynoted at the Milagros Day Worldwide Summit during Covid-19, I became very concerned that women were being quarantined with their captors and needed therapeutic interventions online. When Rev. Nettie Jorinda Bullitt came forward with funds, I immediately suggested that Milagros Day Worldwide should be the Charity Partnership to receive money for domestic abuse survivors in need. This collaboration continues to help domestic abuse survivors rise while supporting health, wellness, and trauma support for women in need. The Global Sisterhood shares Dawn Diaz's belief that everyone has something in their past that they are working through and we shouldn't have to face it all alone.

Advancing Economic Empowerment

"The Global Sisterhood has inspired us to do for other women in our community and gives us the drive to give back through our non-profits. The Global Sisterhood has enabled us to connect with other amazing women, to network with trailblazers in business and philanthropy, and to give back to our community."
—Kemi Kanani, Director of KVDPA & ARUMAS (African Rural Management School) College for Entrepreneurship in Tanzania

There are direct links between women's economic empowerment, poverty alleviation, and sustainable development. The Global Sisterhood's charity partnerships support women entrepreneurs, artisans, and small business owners through access to training, financing, and market opportunities. There must be investment in women's education, skills development, and leadership in order to unlock their full economic potential and promote inclusive growth. Our school for entrepreneurship in Tanzania is a shining example of the power of education on women.

Karagwe Vijana Development and Poverty Alleviation (KVDPA) believes that, if you empower women and support ladies you change the whole community. KVDPA is one of the many sponsored projects of the Global Sisterhood. Its main target is the most vulnerable women and youth in rural areas in Africa. In this community, local women are mainly the breadwinners in the family. They farm, collect firewood to sell, and provide food for the households' consumption, and they are responsible for paying school fees and tuition fees for their children on top of that. Feasibly supporting the household without including women is not sustainable in averting poverty. They must be included, and this is where the Global Sisterhood has stepped up to help. KVDPA, with the support of the Global Sisterhood, empowers women by promoting self-employment as well as providing vocational training aid in the rural area of Karagwe through women and youth groups.

This collaboration began over ten years ago when I interviewed Kemi for Empowering Women Radio for my internationally bestselling book trilogy *Common Threads*. At that time, I also interviewed Ruby Dawn Surgest, a fashion designer from Pittsburgh, and a beautiful connection was formed between the budding, sewing entrepreneurs in Tanzania and the Pittsburgh fashion Fair Trade retail store Ujamma Collective. Soon thereafter Ruby Dawn, a member of the Global Sisterhood, went to visit the ladies in Tanzania and taught them sewing skills. I wore a colorful design from Tanzania on stage and Jas Booth from Final Salute (an organization that helps veterans who are homeless) modeled designs at the Global Gala and Mastermind Fashion Show.

We were able to continue to support the women and children of Tanzania who have created an entrepreneurship program. We have sent sewing machines and computers via our Global Ambassador to help support the growth of women's businesses. With our support, they created school uniforms, reusable sanitary napkins, and a clothing line that is sold near our headquarters in Pittsburgh, PA as well as in other places around the world. They now have an extensive curriculum including but not limited to hospitality, culinary arts, and business courses. It is through education, entrepreneurial training, resources, and networking that we are able to help these women support not only themselves but their families and communities.

As Kemi elaborated, "We are thankful to The Global Sisterhood and Dr. Shellie Hipsky, for supporting the construction and creation of our entrepreneurial college ARUMAS. They greatly contributed to empowering rural women in Africa to learn about business." Without education in the rural area that the college is in, young women can be subjected to being child brides or "hawking" which means begging on the streets. It is through teaching the women and girls how to create income and even their own sustainable businesses that they become economically empowered in their homes and communities.

Empowering Through Education and Leadership

"The Global Sisterhood embodies the true meaning of community and family. Through Dr. Shellie Hipsky's Global Sisterhood, we've had the honor of knowing and co-creating with powerhouse women worldwide; plus, they empowered us financially."
—Haseena Patel,
Co-Founder of LNGB School of Leadership in South Africa

There is a transformative power in education whereby women and girls can be empowered to realize and bring to fruition their dreams and aspirations. We support charity partnerships that support girls' education, literacy programs, and leadership development initiatives to break down barriers and expand opportunities for women's advancement. There are ripple effects of investing in girls' education on families, communities, and societies as a whole. Since I was an education professor, we have worked with multiple charity partnerships that provide educational services ranging from the Autism Caring Center to the Homeless Children's Education Fund. However, I'd like to explain what our Charity Partner LNGB School for Leadership in South Africa does to empower young ladies.

Leave No Girl Behind International (LNGB) is a non-profit girls' empowerment organization founded in 2013 and based in South Africa, dedicated to empowering girls and young women around the world to find, respect, and embrace their voices, talents, and unique potential through leadership. The organization was founded by activists and sisters Haseena and Shameema Patel.

The organization works to reach girls before they become statistics. The focus of LNGB International is to develop girls through leadership training, thus helping to break the cycle of teen pregnancy, HIV, self-harm, and abuse in all its forms, as well as prevent child trafficking, child marriage, female genital mutilation, and other human rights violations.

Millions of girls worldwide, both in developing and developed countries, lack the resources to explore their strengths and capabilities and develop their potential. Often, the adults in their lives also lack the resources to help them.

Their mission is to provide the environment, opportunity, and tools for every girl who uses LNGB resources and programs, to find her voice, expand her world, explore her abilities and talents, contribute to her community, and develop the skills needed to be independent, goal-oriented, and financially stable as an adult.

I have been mentoring and working with the girls in the academies in South Africa in Haseena's Empowerment Circles for years. It was actually the Empowering Women Radio show in which Haseena Patel was listened to by Hena Gul in Pakistan which was mentioned at the beginning of this chapter. Haseena stated this regarding our charity partnership: "The Global Sisterhood has provided opportunities for our girls to learn from strong, successful women, including Dr. Shellie Hipsky herself! These experiences have been invaluable for our girls. The support from The Global Sisterhood has made it possible for us at LNGB International to touch the lives of more girls and bring them opportunities they would not otherwise have had! For this, we are deeply grateful."

It's been wonderful that Haseena Patel, her sister, and her mother have come all the way from Africa to the States to link arms with the Global Sisterhood more than once. They flew in from South Africa to the States to present a powerful Inspiring Lives Talk at the Global Gala and Mastermind in Pittsburgh, PA. In 2019, Haseena gathered The Global Sisterhood together for the first Sheroes Event in New Jersey. The Next Generation presented a check to Haseena to cover the beginning of the LNGB Leadership School which has had a profound effect on the quality of life and trajectory of the hopes, dreams, and leadership skills of the teenage girls in South Africa. Support for the LNGB Leadership School is ongoing and as an alumni of the school recently said, "Thank you to the sponsors from The Global Sisterhood because the LNGB Leadership School changed my life. And when I am older, I want to give back to LNGB as well because I am living proof that it works!" Education and leadership will always be important to the Global Sisterhood.

So, what does it take to have an impactful Global Sisterhood? Women through The Global Sisterhood and charity partnerships respect the importance of collaboration, solidarity, and collective action in driving positive change and building a more equitable and inclusive world for women and girls everywhere. We do all that by doing, "Whatever it takes!" As our Global Ambassador Rev. Nettie Jorinda Bullitt who will be joining me with our charity partners in Africa during our Global Sisterhood Giveback Tour this summer explained, "The Global Sisterhood does whatever it takes to support our sisters around the world when we channel our energy and experiences as women committed to supporting sisterhood endeavors!"

Iman Kamel

Founder and CEO of The Holographic Being H.O.P.E

https://www.linkedin.com/in/iman-kamel-1a720425/
https://www.holographicbeing.com
https://www.holographicbeing.com/work-with-me
https://www.youtube.com/@holographicbeing

Iman Kamel, founder and CEO of The Holographic Being H.O.P.E, is a multidimensional force of nature driving exceptional growth. A champion for personal empowerment and global change, she empowers visionary leaders and entrepreneurs to shatter limitations and unleash their hidden potential. An award-winning filmmaker ("Nomad's Home" and Egyptian Jeanne d'Arc), intuitive mentor, and captivating keynote speaker, she ignites audiences with her infectious energy, playful spirit, and razor-sharp insight. Her global perspective, honed at the Fletcher School of Law and Diplomacy, earned her recognition as a World Economic Forum "Iconic Woman Creating a Better World for All." A celestial encounter and profound initiation with Egyptian Neteru at the Dendera Temple sparked her unique approach, integrating Visionary Akashic Records readings to guide thousands of clients towards unparalleled clarity, power, and expansive unfolding.

SEKHMET'S FIRE: EMBODY YOUR VISION

By Iman Kamel

"The wound is the place where the Light enters you."
—Rumi

A Pilgrimage to Remember

Under Hathor's gaze, the sun's first rays pierce the morning mist, gilding the towering columns of Dendera Temple. Each hieroglyph, a riddle etched in sun-warmed stone, beckons me closer. The scent of jasmine incense mingles with the dry whisper of desert sand, a symphony of scents both familiar and otherworldly. My chest tightens with a yearning that transcends the accolades of my career, a world traveled. It's a hollow ache, a thirst for something deeper that glitters beneath the surface of this sacred space.

The temple's embrace is both comforting and unsettling. Its massive columns dwarf me, their shadows dancing in the radiant light, revealing a path that spirals downward. Each step into the cool, damp air feels like a descent into a forgotten tomb—a tomb within my own soul. The Osirian Temple, steeped in the shadows of the underworld, becomes a cradle for my unspoken longings. The sun, a relentless blaze on the parched lake bed, seems to mirror the fiery hunger that burns within.

Emerging from the depths, I ascend towards Hathor's open-air chapel, each step lighter than the last. A melody of birdsong greets me, a counterpoint to the hushed whispers of the underworld. A gentle breeze, fragrant with desert blooms, brushes against my face, a promise of renewal. In this sunlit space, hope flickers, a tiny flame against the vast canvas of my inner landscape.

Encounter Isis

And then, it happens. The air itself shifts, shimmering like sunlight through gossamer wings. A profound tenderness envelops me, a boundless, maternal strength that washes over me like a warm, life-giving embrace. It feels like the warmth of a mother's love, the whispered reassurance of an incantation.

A gentle hum resonates deep within my chest, stirring a forgotten melody within my soul. This is the essence of Isis, queen of the heavens and protector of women and children. Her power courses through me in measured pulses, awakening hidden reserves of courage and resilience. Images flash through my mind: Isis gathering the scattered pieces of her murdered brother and husband Osiris, her unwavering determination echoing my own resolve to overcome adversity. Her whispers, carried on beams of sunlight, fill me with a profound knowing: Joy will be my wellspring, a reservoir of strength to carry me through challenges yet unseen. It's a promise etched deep within me, a truth as timeless as the stones beneath my feet.

A Turning Point

The echo of my earlier initiations lingers, a reminder of the metamorphosis I yearn for. Can I truly embody the boundless potential I sense within? This question, born amidst Karnak's shadowed Hypostyle Hall, fuels my continued journey. My path leads me back into the embrace of the ancient. During my sabbatical in Luxor, I wander the remaining hallways of Karnak, my fingertips tracing the stories etched into the stone.

Two Years Prior: Sekhmet's Encounter

A sanctuary dedicated to Sekhmet, the lion-headed goddess of fierce power, calls me forth. Entering her space is a step into another realm.

The small chamber plunges into near darkness, the sudden shaft of light illuminating her statue even more startling. The very air crackles with an energy that sends shivers down my spine. The stillness is broken only by the echo of my footsteps on the ancient stone. A hot desert wind seems to have found its way into the sheltered space, carrying the distinct scent of sun-baked earth after a rain – a reminder of her dual nature, destruction giving way to creation.

Standing beneath her watchful gaze, her sun disk gleaming, I feel the full force of her unwavering strength. It's as if an unseen force examines my body, emanating from her statue – something akin to a strange, futuristic instrument. At first, I question myself – Is this the intense heat of the day fueling a hallucination? Yet, as the experience unfolds, fear dissolves, replaced by a fiery energy that courses through my veins, a wildfire of potential unleashed. Intermingled with the heat is a grounding calmness, a sense of unshakeable resolve.

My gaze is drawn to a simple amulet lying forgotten in a crack in the floor – a river stone with a hole worn through by time itself. The energy coursing through me seems to ignite something within this simple stone. I wear it around my neck, a constant reminder of the strength I discovered within her fiery sanctuary.

Emerging from Sekhmet's sanctuary, the world vibrates with a new intensity. The relentless Egyptian sun demands a slower pace, a time for contemplation.

My feet carry me to a gnarled fig tree, its dappled shade a sanctuary against my heated skin. Leaning against the sturdy trunk, I feel the echoes of Sekhmet's fiery energy soften into profound peace. The earthy scent of soil and the subtle fragrance of blossoms carried on a gentle breeze weave their way into my soul.

Akashic Experience

Yet, as my path winds through the ancient landscape, an unexpected encounter changes everything. A chance meeting with a woman skilled in the Akashic arts blossoms into a profound experience. Entering her space, I'm no longer in a consulting room; it is a sacred chamber. The air crackles with anticipation, laden with the lingering scent of incense that curls and twists like a living entity. The experience is a revelation, a vibrant tapestry of possibility pulsing beneath my closed eyelids.

My breath catches in my throat as it becomes more than a revelation of luminous depths; it is a celestial meeting with the Neteru, the Egyptian goddesses and gods. A warmth washes over me, a gentle pressure against my temples as if unseen hands guide my inner vision. It's as if the air has transmuted, vibrating with an energy that thrums against my skin. Their whispers, soft yet insistent, fill my ears – a symphony of sounds that resonate deep within my soul. Is it music? Is it the chanting of an ancient temple ritual? It's impossible to define, yet it's as familiar as my own heartbeat. The scent of incense intensifies, the earthy notes of frankincense mingling with the clean, purifying scent of burning sage – a testament to the enduring power of creation. This is more than a reading; it's an initiation, a sacred ceremony unfolding within the modern space.

Seeking clarity in the torrent of visions, I silently call upon Seshat, goddess of wisdom, writing, and keeper of the Akashic Records. A subtle coolness cuts through the swirling heat like a gentle breeze through a sunbaked courtyard. Guided by her invisible hand, the visions shift and reveal their true meaning and purpose. Specific figures begin to emerge from the luminous depths. A powerful woman, reminiscent of Hathor in her regal bearing, exudes an aura of wisdom and compassion. A skilled artisan, his hands echoing the creative power of Ptah, molds raw materials into objects of both beauty and purpose.

A child, eyes alight with the mischief of Horus, gazes up at me with an expression of pure trust. Each figure embodies a different aspect of my potential, guided into clarity by the Neteru themselves.

The feeling of being overwhelmed gradually gives way to awe, a quiet wonder at the vastness of possibility contained within these timeless records. It's more than just seeing potential pathways; it's a deep sense of recognition. The healer, the leader, the teacher, the creator – these are expressions of my true nature. I am seeing my future and remembering the multitude of lives and experiences that have shaped who I am destined to be.

The Akashic journey reaches its crescendo. The image of myself guiding others into their own records returns, clearer and more powerful than ever. The responsibility of this role fills me with a profound sense of purpose. I feel Seshat's wisdom guiding my heart, reminding me that every person holds within them a universe of untapped potential. Stepping into this sacred space becomes an act of both service and empowerment. The visions fade, yet the threads of connection linger. I am more than a witness to my life's potential; I am an active participant, a weaver of my own destiny. The Akashic Records ignite an unwavering determination within me to turn those possibilities into realities.

The visions fade, but the essence lingers. The scent of sage, a reminder of purification and fresh beginnings, follows me as I step back into the modern world. It's a bittersweet return. Am I the woman I see in those luminous depths – the one guiding others towards their own power? The Akashic experience changes my perspective. My films strive to give voice to the unseen, to showcase the transformative potential within ordinary lives. But now, they feel almost...incomplete. Within the Akashic tapestry, I witness the symphony of human experience, a vibrant world of textures, emotions, and possibilities far beyond the confines of a screen. That richness, that boundless potential, calls to me now. My filmmaking yearns to evolve into something more, something multi-sensory, an immersive experience that invites audiences to not merely watch but to feel the transformative power within themselves. Perhaps this is what it means to be a Holographic Being – using every facet of my experience, every skill within me, to create stories that resonate on the deepest level.

Seven years in the making, my debut film *Nomad's Home* chronicles the lives of Bedouin Women in the Sinai desert. It is a passion project born from my connection to Egypt and a desire to uplift a marginalized community. Sinai is a living character; its blazing sun and swirling sands are a stark backdrop to the women's stories. Witnessing the Bedouin way of life, especially my encounter with Selema, proves transformative. A social entrepreneur defying tribal norms to create her own path, she embodies a fierce resilience that resonates deep within my soul. Our unlikely friendship, a collision of cultures between myself, a cosmopolitan woman raised in bustling Cairo, and Selema, deeply rooted in tribal traditions, fuels a yearning to understand the forces that shape us and the boundless potential lying within us all.

The Revolutionary Spirit

The success of *Nomad's Home* is a stepping stone, yet the true journey lies beyond. I'm a woman with Egyptian blood coursing through my veins. In 2011, protests erupted in the streets of Cairo – footsteps away from the home where I savored stories as a child – and the Bedouin woman's rebellious spirit blazed within me.

Yet, it's more than rebellion that fuels this uprising. The air crackles with anticipation, a potent mix of fear, anger, and resolute defiance. The rhythmic chanting of the crowds sets my own heart pounding. My senses are overwhelmed – the acrid scent of burning tires, swirling dust, and defiant cries rising from the crowd. In this historic surge, I feel warrior women surging through me – Sekhmet's fiery strength and Isis' resilience in overcoming adversity. It's about finding joy amidst uncertainty, a flash of Bastet's playful spirit reminding me that even in darkness, life persists.

Ignited by the Revolution

The revolution ignites a hunger within me for grand projects that extend beyond the power of film. I yearn to bridge divides, not merely through storytelling but through a multifaceted, action-oriented approach that fosters real-world change. Yet, even amidst the whirlwind, the storyteller in me cannot be silenced. During a screening of *Nomad's Home* in Cairo, surrounded by artists and activists sharing stories of female courage, a vision emerges: A film celebrating the unsung heroines of the Egyptian Revolution, an "Egyptian Jeanne d'Arc."

But my ambition transcends a single film. It's a yearning to understand the levers of power and to enact change on a global scale. Driven by this desire, I take a bold step. I immerse myself in the rigorous world of international relations at the renowned Fletcher School of Law and Diplomacy. There, I find myself among a diverse cohort of financiers, diplomats, and leaders, each offering a unique lens on the world's complex challenges.

A Tapestry of Experience

These diverse voices weave a rich tapestry within me. My Egyptian heritage grounds me, while my filmmaking experience allows me to see the human stories behind the headlines. The Fletcher School hones my diplomatic skills, equipping me to navigate complex situations. Every thread of my being feels essential, a vital piece of the puzzle. It's here, amidst the whirlwind of the revolution and the intellectual ferment of Fletcher, that the true potential of integration becomes clear.

Limitations are self-imposed. Filmmaking, diplomacy – these are individual threads, yet I yearn for a tapestry, a way to weave every fiber of my being into a potent force for change.

This desire for a more holistic approach is the seed of the Holographic Being vision. It's the understanding that true power comes from embracing the harmonious integration of all my diverse skills and experiences.

A Call to Evolution

Even as my films garner acclaim, a hunger lingers. The awards and accolades feel like stepping stones on a path not yet fully revealed. The vibrant tapestry of human experience I've witnessed through my lens – from the resilience of Bedouin women to the courage of revolutionaries – beckons me toward a deeper purpose.

The world beyond the silver screen calls to me – bustling markets where spices mingle with laughter, ancient temples where whispers of the divine linger, and the quiet wisdom found in the eyes of a stranger sharing a meal. It's in these moments of connection, of shared experience, that I find the true alchemy of life.

In my travels, I am drawn to the bustling heart of the Sichuan market, where the air is thick with the scent of ginger and chili, the sizzle of onions on open flames, and the warm laughter echoing through the stalls. This overload of senses transports me back to the heart of Cairo, my childhood kitchen transformed for a celebration. The air crackles with anticipation, a symphony of aromas swirling under the low hum of the ceiling fan. The earthy scent of cumin, the sweetness of simmering dates, and the sharp tang of freshly chopped parsley fill the air. My mother, a culinary alchemist, reigns over a vibrant domain of sizzling spices, bubbling pots, and mountains of jewel-toned produce. My aunts move with practiced ease, their hands a blur as they transform simple ingredients into culinary masterpieces. Laughter, chatter, and the heady scent of spices fill the air.

This is a ritual, a celebration of connection, and a testament to the alchemizing power of shared experience. From bustling Asian markets to the quiet rhythm of a Madagascan village, I sense this same spirit of shared creation, the metamorphosis of simple ingredients into something extraordinary. This is a universal language, a celebration of life, that transcends borders and cultures.

My role within this celebratory chaos of the banquet, my father proudly in the center of his antiques and artistic pinnacle surrounded by diplomats and artists, is one of both observer and participant. Cousins pull insistently at my sleeves, begging for one more story or a playful tickle. My laughter joins the rising crescendo of voices, a testament to the pure joy such gatherings ignite within me. It's more than the delicious dishes placed before me – though I savor each bite, delighting in the contrast of textures and the burst of flavors on my tongue. It's about the warmth of belonging, the knowledge that I am part of something larger than myself, a vibrant tapestry woven from shared stories, laughter, and a deep connection to our heritage. These experiences fuel my passion for diplomacy, my understanding of the power of human connection, and my belief in the ability of individuals to foster change. Even amidst the whirlwind of personalities and the inevitable moments of familial drama, the underlying current of love and acceptance remained. It was in this kitchen-turned-banqueting antique hall where I truly grasped the transformative power of hospitality, the alchemy of shared food and conversation, and the ability of these simple acts to forge lasting bonds.

It's this "blood and water" alchemy, infused with love and shared intention, that I sense in the Moscow market, in the hands of the sushi chef, in the silent rhythm of the Egyptian weaver. This is the wellspring of nourishment I yearn to tap into, an empowering energy I long to share. I yearn to foster an environment where the ordinary becomes extraordinary, where individuals with seemingly disparate skills and backgrounds unite to create a feast from humble beginnings. Just like those bustling kitchens fueled by passion, I want to create a space where strategic thinking meets mythical vision, where the multi-disciplinaries collaborate to turn challenges into opportunities, and limitations into stepping stones. It's here that the potential for authentic leadership and radical evolution is ignited.

The Akashic Revelation

My own Akashic journey unveils a truth that transcends my personal evolution. Within these radiant records, I glimpse the potential for others to experience a similar awakening. It's a lived experience, a profound encounter with the blueprints of their souls, that I yearn to share. Driven by a certainty forged in the fire of Sekhmet, I experiment, carefully guiding loved ones and trusted colleagues into their own Akashic histories.

Their shifts are profound: Dormant passions reawaken, hidden talents ignite, and a deep sense of purpose emerges. As their lives unfold with newfound clarity and direction, the ripple effect of their personal growth fuels my own as a guide. What began as a spark with loved ones and colleagues expands organically, as hundreds seek my guidance in accessing the Akashic Records, their blueprints for evolution.

My role within the Akashic realm deepens with each successful journey. The initial awe of my own experience shifts into a grounded, intuitive understanding of the process.

The Birth of a Vision

Word-of-mouth spreads like wildfire. A symphony of voices, each sharing their own unique stories of evolution, echoes through the digital landscape. The whispers grow into a chorus, a demand for a deeper dive into the Akashic realms. It's no longer just about individual sessions; it's about creating a movement, a ripple effect of awakening.

I find myself in bustling workshops, my voice weaving through the shared energy of seekers, their faces alight with a hunger for self-discovery. The Akashic Records become a living tapestry, each session revealing the intricate patterns of lives intertwined, of destinies waiting to unfold. The energy of Sekhmet's fire crackles in moments of breakthrough, while Seshat's gentle wisdom guides us through the labyrinth of self-discovery. Isis's nurturing warmth holds space for the tender unfurling of hidden wounds, while Bastet's playful spirit reminds us that even in the depths of our being, joy can be found.

But the world is vast, and the call for change echoes far beyond the walls of those workshops. A greater vision stirs within me, a vision of a platform that could reach beyond borders, weaving together ancient wisdom and modern tools for self-empowerment. This vision becomes a burning desire, a fire fueled by the stories of evolution I've witnessed, the collective yearning for a deeper connection to self and purpose.

And so, "The Holographic Being Accelerator" is born, a beacon for those seeking the tools to become architects of their own reality. It's a testament to the evolving power of the Akashic Records and the unwavering belief that every individual holds within them a universe of untapped potential.

Descent into the Underworld

The whirlwind of activism and creative inspiration grinds to a sudden halt. The path forward, once a vibrant highway, narrows into a dimly lit tunnel. Relentless fatigue, once a mere annoyance, now becomes an oppressive weight. My body, a vessel I'd always trusted, rebels, revealing its fragility. This illness is a forced surrender, a visceral confrontation with my own mortality that leaves me stripped bare.

Fear becomes a constant companion, accompanying the pain that wracks my body. Yet, even as my voice falters, a flicker of defiance remains. It's a stubborn ember, fueled by the voices of my ancestors whispering from the shadows. As each wave of illness washes over me, Anubis, the jackal-headed god of the afterlife, stands sentinel beside me. His silent presence is a stark reminder of the journey I've embarked upon, a journey beyond my control, a humbling reminder of my place in the grand cycle of life.

Confronting Death

The silence of this forced retreat is both terrifying and humbling. Questions I'd long avoided echo in the stillness: Have I truly lived? Have I made a difference? The answers remain elusive, shrouded in the fog of pain. Yet, Anubis waits patiently, a gentle guide through this labyrinth of uncertainty.

My body wages war against the illness, a losing battle. Each agonizing wave of pain etches the truth of my vulnerability into my very being. Tears flow freely, washing away the masks I've worn, leaving me raw and exposed. In this state of utter surrender, a shift occurs. The fear of death doesn't vanish, but it evolves into a fierce appreciation for the preciousness of life.

The Nile River Ritual

Supported by a circle of 12 women, bonded by this sacred journey, I stand trembling on the riverbank. My body aches, and fear gnaws at my resolve, yet a flicker of defiance remains. As I enter the cool embrace of the Nile, it's as if the river itself recognizes my struggle. The women encircle me, their gentle hands offering support as I float on the surface. Their touch is a balm, their presence a shield against the fear. As water pours over me, a tremor ripples through my soul. This fragile body finds strength and determination to emerge from this crucible. A surge of energy courses through me – Sekhmet's fire is a catalyst for healing and rebirth.

Coming Forth By Day

The sun kisses my skin, a warmth I haven't felt in weeks. It's a balm, a golden reminder of life's persistent pulse. I step onto the balcony, each footfall a small victory, and inhale the scent of jasmine blooms carried on the desert breeze. The laughter of children playing below echoes up, a symphony of resilience. My fingers trace the rough texture of the stone wall, a grounding touch after weeks of disconnection. The world feels alive and vibrant – the deep blue of the sky, the sun-baked rooftops, the rhythmic call of a distant muezzin.

A wave of gratitude washes over me. This fragile body, once wracked with pain, now cradles a newfound strength. The echoes of ancient whispers mingle with the city's pulse, reminding me of the wisdom embedded in my bones. This illness, this descent has stripped away illusions of invulnerability, leaving me raw, open, and profoundly connected to the flow of life.

The Lotus-Born Heart: A Journey of Unfolding

My upcoming book, *Quantum Leaps and Lost Socks*, is an invitation – to awaken to the whispers of your own soul. It's a tapestry woven from my own lived experiences: A kaleidoscope of memories, encounters with ancient deities, and explorations into the depths of human potential.

This tapestry, with its rich hues of both joy and sorrow, pain and liberation, is the fertile ground from which the Lotus-Born Heart has blossomed. It's a framework for personal alchemy, a five-phase journey that mirrors the lotus's own emergence from darkness into radiant bloom.

Each phase is a petal unfolding: From the "Primal Mud," where hidden potential stirs beneath the surface, to the "Seeking Light," where a spark of purpose ignites within, guiding us out of stagnation. The "Luminous Ascent" beckons us upwards, as we shed limitations and embrace our authentic selves. In "Radiant Blossoming," we discover our unique gifts, our voices rising in a chorus of purpose. And finally, "Sacred Seeding" calls us to become a fertile ground for others, spreading inspiration and cultivating change.

This is a lived reality, a journey I've witnessed countless times, in the tears shed in moonlit temples, in the laughter shared around crackling fires, in the quiet moments of self-discovery under desert skies. It's a cyclical dance, each unfolding revealing new depths, possibilities, and layers of the radiant self. It's a journey *you* are invited to embark upon.

The Alchemist's Invitation: Your Transformation Awaits

Within these pages, you'll uncover the wisdom whispered by forgotten priestesses, the ancient echoes that still resonate within the stones of Egypt. You'll find solace in the realization that your struggles are a fertile ground for growth. And you'll uncover the tools to ignite your inner fire, embrace your unique brilliance, and create a life that radiates with purpose and meaning.

The stories of those who have embarked on this journey are a testament to its power. Nathan, a successful entrepreneur and yogi, arrived at a crossroads, burdened by conflicts and a gnawing sense of not belonging. "I came into the program lost and disconnected," he confides. "But through Ima's guidance and the support of the community, I found the courage to be my authentic self. This unleashed a wave of creativity...a leap in my career...a profound shift from trying to understand the universe to making love with it."

The Holographic Being: A Tapestry of Light

Nathan's words echo a truth I've discovered through my own journey – we are a tapestry of interconnected aspects. This is the essence of the Holographic Being: A dynamic, multi-dimensional expression of our true selves. It's the understanding that within each of us lies a vast potential waiting to be unleashed, a unique blend of talents, experiences, and wisdom that, when integrated, creates a life of purpose, joy, and profound impact.

But the Holographic Being is more than an individual concept; it's a cosmic blueprint. Just as a hologram contains the whole within each of its parts, so too do we each carry the blueprint for a new world within our very being. When we embrace our multifaceted nature, we become conduits for a collective awakening, a symphony of interconnected consciousness that ripples outward, transforming our communities and, ultimately, the world.

It's a vision that calls to us from the ancient temples of Egypt, whispers through the Akashic Records, and echoes in the hearts of changemakers across the globe. It's a vision of a world where we no longer fragment ourselves, but embrace the totality of who we are, stepping into our full potential as creators, healers, leaders, and visionaries.

A Journey of Unveiling: The Alchemy of Self

The Lotus-Born Heart is not merely a framework; it's an invitation to this awakening, a melody of transformation that echoes within your soul. It calls you to shed the masks that no longer serve, revealing the radiant wholeness of your Holographic Being.

It invites you to reclaim your birthright: The unbridled creativity, the focused clarity, and the unwavering sense of purpose that lies dormant within. It beckons you to embrace the ancient wisdom that flows through your veins, the knowledge that you are a vessel of infinite possibility.

Your Journey Begins

In this sacred space, we draw upon the wisdom of ancient Egypt, the Neteru's guidance, and modern tools for self-empowerment. We explore the depths of your being, discovering the hidden gems of your soul. We dance with your shadows, transforming limitations into fuel for your fire. We celebrate your unique brilliance and your innate capacity to create a life that is both fulfilling and impactful.

If you feel a yearning within, a whisper of something more, I invite you to join me on this journey of unveiling. The path of the Lotus-Born Heart awaits... Dare to blossom.

Jacinth Nicko

Virtual Assistant

https://jazzonedayatatime.wordpress.com/

Virtual Assistant, Businesswoman, Writer I'm a working momma and still manage to keep crossing things off my bucket list once in a while. Whenever I'm extremely happy or sad, I always write! Not to mention my quiet obsession with poetry. I'm an old soul, from music to books and even movies.

THE JOURNEY OF PERSEVERANCE

By Jacinth Nicko

Growing up in an unstable and non-nurturing environment had a significant impact on my formative years. Yeah, that was my life. This book? It's my way of unpacking to dig into that experience—exploring its lasting effects and the ways I've found to heal and keep moving forward.

I recall observing the neighbor's child who was celebrating their seventh birthday with party hats and clowns. As I approached my own seventh birthday, filled with curiosity and innocence, I turned to my sister and asked what would happen on my day. I can vividly recall the expression on my sister's face, hesitant to disappoint me, as she softly replied, "I don't know yet." As a kid, I dealt with a lot of tough stuff, so I created my own little world. I'd spend time writing, reading alone, and even singing like life was a musical. Finding a cozy spot where I could feel better was the key, especially when feeling abandoned. So, I built this refuge where I could find comfort amidst the hardships of abandonment by those who were meant to be my pillars of love and protection. But as I've grown older, I've come to realize that the wounds of the past don't have to define me. I've learned that healing is possible and that it's okay to acknowledge the pain and trauma of the past while still striving to create a better future for myself. Fast forward, I decided to consistently strive to learn and adapt. However, from my teenage years into adulthood, I've encountered numerous betrayals from people who I loved. Despite these setbacks, I refused to let them hold me back. Instead, I chose to take the high road and continue moving forward, focusing on growth and resilience.

During college and my 20s, I held down a 9-to-5 job while dabbling in various business ventures here and there. However, when the pandemic hit, everything changed. I transitioned to freelancing as a virtual assistant. It felt like a surreal dream as I reminisced about seven or eight years ago when I prayed to God for a job that would let me work remotely while still being able to fulfill my duties as a mother to my daughter. I often observed freelancers happily working on their laptops wherever they went. Now, reflecting on the journey, I realize that God has answered my prayers in the most unexpected way, granting me exactly what I had asked for. Now, I can finally say I love my job and what I do.

I've been fortunate enough to cross paths with some truly remarkable individuals in my lifetime—people who have inspired, challenged, and helped me become the person I am today. One such person is Anisa Crespo, whom I consider to be God's instrument in helping me survive a certain period of my life, and she continues to be so until now, though we are across the globe from each other. I fondly refer to her as my angel. Furthermore, I recall my lifelong passion for writing. From a young age, I've always poured my thoughts onto paper with the dream of one day publishing a book. Remarkably, one day, Anisa Crespo asked me if I would like to be a part of and contribute to a book, sharing my story in the hope of inspiring others. Truly, dreams manifest in God's time!

The struggle never truly ends, even when we achieve one of our dreams. But with each experience, we gain perseverance and develop endurance. In 2021, I faced heartache when I lost my aunt, my closest confidante in the family, because of COVID-19. This sorrow came just four months after my mom fought off the virus herself. I spent almost three weeks in the hospital, looking after my mom while praying hard for her recovery from a life-or-death situation. I was so desperate I turned to God, holding onto my Bible and crying my heart out. It's pretty amazing that one morning my prayers actually got answered. My mom beat the virus and we went home. It was my aunt who picked us up from the hospital, unaware that she would be the one to leave us just four months later. One anxiety after another, trauma following trauma.

In the midst of the ordeal, I decided to surrender all my pain and questions to God, grappling with my numerous "whys." I have learned the hard way that pain comes from all sorts of stuff—loss, betrayal, disappointments, lost time, you name it. Dealing with it takes guts, honor, and a whole lot of self-love. When you're hurting, that's when you gotta show yourself some extra love. Do whatever helps you cope.

At present, I live day by day. However, each day I choose to remain hopeful and dedicated to my life's purpose: being the best, most nurturing mom I can be. I understand that I won't be the perfect kind of mom, and I never will be, but I'm committed to striving for it for the rest of my life. Also, I aim to ensure a comfortable life for my daughter by funding and supporting her dreams and eventually saving up for my retirement. This way, I hope to make up for the time I've lost due to life challenges by indulging in activities like reading, traveling, writing, and sharing blessings with others, from place to place and even around the world. That's my ultimate dream.

I read somewhere that the best time to love yourself is when you are in pain. Also, at the end of the day, we have to face the music, feel the pain until it loses its power, and then move on. With our renewed strength and resilience, let's keep going. Learn to roll with the punches of life, knowing we've got what it takes to tough it out, heal up, and come back even stronger to thrive once more. With a heart full of gratitude and hope, I hand over what's to come to God, trusting that His grace will shape every page of my life. To God be the glory!

Janet Clark

CEO of The Freedom Shift, LLC

https://www.linkedin.com/in/janetclarkwin/
https://www.facebook.com/janet.m.clark2
https://www.instagram.com/janetclark777/
https://www.thefreedomshift.com
https://bit.ly/winwithjanet

Janet Clark, CEO of The Freedom Shift and founder of WIN: Women's Impact Network, is leading a movement to help mission-driven women entrepreneurs discover, fund and launch their own mission. After a 30 year in corporate career and 20 years as an entrepreneur and business coach, Janet recognized the systemic barriers faced by women who want to create a life of freedom. In 2023, she retired from high ticket coaching and founded WIN, an initiative empowering women to rise together and support one another. Under her leadership, WIN has become a driving force for women to collaborate not compete and focus on abundance over scarcity. Through her podcast, The Freedom Shift, Janet teaches women entrepreneurs how to activate their Divine Feminine to create more time, lifestyle and financial freedom. She advocates for faith, family and freedom and inspires women to step into their higher calling. Janet is leading a movement of women living their lives on purpose to build a lasting legacy of Health, Wealth and Freedom for their future generations.

FROM WINE TO WIN: LETTING THE "E" GO.

By Janet Clark

"I am open to miracles. I believe in miracles.
I have experienced miracles."
—Janet Clark

I was glued to my screen, pure disbelief coursing through me. I blinked as if trying to wake up from a dream, then hit that refresh button again just to be sure. And there it was, bold as day: $102,508, my year-to-date earnings from a side gig I'd been working at just a few hours a week while running my existing business.

Of course, I had been getting checks every month, so I knew I was "making money" but the fact that I earned six-figures in my first year just blew my mind. If someone had whispered this possibility into my ear a year ago, I'd have dismissed it as sheer madness. It wasn't possible just from social media. Making money is supposed to require hard work.

It truly felt like a miracle.

I didn't get into it to make money; it was all about the mission, to take a stand for entrepreneurship and the American Dream. I simply said "yes" to switch my shopping away from big box stores that were stomping out small businesses and start shopping at a US-based company that supports entrepreneurs.

What I discovered is that the company pays lucrative referral commissions for those who enroll others, and there were many coming through social media who also wanted to make the switch. So, I decided to become an enroller, and WOW.

This unexpected $102K was shocking to me. You see, I had always believed that making money required hard work and lots of planning and executing on a plan. But this experience shattered that notion.

True empowerment doesn't come from any outward force; it comes through the grace of God. We are already empowered beings. God created each of us with unique gifts, talents, and life experiences - these are the true sources of our power.

As I peeled back the layers around this $102K miracle, I understood it was meant to be a startling reminder that when we surrender to our highest calling and operate from genuine service, the Universe will conspire to handle the "hows." Our role is to show up fully as who we were meant to be - divine, powerful creators, bringing our visions into reality.

This is the story of my journey to embrace the truth of my own God-given power. A path that was grounded in Faith, Family, Freedom, and Failures. Along the way, I discovered the keys that allowed empowerment to flourish and a new legacy called WIN (Women's Impact Network) to come forth.

From my devout Catholic upbringing to hitting rock bottom after corporate life, you'll walk the path that took me from numbing myself with glasses of wine to unapologetically claiming my power as a force for women's empowerment.

By the end, you'll understand how failures can be powerful catalysts to discover our deepest truths. You'll see how prioritizing family cultivates unshakable self-worth, how faith ushers in miracles, and how the highest freedom is realizing you were already empowered...you just had to be reminded.

Buckle up for a journey full of hard-won lessons, unexpected blessings, and the ultimate discovery of my true mission, to be a Woman of Impact. This is my path to WIN.

"Family means everything to me,
it's the purest form of unconditional love."
—Janet Clark

I was blessed with a loving, secure childhood home that provided the fertile soil for my earliest seeds of empowerment to take root. As the oldest of five children, I relished the nurturing role entrusted to me by my mother who named me Janet, which she said meant, "God's Gracious Gift" setting the tone for my lifelong search for God.

While I embraced my role of "big sister protector" wholeheartedly, I also craved independence and time for myself. My parents were in some ways controlling and at other times gave me lots of autonomy to do my own thing.

School was my sanctuary, a place where I thrived academically. I took pride in helping my little sister learn to read and actually enjoyed doing homework. I loved babysitting and earning my own money. I remember earning money by taking my siblings or the neighbors' babies out for walks when I was only about eight or nine.

Our extended family was vast with numerous aunts, uncles, and 26 cousins woven tightly into my childhood. We were an extremely close clan, spending summers together at our family camps - swimming, cookouts, and playing charades and card games.

In those youthful years, I was fully convinced that my warm family dynamic was the norm. How could I have known the tightly-knit, unconditional love surrounding me was, in fact, an incredibly rare gift? Both of my parents maintained remarkably close bonds with their siblings, infusing our household with an air of loyalty and unconditional love that became a big part of my core values.

Of course, no family is perfect. There were moments I felt unseen, unheard, or unfairly criticized. Yet, even when I felt slighted or misunderstood by my parents' boundaries and rules, I never doubted the security of their love.

For me, everything in life revolved around getting married and being a mom one day. Babysitting was my superpower from age 10 - I had a natural knack for connecting with children and some natural organizational skills. Nothing fazed me when it came to nurturing and caring for kids and tidying up the house.

Starting my own family and becoming a mother myself was a joy unlike any other. My first son was like a new toy - happy, funny, and an unstoppable bundle of energy. At just nine months old, he went from teetering to full-on running. I loved motherhood so much that I was pregnant again before he turned one, shockingly delivering twins when my firstborn was just 16 months old! We had no preparations for two babies - not even a second car seat in our Volkswagen Beetle.

Despite the chaotic bliss of raising three infants with limited means, I was utterly delighted to be a mom. To me, they were miracles. Yet, I also realized I wasn't totally cut out to be a stay-at-home mom. As nurturing as motherhood felt, I needed more outside stimulation to challenge my mind. We also needed money, so I worked a part-time retail sales job at AT&T that allowed me to be home a lot while also engaging my entrepreneurial spirit and business mind.

Over the years, I continuously adjusted, trying to create the best of both worlds as our family grew with the birth of our fourth son. While juggling work and four kids in five years brought immense challenges, my husband was supportive as I followed my intuition for crafting our lives. I was definitely the "driver" in the family, and he was consistently in the background, keeping things from falling apart.

My children are truly the light of my life and my greatest accomplishment. They are now all married with 10 grandchildren between them. My grandkids shine an even brighter light that fills me with immense joy and blessing in my role as "Gabby."

In hindsight, I recognize that my path was strewn with many building blocks and challenges designed to fortify my self-worth, autonomy, and personal empowerment. The responsibilities heaped on my young shoulders gave me grit and resilience.

I truly believe that unconditional family love is the best gift we can give our children. I grew up with my kids, but their needs came first. Teaching them that they were empowered to become the best version of themselves was my responsibility, and I took it seriously.

While my family foundation was strong, woven through cherished memories and nurturing lessons - it was just one thread in a larger tapestry. The next piece woven into the fabric of my empowerment was Freedom.

> *"I hate stupid rules. Everyone should do whatever*
> *the hell they want."*
> —Janet Clark

From the earliest age, I rebelled against rules and constraints. I was a free spirit in many ways. As an adolescent, I loved the liberation of leaving my family's house to go hiking in the woods, swimming, or riding my bicycle to explore far-off places. With my mom preoccupied with caring for my younger siblings and maintaining our home, I had plenty of unsupervised time to roam and discover a sense of independence.

I was the only one among my five siblings who had my own bedroom growing up. While my two younger sisters shared a room, and my two brothers shared another, I treasured that personal space where I could escape the household commotion. It was my sanctuary for reading, doing homework, talking for hours on the phone, and simply feeling free to be myself away from the commotion in the house.

When I met my husband, Steve, at age 15, I felt an immediate kinship as someone who also craved autonomy. My family had recently moved, and I was struggling to find my place among peers who had grown up together in that community. Like most teenagers, I felt my parents were too overprotective, too rule-bound, and not attuned to my emotional needs. So, being the solution-oriented and

goal-driven person I was, I decided the obvious answer was to skip college, marry Steve, and begin my independent adult life.

This decision wasn't exactly what my parents envisioned for me, but I had a fierce determination to live life on my own terms. Directly out of high school, I transitioned from my part-time job as a telephone operator to a full-time engineering position at New England Telephone. Once I got a taste of that exhilarating independence – making my own money, buying clothes and makeup, and saving for our upcoming marriage – I felt free.

We bought a house and married when I was 19 and Steve was 23. I loved every part of building our new life together, except for the fact that Steve was laid off from his job the day before our wedding. But even that hurdle didn't faze our youthful optimism and commitment. I simply added a part-time waitressing job to my full-time job schedule while Steve found a transitional position that required long hours. We knew we were on our own and relished the idea of crafting our future through our efforts.

That mindset drove us through those early years as we worked toward our next goals of starting a family and purchasing a larger home. I thrived on attaining self-sufficiency and never expected or wanted financial assistance from our parents. To me, that ability to stand on our own two feet defined true autonomy.

As my children came along, I found ways to balance work and family by pursuing sales roles that offered higher earning opportunities, over and above a salary. What I loved most about sales was the unlimited income potential based on commission – there was no cap on how much I could earn through my own efforts. Once I realized that, I was hooked on sales as the ultimate path to personal and financial freedom.

I took full advantage of the educational opportunities offered by my employer, AT&T, earning both my bachelor's and master's degrees while working and raising my family. Education was how I continuously expanded my sense of empowerment, confidence, and possibilities. AT&T felt like an extended university, with abundant training programs, and even tuition assistance that allowed me to attend college for free. I maximized every opportunity because it led to greater freedom. Yes, it was challenging to raise four children, maintain a corporate job, and get a college degree simultaneously, but I was empowered.

I ultimately took an early retirement from AT&T at age 45 after 25 years. Part of my decision was driven by culture changes I disliked within the company but I also wanted to pay closer attention to our oldest son who was 15 and facing some challenges. I felt he needed greater parental involvement to redirect his life in a more positive direction. Thank God I had the freedom and financial means to step away from corporate America when my family needed to take priority.

After AT&T, I started a business called Dynamic Discoveries, selling motivational products in mall kiosks. My business partner and I hired our kids to work for us, using it as a platform to teach them critical interpersonal and sales skills.

This was a great time for me to involve my three teenage sons and husband in something that was fun and educational. Those entrepreneurial years empowered us all, although the expensive overhead of mall rents, inventory, and payroll left us with extensive credit card debt. And then my partner decided to walk away and leave me with the $100,000 owed because it was all in my name.

All that debt from Dynamic Discoveries weighed heavily. Yet, rather than allowing anger or negativity to consume me, I persevered, using my newly-earned master's degree to land a six-figure corporate job that provided a car, a prestigious title, and the income to pay off all that debt within a year.

My new job had me doing a fair amount of traveling to New York City. While I loved living in the Massachusetts suburbs, I fell in love with the vibrant energy of New York. I loved the anonymity and the non-stop hustle and bustle of the city.

I continued to get better positions at a few different companies during the dot-com boom, allowing me to spend more and more time traveling to NYC, living it up on lavish expense accounts, and surrounding myself with successful, fun-loving professionals. I was earning a lot of money and enjoying a faster pace of life.

Yet, as freeing as that pivotal phase felt, it was also the beginning of my disillusionment with big corporations. I witnessed too many unethical practices – inflated numbers, cooked books, and a lack of authentic commitment to employees and customers. It was a harsh awakening that taught me large companies cannot be trusted, no matter how prestigious. They exist to line their own pockets.

Fortunately, that loss of faith in corporate coincided with my entrepreneurial skills being sharpened through roles that involved building new business divisions from

scratch. I spent years honing my ability to open new markets, recruit talented teams, and generate results through self-directed effort. When I finally decided to exit corporate life, I felt prepared to embark on a full-time entrepreneurial path aligning with my deepest values and need for freedom.

> *I believe in the American Dream. We get to create our own life of freedom: financial freedom, time freedom, and lifestyle freedom.*
> —Janet Clark

After decades of climbing the corporate ladder, I finally said goodbye to that chapter of my life. It had provided me with a great career, full of valuable lessons and growth experiences - even surviving being fired twice for standing up for my principles. But I knew it was time to leave that world behind and become an entrepreneur.

I started an independent sales agency called Integrated Communications. Within two years, I built it into a successful six-figure company generating monthly recurring revenue. I was debt-free with two homes, spending most of my time at our beachfront condo on Cape Cod. I was also managing a women's gym and teaching spinning classes on the side. With the boys all out on their own, some with grandchildren on the way, I had achieved the trifecta - health, wealth, and freedom.

But something vital was still missing...purpose and passion. I had fallen into the habit of drinking wine every night to numb myself. It was creating issues in my marriage as my husband grew concerned about how it affected my moods and behaviors. I would get annoyed with his attempts to control my life when really he was just looking out for my wellbeing. Needless to say, it put a strain on our relationship.

I vividly remember speeding down the highway one crisp fall day, the vibrant New England foliage blurring past my window. I felt irritable, depressed, and completely discontent with my life. There I was, on my way to visit yet another small company, to sell yet another technology solution in yet another drab office park. That's when I blurted out loud: "What the hell is wrong with me? I'm just not happy."

As if in direct response, a voice came over the car radio promoting a program called Positive Changes Hypnosis. I knew nothing about hypnosis but those two words - Positive Changes - grabbed me. I instantly understood that was exactly

what I needed. Thus began my journey into the next level of personal and spiritual empowerment.

It was time to radically change course and get my life on track toward serving a higher purpose. Through hypnosis, I lost weight and decided to sell my business interests to start anew as a business coach. I also realized that I needed to quit drinking wine and deal with my unhealthy coping mechanisms, which led me to join AA.

I named my new coaching business The Freedom Shift - an embodiment of the profound personal shift I was experiencing leading to a true sense of freedom and self-actualization. I offered business coaching in the area of sales. Over the next 15 years, it grew to multi-six figures annually and supported me as I grew and evolved in the online space.

Running that business was fun and challenging and required a lot of work as a solopreneur. I loved it. and it felt very freeing as I was able to work when I wanted, from any place, and I had plenty of free time to travel with Steve.

My life was pretty free during those years except for my dad getting Alzheimer's and my mom needing support. We decided to move to Florida and bring them down there with us. I had the flexibility in my schedule to manage their care plus travel back and forth to be with my expanding group of grandchildren.

Most importantly, I lived my life according to my values and was able to create a life that worked for me. I truly loved my work because I was also helping other entrepreneurs. Money was flowing in, and I was deepening my spiritual life too. While the business moved me in an empowering new direction, this was merely the first step toward an even deeper transformation.

After 15 years, I decided I wanted to wear less of the entrepreneurial hats, so I gave up coaching and primarily did sales and enrollments for another coaching program and they handled the fulfillment. That left me with lots of free time just as Covid hit.

And that's also when my spiritual life took on a new intensity.

"God answers my prayers. I just don't always see it when it's happening."
—Janet Clark

Both of my parents and my entire extended family were devout Catholics. They had a strong belief in the Holy Trinity, and my mom instilled in me a deep affection for the Blessed Mother. My faith has been the guiding light throughout my life's journey, even when I zigged and zagged off the path along the way.

My connection to these religious beliefs played a significant role in my decision-making processes over the years. It was a spiritual anchor that guided me through turbulent times. Over time, my beliefs transformed into a more personal connection with Jesus, but the essence of my faith remained constant.

There was a period when I veered away from the church during my dating years and before having kids. My husband wasn't religious - in fact, he struggled with organized religion after hearing stories of abuse within the church. I also felt disillusioned by the church's rigid rules, institutionalism, and sexual abuse. However, my core faith never wavered.

When my children were born, I wanted them baptized and raised with the same deeply rooted Catholicism I had known. I brought them to church, ensured they received the sacraments, and even taught CCD classes. Yet in many ways, it felt more obligatory than pure, fulfilling childhood obligations rather than nurturing an innate love for God.

The church ultimately let my children down as it had me. They never quite felt that spiritual pull or learned to love the faith in the way I once did. So, once they were grown, I slowly stopped attending church myself. I still prayed to God and the Blessed Mother when I needed something or felt afraid, but that consistent bond, that truth that God was always with me, had faded into the background.

I suppose you could say I lost my way for a while. I remember feeling that clearly in my early 50s despite having achieved most of the goals I'd set for myself in life. I had created the life I always wanted and prayed for, one filled with personal and financial freedom. Yet I couldn't shake the feeling that something vital was still missing.

I had worked tirelessly to hit those benchmarks, but once I achieved them, I felt hollow. It stemmed from living out of alignment with my true values. It was a

harsh realization that what I'd created lacked genuine fulfillment and passion. I was at a crossroads. What now? The old saying "Be careful what you pray for" resonated deeply. I had to accept that the life I'd built wasn't bringing me the perfect joy I expected.

In that sobering realization, a profound desire for spiritual change stirred within me once more. It was time to embark on a new inner journey, one that would test my courage and redefine my sense of self. The road ahead was uncertain, but the call of my restless soul grew louder with each passing day.

I tried to numb that gnawing ache through food, alcohol, trips to NYC - anything to escape the mundane life I had trapped myself in. I felt stuck and bored, going through the motions on a loop. It hit me that the change I so desperately craved had to begin within my mindset and thoughts. I wasn't thinking deeply enough about what was happening in my life.

That spiritual awakening came through an unexpected channel – the first being hypnosis which led me to AA where I worked through the 12-step process and learned how to let go of built-up resentments and past hurts.

As frightening as it was to confront those shadows, an even more powerful light began to pierce through. I learned how to meditate and a familiar voice, the same one I had felt reverberate through my soul as a child, whispered to me "Come back to Jesus," and in my mind, I saw God handing me a Bible.

This profound experience startled me so much that I shared it with my sister. I remember telling her that I had no idea how to understand the bible or to have a relationship with Jesus. That's not something I learned in the Catholic schools or from my parents. They taught us the Catechism and that Jesus was the Son of God who was crucified, not someone to "be with". I was bewildered by the message but open to a spiritual rebirth.

Again, the answer came over the radio while I was driving my car down the highway. I was heading home to Cape Cod to visit my parents on a Sunday afternoon. The usual station where I listened to conservative talk radio was airing a syndicated show about health, only this one was about Spiritual Health. The guest was Mother Clare Watts, an ordained priest in a mystical Christian order called OCS, the Order of Christ Sophia.

She explained how she had grown up as the daughter of Baptist missionaries but she rejected Christianity. She had traveled a path through Sufism and Buddhism and spent many years living in an ashram. Then she said the words that I couldn't unhear: "All those roads led **back to Jesus**." She went on to say that she ran schools where they taught students **how to understand the Bible** with their own personal teacher. Oh my God! I couldn't write that information down fast enough!

I called my sister, Linda, immediately and let her know we were heading to the Center of Light on Tuesday night to find out what it was all about. That was the beginning of my 10-year association with the Order and Mother Clare. The incredible spiritual growth and building an intimate relationship with Jesus that I experienced over the next 10 years was profound, but a subject for a book of its own. Let's just say it was a miracle.

It seemed that God answered my prayers by sending me messages over the airwaves! First, it was Positive Changes over the radio, then Mother Clare being aired on the radio, and most recently, a YouTube podcast that brought me full circle back to the Catholic Church. My life is so entwined with Jesus now, as my mentor and friend, that every day I wake up feeling blessed and divinely inspired to make a bigger impact.

My faith is rock solid. I love attending mass and receiving the Eucharist every day. I read my Bible scriptures, pray and journal every morning, and then go to church to start my day. I love God, I love Jesus, and I love the Blessed Mother deeply. And I feel the presence of the Holy Spirit giving me guidance and wisdom. I don't go anywhere without them and my life is much more happy, joyous, and free.

> *"WIN is my legacy, a movement of empowered women fulfilling a higher calling through collaboration".*
> —Janet Clark

Going back to where we started and my side gig earnings during the chaos of Covid, a new voice over the airwaves ignited a fire within me. This time it came from an Influencer I was following on YouTube.

"Why support conglomerates that destroy our freedoms and health while stomping out small businesses? Why not choose a US-based manufacturer that supports American families?" The question resonated deeply, sparking a resounding "Hell, YES" within me. Little did I know this decision would evolve into my life's mission.

It's not about the products or the company - though they do align with my values of Faith, Family, and Freedom. It's about empowering women to fund their missions, to create a meaningful impact in the world. So, I invested not just money, but my heart and soul, to build WIN: Women's Impact Network.

Through WIN, women link arms, earn substantial income, and build mission-based businesses. I offer my coaching for free, funded by our partner, The Wellness Company, because I believe that through the power of collaboration and abundance, we will change the world.

At WIN, we've created our own economy—a community committed to individual missions, united in our pursuit of Health, Wealth, Freedom, Fulfillment, and Peace of Mind. Together, we embody the Divine Feminine energy of collaboration, abundance, and nurturing.

I invite you to join us, to be part of something greater than yourself. Together, we will make the world better for our children and grandchildren. I can't do this alone; it takes all of us working together to WIN.

Join the movement of mission-driven women at WIN and let's rise together: http://bit.ly/winwithjanet

Janice Cruz

LoveDose Coaching
Coach

https://www.linkedin.com/in/janice-cruz/
https://www.facebook.com/CoachJaniceCruz/
https://www.instagram.com/coachjanicecruz
https://janicecruz.com
https://podcasters.spotify.com/pod/show/selflovescience

Janice Cruz, a self-love coach, woman leader in tech, Latina, mother, entrepreneur, and cancer survivor, integrates her diverse experiences into a narrative of empowerment. Throughout her journey to heal from illness, she uncovered the transformative force of self-love. With a decade of expertise in technology, test engineering, and agile practices, Janice applied testing principles and root cause analysis skillfully to uncover paths to wellness. This profound realization led her to her life's mission: to spread joy into the world by guiding others in embodying the principles of self-love to lead themselves to a life so exciting, they wake up every day excited and profoundly grateful for the chance to be themselves once again. From navigating corporate landscapes to battling illness, she utilized every facet of her identity to inspire and uplift. With unwavering determination, Janice empowers individuals to embark on their own journey of self-discovery and unwavering self-love, forging a future illuminated by authenticity, strength, and boundless compassion.

EMBRACING THE PATH TO SELF-LOVE AND HEALING

By Janice Cruz

My daughter held the surgical glove that had been blown up for her to play with. I'd left her toys in the car. Good moms didn't forget toys. Tired moms do. The surgeon came into the room, stopping all the air in it. I was worried I'd be in trouble for playing with medical supplies. She pulled a marker out of her pocket and said, "You know what this needs?" She then drew a happy face on it. She let me know the results weren't in yet but decided it best to explain the stages and grades of how cells can grow uncontrollably and what each of those means in terms of possible outcomes.

I didn't look back at the oncology surgeon's office. She'd call when she'd call. My daughter kicked her little legs quietly in the back of the car and munched on her star puffs. I YouTubed something along the lines of how to heal breast cancer. I was headed out of town and had a 12-hour drive to figure it out.

I needed snacks for the impending doom road trip, so I stood in front of glowing green produce, confused by how to feel while waiting to hear if the palpable lump in my right breast was cancerous. The phone rang to notify me that I was, in fact, a statistic. I laughed and commented how annoying it was; this inconvenience. My heart pumped loudly because I wasn't sure where to pour the pain out from. I'd spent the previous 17 years mastering the art of suppressing tears and hiding anything that resembled softness. I believed that this world ate people like me alive until we blended in with our banter and prose, and disabled the signals our bodies send to warn us when we are being cut open by people, jobs, significant others, and vices.

I couldn't cry out loud in the car because I didn't want my child to know that I was a human or that big girls cry. It felt like my tears were ripping new pathways through my ducts to find their way out of my face. I was ashamed of these tears. Where was the girl who spent a lifetime suppressing hurt and choking back the words she should have said, forcing them to shoot pain into her right breast, right beneath the surface where they were becoming visible by oncologists?

By the time I reached my destination, I'd learned about adjuvant care, sulforaphane, the warrior fast, organic food, clean water, natural healing, and everything that every conspiracy theorist and esteemed doctor had to say about the poisonous origin story of chemotherapy and cancer. My head pounded with a migraine as I thawed breastmilk out with hot water from the hotel coffee machine. I said out loud, "I did this to myself." It was a matter of fact. Some deep wound ripped itself open just to assure me that I gave myself cancer. I wonder now, as I move through the world, meeting other people thriving after cancer, but never dare to ask. I wonder if they also used to think that maybe if they got sick, they'd finally write a book, quit their job, put their musical into production, or even just tell people they've been writing a musical most of their lives. I wonder if, like me, they'd prayed to get sick, to be whisked away to a hospital where they could be isolated, with no responsibility, no visibility into how the world kept beating them up, and where people come into the room just to see if they were ok. I pulled in everything I'd learned about how thoughts come into being, the placebo effect, and the law of attraction and concluded that I got what I asked for. I believed I somehow deserved this outcome.

There was this cellular sigh of relief because I realized that this was the first time, in as long as I could remember that I could put myself first. For most people and their family and friends, an illness diagnosis is terrifying in the way it appears from around a corner like a stranger hiding in the shadows. Not for me. Yes, I was scared and looked for every hidden door I could run through to get away from what was happening, but I could also feel my spirit being lifted off the floor where it had resided as a doormat to everyone in my world. I thought about how every minute of every day was now just for me and my child, no one else. I felt free as the handcuffs to my past life had fallen away and shattered into a puff of smoke. None of the things I once worried about or feared could be given the gift of my attention anymore because I needed it all. The problem was that I had no idea how to care for myself.

Imagine a thick and sticky feeling of shame that forces all of your body to cave inward. It forces your head to hang at a 45-degree angle and makes you wrap your arms around your chest like a straight jacket because it's the only protection that remains for your heart. It's like being trapped eternally in the moment before your heart explodes out of your chest. I call this "the muck." This is how I felt every day. It's a viscous, dark sensation of nothingness, ugliness, and not-enoughness. It's the feeling of a soul wilting like flowers whose needs for survival you've tried to understand for a lifetime, only to watch the leaves rot and fall from the wetness of overwatering.

If you watched me from the outside, you'd say that I lived an average life, with average income, and averagely toxic destructive relationships. You'd have said that I was a woman who partied and desperately wanted what I call freedom, and a therapist would call an escape. The life I lived before that diagnosis hurt so badly that my response to cancer was "Thank God, my prayers were heard." I wasn't sure I even believed in God. Sometimes I stared into the void and felt that solace of being small as an ant in comparison to whatever was out there but it would pass. I prayed, night after night, for relief from my pain. I asked the universe to take it away, to take me away from it all. And on that day, it did.

In 2019, I started what I now refer to as "the incubation period." My extremely stressful circumstances forced me to pour into myself at an accelerated pace and high level of intensity. It was life and death. I was also pretty isolated. I'd moved away from a toxic home and into my childhood home with my parents where I felt peaceful and at ease. I cut off all access to anything that could steal my energy. You don't know what you're made of until you fall completely apart. You pick the pieces up, examine each one for its usefulness, and decide, which parts of you to trash and which will be glued together with gold. Sometimes, you need to fall apart so fiercely that those pieces can never be put back together; otherwise, they'd become the vessel to hold your pain again. All the old parts of me withered away, and I was nothing but a seed with no awareness of the sunlight right above the surface, ready to fill me with life.

While going through all of this, I was working as a lead test engineer and spent all my days identifying defects in systems, searching for root causes, understanding the mechanics of how things should function, and learning how to execute without issues. We rarely deployed without issues, just to keep it real. I'd developed systematic approaches to solving problems all day. If you know anything about memory, you know that when a heightened emotion is achieved in conjunction with an experience, your brain will commit it to memory. As a tester, mistakes can have big consequences, so when we make mistakes, it becomes a line item on a test plan to ensure we can prevent it from happening again. On great test plans, many line items eventually become obsolete because great systems are built while they're in place. I applied this same methodical thinking to healing from cancer.

I read medical journals, watched YouTube university videos, and purchased every book and cookbook about healing cancer that I could find on Thrift Books. My unwavering curiosity allowed me to approach information neutrally. I remained cautious of what information I allowed to influence my process while remaining receptive to all possible solutions. Having worked with intelligent, creative, nerdsome developers meant I'd spent the preceding years of my life learning from brilliant people. I'd learned about simulation theory - which states that the world is basically an advanced civilization's video game. I walked through the world imagining that I was in a role-playing game where anyone I met was a character with stalls of trinkets or golden nuggets of information about my mission to heal. This provided me with level-ten entertainment value and helped me develop an exceptional level of resilience. Imagine meeting a rude person and having the ability to believe they're just a video game troll!

I also believed that I was surrounded by teachers. I needed answers, and I had no attachment to where or whom a theory came from. I soon found myself in conversations with people who, under no other life circumstances, would I ever have engaged with. I told everyone what I was up to, so strangers of all religions and values prayed for me to their various higher powers. I didn't know which of these would be the key to completing my mission, so I always said yes when prayer was offered. Strangers have prayed for me in grocery stores, elevators, meditation retreats, bookstores, group therapies, family parties, over the phone, via text, through social media, and in rooms where I was present only in the minds of others. I have shared tears with people whose names and faces I can no longer recall. Strangers opened their hearts to me and shared their stories about how they'd also been impacted by illness. I learned that suffering and healing were all around me. I committed, in those moments, that I would always treat others with peace. You'd be amazed by how much you can learn from the world, how beautiful people really are, and how many friends you can make when listening becomes your superpower.

The booster pack of my commitment to learning more about healing was that I was fueled by pure survival instinct, which happens to be the source of infinite motivation. I learned that people heal through food, forgiveness, joy, sunlight, exercise, treatment, and love. Because I was so thoroughly testing the process of healing, I tried nearly everything that everyone told me to do. Thankfully, test engineering also requires you to determine how relevant each test scenario is. So, when I stumbled across people who blended liver into smoothies, I could easily say "Hell-to-the-no!".

I soon realized that I couldn't learn fast enough. As in, my brain's data processing system was limited in comparison to my appetite for consuming new information (as were the number of hours in the day). I revisited a SuperBrain course that I'd purchased, which helped me to speed read. I applied concepts from some modern thought leaders such as the concept that even reading short amounts of content would still contribute to knowledge expansion. The ability to learn is cumulative, so every new enhancement I made to my approach made my thinking more expansive, meaning I could ingest information en masse without burning through valuable minutes of life.

I read books that studied spontaneous remission and what patients did to contribute to said spontaneous remission. I made devastating mistakes along the way as well. The thing about unwavering faith is that it can also lead to big failures because sometimes you forget that you're still human with the ability to fall. I believed with a fiery passion that I could heal cancer with juice. You can imagine how pissed I was watching my chemo nurse rip the alcohol swab open to clean my port. My best friend sat beside me, and while we both watched the needle move in slow motion towards me, she remembered her duty and disrupted the moment by feeding me something more engrossing than fear, which is juicy gossip. That is what friends are for.

In the infinite piles of books that I was reading about healing all things, I picked up a book about a miraculous cancer healing story. There was a single concept in the book that baffled me. The author wrote about her near-death experience where she realized that had she learned to love herself, she would not have gotten ill. I didn't know that, while on a mission to cure illness, my seed of purpose was being watered and growing slowly. The purpose that God has for me, the gift I carried with me from the ether and before being planted on Earth, was about to emerge and fill the forest I'd just burned down with radiance, vibrance, and a life worth waking up to.

I became fixated on this concept of self-love. I had no life lessons on this. I wanted to cut it open like plants during science class, to know which parts were the keys to unlocking my power to heal my body. I Googled and I read, but there are no medical papers about self-love, just memes of women holding coffee cups in front of the ocean on Sunday mornings. I sat in bathtubs, brows furrowed, soaking in magnesium and pure castile soapy water, and pounded my fists on the water in frustration wondering, "Is this self-love?" I read and searched for the methodical approaches to self-love but no one had any formulas I could test. There were no test plans or acceptance criteria that would help me understand what it meant or how I could confirm that I'd achieved mastery of this concept.

Self-love was like poetry whose words breathed deeply in and out of your dreams, waiting for you to reach your hand in and grab them, only to find that they disappeared with dusk. It was an energy that fueled the universe and powered the Earth, but it was nowhere to be found. It was an abstraction that people claimed to practice, but to me it was bullshit. Still, there was research to be done and data to be collected. Since intelligent design made me a data analyst with the curiosity of a scientist with obsessive-compulsive tendencies mixed in and a relentless drive to be right, it was game on. My new mission was to learn what this love of self meant and how it could theoretically heal my body.

I wrote down everything I love to do: go to used bookstores, write poetry, write songs, spend time with friends, take hot baths, sit still, read, walk around the pool, fall in love, ruminate, be introspective, learn, grow, talk, sing, do yoga, go for a run, do nothing, visit antique shops, sit in melancholy, wonder at the vastness of the stars, brunch, experience the newness of food, explore my city, coffee shops, try new tea, go to Asian markets, eat exotic fruit, and so on. I did everything on the list, and then I would write down my journal entries (my scientific observations and findings, if you will) to try to decrypt the patterns of what I had done to become a woman who needed to escape through illness. I spent all of my time trying to figure out what was wrong with me and why my body gave up on me. I looked self-love in the eye and challenged it. "If you're real, prove it."

I realized that I really enjoyed all of those things but I felt like I should love different things. I enjoy short walks but thought that meant I was lazy because fit people enjoy CrossFit and marathons. I love baths, a simple pleasure that someone once called swimming in a pond of your body's dirt. That hilarious observation made me think I should become a shower person instead, even though sitting in a steamy hot tub makes me feel like a princess. I enjoyed being treated with love, affection, and respect, but my upbringing taught me that all men are lying, cheating trash buckets, so the best thing to do would be to pick your favorite bucket of emotional trauma and date him for seven years. Everything about me that is good, kind, and authentic, I shoved down into the darkest spot in the back of my brain so that I could live a life that suited others. "Hello, world, here is your doormat. I shall do as I think you please."

I realized that I hated myself and all the things I'd built my life around. The problem was that it wasn't even me. The woman who allowed herself to be emotionally abused by men, jobs, and most horrifically by herself, did not look like me in the slightest. I was so angry that I'd spent thirty-two years of my life trying on masks and personalities so that no one would feel uncomfortable around me. I began to hold my middle finger to my ceiling to cuss out a God who I barely believed in at all. How could this world make mothers sick? In those moments, having faith equated to saying, "Just in case it's my time to go, I'm going to make sure I have a clear conscience." I journaled about forgiveness and found a resounding ugliness from years of accumulating and absorbing the ugliness of others that had grown inside of me. Before that, forgiveness was the gateway to allowing cheaters and abusers to re-enter my bed. Letter by letter, as I tore through pages in notebooks, all of the peace I'd been meant to bring to the world found its place within me.

While choking down green juices, jumping on a mini trampoline, getting reiki over the phone, taking vitamins A through Z, staring in the mirror and calling that no-eyebrowed, free Brazilian-waxed, bald-headed woman pretty, using emotional freedom techniques, tapping my eye sockets, and singing out loud in my yard for the neighbors to enjoy, I never quit. I didn't believe I would heal but somehow, every day, I picked up my mustard seed and tried again.

All the way in the back of that darkness, there was a spark with the slightest flicker. It was a brilliance that existed just outside of my peripheral vision, a tiny glimmer that every so often had me turn my head to ask, "What was that?" I couldn't see it because it was covered in hurt, life, masks, facades, and impatience. It was love that powered this vessel. I reignited it by increasing my happiness and preventing negativity from entering my life. I walked out of rooms with stressful conversations happening, unfollowed toxic social media accounts, and stopped watching the news. I prayed over every part of my body, thanking it for everything it could still do even while broken. Little by little at first, but then with a fire that could burn down a city, that spark of love began to radiate outward. It collected power from everything around it that I loved. It was like lava, consuming everything in its path on a mission to become a mountain.

Each night, I stared in the mirror at this blank slate, wondering who she was without everything she ever leaned on to feel beautiful. She was 100 lbs, freshly single, living with her parents and her child, and missing part of her womanhood after a mastectomy. Every single part of her past life was wiped away, and nothing and no one could ever force her to go back. I began repeating affirmations every night like this. Funny thing about affirmations in the mirror - remember the muck? Yeah, the muck doesn't like to be called pretty. I told myself that I was surrounded by love, brilliance, success, and beauty, that I was pure love, and that I was already the woman who moved the mountain. The first few times I read these things to myself, that dark, thick, ugly muck that had weighed me down like bricks on my feet in an ocean, would bubble up to the surface, looking for its way out. It felt gross, like lies. Every nice thing I said to myself was rebutted with "This is stupid."

I realized that I'd heard that same thought thousands of times throughout my life. I wondered if our minds had these eight-track tape players that were just running the same audio over and over. I looked at my thoughts like they were in a movie and decided it was time to clean up the street. On day one, I only believed one of 55 affirmations. That I was surrounded by love because I was, in fact, surrounded by love. I lived with my parents, my child, my sister, six dogs, three cats, and three turtles. The turtles didn't love me or know I existed but someone loved them, so by default, love was in the air. With every forced repetition, I drowned out those destructive beliefs and found myself skipping towards the mirror.

I began floating everywhere. I was lighter, happier. I realized that I deserved everything on that list of affirmations. I also realized that some of those affirmations required me to leave room for proof they were true. My hair had started to grow back in with little coils that I was not born with. It was like God's consolation prize for making my hair fall out. It grew into a curly, silky bouffant on my head. I went to a girl barber and got some dope designs shaved into my head. When I emerged into the world, I radiated authenticity, joy, love, peace, happiness, faith, and exhilaration, and I believed that the world was filled with new opportunities for happiness.

I was worthy of sunshine. I found the more I was myself, the more amazing people I found myself surrounded by beauty and excitement. I was utterly in love with the woman I was born to be. I wondered how I could be so lucky to live this life as myself again, over and over. I attracted successful, amazing, brilliant, incredible people into my life.

One beautiful summer day, I felt that overwhelm that used to accompany my downward spiral days, but it was in reverse. I found that every experience I had that day amplified the joy even more. The joy kept compounding, growing, and in a moment it was too much for my body. I felt like I cracked open and my spirit poured out into the sky. I was free. The feeling of self-love made me see that it was always my purpose. Since the precipice of time itself, I was meant to share this experience to help people open that pathway for themselves. I committed that I would always love openly and help people on their own paths to love themselves deeply. No vice on Earth can compete with those feelings and experiences.

That feeling of despondence sometimes echoes into my evenings now, a flicker of a memory of things passed. Sometimes I grab hold of the melancholy because I miss her, and I wonder how she's doing, like an old friend you can sit with and talk to for hours. All the while aware that she doesn't fit into the life you've created, that you will never have what you once had with her. She's something that I can reminisce on while I bustle about a busy schedule of photo shoots, events planning, growing my career, learning, praying, having fun, and feeling joy to levels that can't be measured in anything but poetry.

I remember the times when I longed for joy and happiness that I wasn't sure existed. Now, as I sit in my glider chair staring at the plants in my little porch garden, I wonder how I got to be this lucky. Since my diagnosis, I've graduated with my master's degree, obtained six professional certifications, been promoted, started a podcast, began public speaking, and joined a women's empowerment non-profit, called Women on the Rise with a two-year term as the events director. I have the most amazing friendship and networking groups. I am so happy that every day I wake up with a level of gratitude that allows me to love myself on good and bad days. I believe that I am meant for greatness and that I will continue to be in the presence of greatness in others as I move through the world.

 I often kneel in gratitude because the joy overwhelms me. An instinct that once had me keeling over in pain, begging the universe to free me from this life, is now to share my gratitude with the stars. I send out loving feelings into space just in case it's true that the universe is a prism that reflects on itself. I pray into the future just in case generational blessings can be collected by strangers. I tell myself every day that my grandbaby's, grandbaby's, grandbaby's grandbabies will inherit a generational blessing of deep self-love. They will stand in the mirror, looking deeply into their own eyes in wonder. They will have some lingering feelings that they can't quite place. They will feel this internal knowing that they are worthy and deserving of all the love, joy, and greatness that the world has to offer. They will know that the love they feel and give is infinite and eternal. It feels like waterfalls pouring beneath our feet and uplifting us higher towards the warmth of the sun.

Jenny Fuller

Owner of Jenny Fuller

https://www.facebook.com/deanJenny1
https://www.instagram.com/jennydeanfuller
www.jennyfuller.net

Jenny Fuller is a believer first, a loving wife second and lastly a mother to three busy teenagers. I am truly living out my God filled mission. My mission is to EMPOWER other woman to find their spirtual gifts and to live their God filled life calling. Jenny is passionate about educating others on the importance of faith, nutrition and fitness. She believes with all of these three pillars functioning properly you will be able to create a life you dream of!

NOW YOU CAN EXHALE...

By Jenny Fuller

I am mostly passionate about women getting their houses in order. When I say that, I do not mean your physical house (your body). I am referring to your "heart." God recently pulled me out of chains and bondage, and he has shown me that I need to share this message!

My goal in life is to live like a Proverbs 31 woman - "Many women do noble things, but you surpass them all." Charm is deceptive, and beauty is fleeting, but a woman who fears the Lord is to be praised. Give her the reward she has earned, and let her works bring her praise at the city gate.

1st Corinthians 14:33 and 14:40 tell us God is not a God of disorder, but a God of peace, and we are to make sure everything we are involved with is done properly and in order. God does not bless chaos or confusion.

Get your surroundings in order. Your home is a representation of your life. Develop the habit of finishing what you start and taking care of what you have now.

Getting your house in order the Christian way involves a holistic approach that encompasses various aspects of life including spiritual, relational, financial, and physical well-being. Proverbs 31 1-31, "As the man is the leader of the home, there is a place for the woman, she is to be the teacher her job in the home is very important that is the reason why God did not intend for wives and mothers to work outside the home."

A little less than a year ago, both my husband and I owned two separate companies. We were the typical, small, suburban family who didn't eat family dinners, ate standing up, barely saw each other, complained at night about how hard our life was, and blamed it on other people. I was not praying for my kids' days, my husband's, or my own. I was the typical wake-up-and-live in the rat race of life and could not see my past self. I remember one night I was in a fetal position on my closet floor. I remember thinking there has to be more out there - life should not be this hard!

After about a month of surrendering and just releasing the stress to God, He wanted me out of that business. God has a funny way of pulling you out of things that he is not number one in. And that is what he did. Once he pulled me out of my business, I was able to see how many of my family and close friends needed my prayers! See, when we are in our own mess or our own stress, we are incapable of seeing what others need. We are too self-absorbed only thinking about ourselves.

Slowly, He started showing me who I needed to pray for and how to get my house in order. The three areas that He has shown me are **spiritually, financially,** and **physically.**

Let's start with the **spiritual**. How do we get our house in order (and our hearts) SPIRITUALLY? First, you need to invite God into every aspect of your life, including your kids and husband. He will begin to show you where you need to work. Repent to Him anything that is weighing heavy on your heart. Remember, sinning keeps us further from God. In your quiet time, ask God, "Who do I need to forgive?" It could be someone from two decades ago. Make sure to clean your heart out. I imagine going in my heart with a vacuum cleaner and just soaking up anything that does not serve me anymore.

Once you get your heart clean and pure, God can go in and give you His spirit. Love, Patience, Kindness, Gentleness, Goodness, Joy, Faithfulness, Self-Control, and most importantly, PEACE. That is what I teach my teenagers when you have a big decision to make - try to feel your heart, God is PEACE. Everything else, if it feels stressful or fearful, is not from God. That is how I want them to learn to make their decisions in life. Discernment is HUGE!

Kids are sponges; they will do what we do. Romans 12:10 says, "In honor preferring one another." Honor means RESPECT. I see a lot of households lose this one piece. Our children will respect us once we first respect them. A lot of parents are still trying to grow up and get their lives together on top of raising kids. As parents, we really do not have time to mess up or, if we do, we must always acknowledge our screw-ups and apologize to our kids, so they can have some good communication skills under their belt. Adults need to act like adults and admit when they are wrong. I feel like this one step would set the next generation up for success.

When I got away from my selfish ways, God revealed that my kids needed me to pray with them and for them. I have started praying daily, and I know God is working in their hearts spiritually. We should prioritize our family relationships. Yes, teens are difficult to talk to, but remember this is not who they are. They have to get refined in this "teen" process, and God gave us "our" specific children because we are equipped with everything they need.

One prayer that has helped me cultivate my relationships with my kids is, "God, please show me who I need to be for each of my kids' needs. What can I do to serve them today?" Try that and see if it changes your heart toward them. Spend quality time with each important relationship to you. Life moves quickly, and before we know it, kids are gone from our homes. We do not get a second chance - once they get a taste of freedom, we lose them! I pray that we instill some really important tools in their toolbox before they go. DO IT NOW! We do not get a do-over in raising our kids. We get one shot! Let's try to make the most of our parenting careers because the next generation needs us!

Some tips that I have done to help get my house in order:

- Alone time with God every morning for at least 10–15 minutes
- Daily walk with my husband
- Family night where we each write our favorite Bible verses out and tape them to the fridge
- Have the 10 commandments up in my kitchen
- Make myself available for them when they need me
- Clean my heart out with any unforgiveness I had trapped inside me
- Start planning my day the night before
- Make dinner or breakfast time with family more meaningful
- Set out intentional dates with my family
- Set away intentional time on my calendar for God's time (make an appointment with God)

Remember this, Job 33:4 (my favorite Bible verse), "The Spirit of God has made me, and the breath of the Almighty gives me life." Think about that for a second. Trade the anxiety, the dread, or the pressure that weighs heavily on your heart for the refreshing truth that God breathes life into you. He doesn't feed you with fear. He doesn't drown you with guilt.

The second way to get your house in order is **financially**. The Bible refers to money more than any other topic, including faith and salvation. Jesus mentions money in sixteen out of thirty-eight of his parables. With so much emphasis on this essential topic, it would be wise to study the significance and connection money has to our everyday lives.

Instead of building up our bank accounts on Earth, scripture encourages us to lay up treasures for ourselves in heaven (Matthew 6:19-21). Our finances can help us have a true treasure in eternity if we invest in making a difference in God's Kingdom. We need to learn to be an investor in life, not a gambler.

I pray that you sit and reflect on your heart about money and see what God wants you to do with your finances. Do you need to get out of debt? The Bible does not teach that going into debt is an exercise of faith. In fact, oftentimes debt is evidence of a lack of faith. The Bible teaches that all of our debts must be repaid. Psalm 37:21 says, "The wicked borroweth and payeth not again."

A person can NEVER be debt-free if they are addicted to instant gratification. We have to learn how to be patient and save for what we want. We can't just expect to have money; we have to RESPECT money. Proverbs 21:20, "A wise man saves for the future, but a fool spends whatever he gets."

Here are five ways you can get your finances in order the Christian way (by Dave Ramsey).

1. Get on a budget, a written plan. "For which of you, intending to build a tower, does not sit down first and count the cost, whether he has enough to finish it." Luke 14:28

2. Get out of debt. "The rich rule over the poor and the borrower is a slave to the lender." Proverbs 22:7

3. Foster high-quality relationships. We become who we hang out with. "Do not be deceived, evil company corrupts good habits." 1 Corinthians 15:33

4. Save and invest. "In the house of the wise, are stones of food and oil." Proverbs 21:20

5. Be generous. "For God loves a cheerful giver." 1 Corinthians 15:33

We will never be the owners of God's possessions, but He allows us to manage, protect, and expand His assets. Money management has spiritual significance. **The power and meaning we give to our money reflect how we manage our lives.** We're all given time, talents, or treasures to work with, and God expects a return on his investment. Each will be given according to our ability.

The last and final pillar is our vessel, **our bodies**. The best way to think about this is your body is not yours; our body belongs to Christ. God created us in His image. So that means we must steward our bodies. First Corinthians 6:19, "Or do you not know that your body is the temple of the Holy Spirit that is in you, whom you have from God, and you are not on our own?"

We need a physical body to become like our Heavenly Father. Our bodies are so important that the Lord calls them temples of God (see 1 Corinthians 3:16-17; 6:19-20). Our bodies are Holy!

I was blessed to grow up in a house where fitness was an important part of our daily lives. Movement has always been in my life. I feel more alive when I am in motion. I have been in the fitness industry for over three decades now. I have even owned my own gym. When I teach classes, I want the people in my class to step away from their distractions (life) and step into their "physical spirit". I want them to feel the connection between their mind and body. I want them to separate themselves from their negative thoughts about their bodies.

We do an exercise in class, and you should try it. Get in front of a mirror and stare at yourself, look into your eyeballs, and look deep into yourself. What thoughts come up? Let them all come up and bring light to your thoughts (I don't like my legs, my stomach looks flabby). All of these thoughts come up and when you bring light to them (acknowledging them), they will go away! The devil had you in bondage in the dark with those thoughts. I teach them that we are not connected to our thoughts! You can actually rewire your brains! What I wanted people to learn so badly was that our bodies are made in His image. If we held ourselves with respect and honor, God would be very pleased. He does not want women shaming their bodies.

To honor God, we should treat our bodies like temples. We should treat our bodies like sacred ground. Something you would never destroy, something you would never allow to become dirty, something you would work to maintain and keep pristine.

This might come as a surprise because God considers our physical health just as important as spiritual health.

Psalm 119:73 says, "You made my body, Lord; now give me sense to heed your laws" (TLB). God set up the principles of good health. He doesn't just want you to have a pure heart. He wants your body to be in shape so He can use you more effectively.

Here are five simple yet effective steps you can take to treat your body like a temple.

1. Read and follow your body's signals. "In order to trust your body as a guide, the first step is to begin to understand it."

2. Prepare and show up for your meals; try to eat what is wholesome and not fried.

3. Take a bath, and keep peace in your heart and mind.

4. Move to feel good every day. Do something active, walk, play tennis, or find something you enjoy. When we sit all day… we are dying!

5. Restrict your screen time - less time on the phone and watching TV, and more time outside in nature.

I know being a mom is busy! I know life is full of distractions and that can derail your fitness and faith goals. There is a HUGE temptation to think, "I'm too busy, I don't have time to read my Bible," or "I'll eat whatever I want and skip my workouts for the next few months and then I'll get back on track in the fall."

Just remember that listening to distractions is going to set you back. Ignorance is NOT bliss; we reap what we sow. If the enemy can steal your health, he can steal your future. Do not let him win!

Mindset is HUGE! Pay attention to the words you are saying to yourself. What comes out of our mouths is in our hearts. So, watch what you say to others, and most importantly, what you say about yourself. What you say out loud will happen. Guard your heart. What matters more than the fun we have or the stuff we accumulate is what we did with the time we were given. We can not get too comfortable with life on Earth. We won't be here forever. The Bible tells us, "If you have been raised with Christ, keep seeking the things that are above, where Christ is, seated at the right hand of God. Set your minds on the things that are above, not on the things that are on earth" (Colossians 3:1-2).

We need to monitor and pay attention to our emotions. A lot of people base their day on how they feel. That is the first mistake.

Try this. Recognize and acknowledge every single thought that trickles into your mind. Pay attention to your fears, listen to your anger, and take note when you are triggered. When we feel fear, that usually shows up as anger. We should notice it, evaluate it, and acknowledge it. Just remember, God wants us to have peace in our hearts; not fear, not anger, just peace that is how the Holy Spirit can reside in our hearts.

I hope that these three areas and tips will help you "get your house in order."

Here are some journal questions that you can ask yourself if you want to find a mission statement for your own life.

1. What do you want your life to stand for?

2. What are you uniquely put on this Earth to achieve?

3. What kind of legacy do you want to leave behind?

4. What gifts, talents, skills, resources, and opportunities has God given you to use to serve Him and others?

5. What is important to you?

The significance of your life carries more value than what others think about you. Whenever you are forced to make a decision between purpose and preference, choose PURPOSE.

Life tip: if you are in a season where you are not seeing much fruit. I know this works because this is exactly what I did. We are all self-centered. If we take our focus off our problems and be good to someone else, God will put His hands on our problems and make things happen that we couldn't make happen. While you are busy helping others in their situation, you're not losing time because God is working on your situation.

Another life tip: learn as much as you can about yourself. Reflect on your upbringing, and bring light to any trauma you might have experienced as a child. Pay attention to your fears, know your triggers, and understand your desires. Who is in your head? If you want to bring more joy into your life, you are going to have to manage what you focus on. Know yourself really well, and then let God clean your heart out, and He will fill it all up with His goodness. Remember, we can only get guidance from a higher power if we are quiet in our minds (our souls). That is when the peace of the Holy Spirit will rest upon us.

My prayer for everyone reading this is that you feel peace in your heart when you read these words. This world is full of broken spirits. People who have given up in life or who have listened to the lies that the devil wants them to believe. Remember, you have someone who loves you so much that He wants to take away any of your problems. You also have someone who wants to kill and destroy you, and if they can't get to you, they will get to your family. We need to filter our thoughts. If you have a thought that is negative or makes you worry, that is from the Devil, not from God. Any thoughts you have of peace, joy, or what just makes you happy, that is from God. God isn't just calling you to do you. He is calling you to do the "new you," the one that God has shaped and refined and made you in His image.

I will end with this… "Your life is your story. Write well. Edit often."

Linda Tucker

Business Transformation Systems Inc
CEO & Business Coach

https://www.linkedin.com/in/linda-tucker-60687a56/
https://www.facebook.com/linda.tucker.96343/
https://MakeYourImpactwithWIN.com
https://www.freedomswitchusa.com/switch-with-lindatucker#form-BE0z2N_wIU

Linda is a daughter, sister, widow, grandmother, business CEO, and lifelong learner who enjoys sharing her empowering story with others. If you struggle with feeling ordinary in a world where everyone around you seems extraordinary, perhaps you'll resonate with her not-so-spectacular journey along a bumpy life road filled with challenges, frustrations, unexpected turns, painful losses and hard-won triumphs. Linda's story isn't about a meteoric rise to greatness but instead chronicles a life lived deliberately, with purpose and resilience. Join Linda as she shares her adventures, life lessons, and insights gleaned along her path to prosperity and gratitude. As a valued member of the Women's Impact Network, Linda continues to inspire and encourage women to share their gifts, talents and energies to enhance lives. Linda enjoys summers in New England, where her children and grandchildren live, and winters in The Villages Florida. Her passions are health, wealth, faith and family.

FROM TEENAGE MOTHERHOOD TO EMPOWERED WOMAN: A JOURNEY OF RESILIENCE AND GROWTH

By Linda Tucker

On October 11th, 1957, I turned 17. Five months later, I married Darrell. He was 19. Four months after our wedding our son, Jamey Carl, was born. And two years later, we had our second son, Matthew James.

I always knew I would be a mom someday but making that decision at 17 wasn't a great idea.

I barely got my high school diploma. I remember arguing with my mother about it. She wanted me to get it but I argued that I didn't see the point. "Ten years from now who will care if I graduated or not?" I argued. Her reply was that I would regret it if I didn't. Because she wasn't exactly thrilled that I was 17 and pregnant, I decided to placate her and talked to my school's guidance counselor. I was in the middle of my senior year and had completed all the requirements for graduation except four years of English. I was told if I could find a teacher to assign me an independent study curriculum, and if I completed the assignments, I could receive my diploma. Luckily for me, one of my English teachers agreed.

Looking back now, I am so grateful that my mother insisted I complete high school and that the school was willing to work with me to achieve that milestone. Having that diploma made a world of difference for me later on.

I learned pretty quickly that the married life I envisioned wasn't happening. Looking back, I'm sure I was suffering from post-partum depression, especially after Matt was born. At the time, I didn't understand much about childbirth, being a mother, or a wife.

After my kids were born, I remember being so in love with them that it scared me. That sounds crazy now but I literally thought that I could love them so much I would spoil them. My crazy thoughts told me I needed to toughen up. They were boys, and they didn't need their mother smothering them. Those thoughts seem absurd to me now because, believe me, you can never love your children too much. Some of my thinking came about because I had two brothers and my father was always talking to them about being "a man." I wasn't particularly close to my mother or my father. My dad was the guy who went to work, came home, watched TV, went to bed, got up, and did it again every day. I got my work ethic from him. He was a good provider for his family of seven that included himself, my mother, and five kids. In later years, to my regret, I employed some of his tough love methods to the detriment of my teenage sons. Luckily, today, I have two grown sons I am extremely proud of.

I was the middle child. I had an older sister and brother and a younger brother and sister. Janet was the oldest and Claudia was the youngest. I was sandwiched between Daniel, my oldest brother, and Timothy, my younger brother. I always felt that I fit the stereotype of the unseen middle child. Quiet and introverted, I never bonded with either parent. If I had to say which family member I was closest to growing up, it was definitely my younger brother, Tim, in the early years. Janet, my older sister, and I grew close only after we married and had kids. We remain close today.

By the time Matt was born, Darrell and I were not in a good relationship. I was feeling fat, ugly, stupid, and alone. Darrell was gone all day working, and in the evenings, he often wanted to spend time with his friends. My friends had moved on in life – gone off to college and were not tied down like me with two kids and a husband who didn't love me. At one point, Darrell told me he loved me but wasn't *in love* with me, and for me, that wasn't good enough. It was the beginning of the end.

Miraculously, Darrell and I were able to buy a house shortly after Jamey was born. A childhood friend of mine had a father who built houses. He was involved with the Farmer's Home Administration, a government program that he helped us qualify for. They were offering first-time homebuyers the chance to buy a home for $1 down, and a mortgage payment based on income.

Since I wasn't working and Darrell wasn't making much at all, our mortgage payment back in 1975 was $81 per month! We got a brand new, three-bedroom, ranch-style home, with a full basement, on one-quarter acre of land in a neighborhood called Sherwood Forest. The neighborhood was full of young families just like ours. I never really felt like I fit it in there though because I was younger than most of the other moms by ten years or so. I also found out I was somewhat of a misfit with women in general. I wasn't into home décor or crafts or other "womanly" pursuits. I was more of an outdoor lover who enjoyed blue jeans and sensible shoes over glamming it up. I wasn't much of a cook but I did learn how to make the basics – meat, potatoes, vegetables, pasta, and rice. I did some baking and enjoyed doing it, but, concerned with the health issues of too much sugar, I ended up giving that up. My dedication to fitness and health has followed me all my life.

Darrell had graduated from a post-high school, two-year, technical institute with a degree in electrical engineering. He had gotten a job at Digital Equipment Corporation (DEC) which at the time was a big name in computers.

Back in the mid to late seventies, computers were uncommon. Personal computers were in their infancy, and Darrell was fascinated by them. He was willing to do any job at DEC just to get a foot in the door. For a couple of years, he worked the night shift and did something that had to do with carbon for computer chips. I didn't fully understand what the carbon was used for, and I still don't, but he would come home covered in black soot. Through intelligence and hard work, he was eventually able to move into field service on the day shift, wearing a shirt and tie to work, and troubleshooting computer issues. He was definitely at the forefront of the computer infusion into every home in America.

Because I was unhappy and feeling left out of life, I decided that I would also learn about computers. If he could do it, I could too. So I enrolled in a local college to study computer programming. It was a yearlong certificate program where I would attend school two nights per week and all day Saturday. Back then, the programming languages I learned were Basic, Fortran, and C. I did pretty well at it and eventually got a job working at a law firm. I was the only computer programmer, and I hated it there. I learned that I wasn't ready to fly solo, and I really didn't like programming. But, I did get a free divorce attorney, and by 1981, Darrell and I were divorced. I was subsequently let go from the law firm (which I considered a blessing).

I used my knowledge of computers to get a job in the accounts payable department of a food distribution company. After a year or so of working in A/P, I transferred to working directly with the operations managers there. It was a cushy job where I drove around from one of their warehouses to another, just gathering timecard data for all the warehouse workers and submitting the data to payroll. Later, I transferred again to working in one of the warehouse offices scheduling incoming deliveries. It was a simple job that didn't require much skill. And I was pretty broke. I had bill collectors calling me all the time and I was worried I would lose my house. Darrell wasn't making great money either but he did contribute child support whenever he could. I was struggling financially and I knew that the only way out of my mess was to change my circumstances.

After a few years at the food distribution company, I decided to set my sights a little higher. I knew I didn't want to be a computer programmer, but I liked that I had a pretty good understanding of how computers worked. Most businesses were just beginning to use computers. In the early eighties, they were still using calculators and manual ledgers.

In 1983 I applied for a job at a local University in the Accounting Department, and I got the job. I was now working in accounts receivable instead of payables. My job was to work with students on paying their tuition. The job was right for me. I was the first person at the University outside of the computing department to have a computer terminal on my desk. I remember people asking me what it was and what it was used for. Prior to getting a terminal connected to the mainframe computers located across campus, all accounting records were entered on paper and sent to the data processing department. The data was transferred to punch cards which were loaded into the computer. Reports were generated and then printed on green bar paper. These reports would take days to produce and would be outdated by the time we received them.

The best part of working at the university was the benefits. They didn't pay great but I wasn't exactly working a high-level job. They did offer free tuition for employees. I wanted to get a degree in business administration but they didn't offer that as an undergrad degree program. So I signed up for public administration instead. With the public administration degree, I would be taking almost all the same business courses, and it offered a five-year path to a master's degree. During my senior undergrad year, I would be taking graduate-level courses which would count towards both degrees. Since this sounded good to me, I enrolled.

At this stage of my life, I was working a full-time job, going to school nights, and raising two kids. I also remarried. My new husband, Frank, at the beginning of our relationship, was a minister and full-time worker at a local hospital. He eventually left his work at the hospital and we invested in a breakfast/lunch restaurant where Frank would be the owner and cook. I kept the books and also helped out with cooking and serving on weekends. Jamey and Matt were in grade school, and they would sometimes come to the restaurant on weekends and help with dishwashing. So, my schedule was jam-packed. I had a full-time job during the week working 8:30 am to 4:30 pm, went to school two nights per week from 6:30 – 9:30 pm, had lots of homework (getting up at 4 am or 5 am to get it done), spent weekends cooking and serving at the restaurant, and managed the restaurant finances while raising two young sons.

I thrived during this period of my life. I got promoted at work from accounts receivable to grants and contracts accountant, and then to assistant controller. I graduated cum laude with my bachelor's degree in 1993 and finished my master's in 1995. Because I attended school part-time, it took me ten years to complete the five-year degree program, but I finally had my master's degree. I had worked hard to get it.

The other good part about working at the university was not only was I able to go to school tuition-free, but so were Jamey and Matt. They were six and eight years old when I started at the university but I had the vision that eventually they would be eligible to attend college.

Jamey graduated from high school the same year I graduated from college, 1993. He got accepted to the university and studied computer science. He got an internship at DEC, the same company Darrell worked at, and upon graduation in 1997 got hired there full-time. He still works with computers today.

Matt never attended the University. Instead, he attended a community college and married Bobbi, a girl he met there. They have a beautiful daughter, Alexis who is now 11.

Frank and I were married in 1983 and divorced in 1993. The restaurant failed, not because of anything Frank did or didn't do, but because we didn't own the building where the restaurant was housed.

The landlord raised the rent to the extent that the business could not be profitable, so eventually, we just shut it down. Our marriage failed because I had changed and Frank hadn't. I had achieved the goals I set for myself but I wasn't done learning and growing. Frank didn't have many ambitions, and I felt he wanted me to settle for less than the life I wanted to lead.

When I left the university in 1997 for a job at a medical center, I was armed with both my bachelor's and master's degrees. The many experiences that the university had provided me with gave me a firm foundation that allowed me to explore new options. I applied for a job in the IT (Information Technology) department at the medical center and was hired as a liaison between the department of surgery and IT. It was a huge financial raise for me.

My role was to make sure that the surgeons had the technology they needed to do their jobs. I joined the medical center at a time shortly after the merged two hospitals, a small community hospital, and a large teaching hospital. There was a lot of rancor among the employees. The small community employees felt they had been swallowed whole and their culture destroyed. The large teaching hospital didn't like the new administration dictating "corporate" rules and stifling their academic license for creativity and autonomy.

I was the newbie who didn't know either entity before the merger. People wanted me to take sides. It was an uncomfortable place to be. I wanted to be Switzerland and remain neutral, but the battle raged around me. My own direct reports plotted against me. Many of the physicians took out their anger over the new rules on me and since my job was to make them happy, I was not loved. My paycheck came from the IT department and my job performance was evaluated by them. I walked a fine line between advocating for the surgeons' needs and enforcing the IT standards. I survived while others didn't. After a major coup where the head of surgery was ousted, I was moved from surgery to IT where I no longer had to straddle the fence.

The IT department was going through some reorganization, and we spent months sitting around, doing nothing while the bigwigs planned their strategies. I was bored to tears. When I got the chance to move from IT to medical records, I jumped at the opportunity and got another salary increase. I was finally earning decent money.

I remarried for the third time in 2001 to Art. He and I had been living together since shortly after my divorce from Frank. Art was 10 years older than me when we met. He was a building inspector, carpenter, and Air Force veteran. He was the father of two children, Diana and Aaron. When Art and I began our relationship, Diana was 23 and Aaron was 21. Jamey was 18 and Matt was 16. Jamey had started living at college so Matt was the only one living with us.

Shortly after Art and I got together, he left his job as a building inspector and was hired by the City of Worcester as a housing rehabilitation specialist. Art and I were a good match for one another. We both loved the outdoors, fitness, our kids, and our grandkids. By the time we married, Diana had four children and Aaron had five. We were enjoying life. Although the grandkids weren't biologically mine, I loved being a grandmother to them.

I stayed at the medical center until 2006 when my first genetic - grandson, Ryan, was born. Rather than have him enrolled in daycare so Jamey and Sherri could work full-time, I wanted to be the one to spend time with him. I hadn't really gotten to enjoy my own kids because of the stress of being a child parent myself, and I was determined that I would be the best grandmother I could be.

I was able to retire from the medical center with a small lump-sum pension payout that would cover my expenses for one year. Art and I had a plan for him to retire in 2000. After retirement, we were going to move to New Hampshire because of our love of the mountains, lakes, and oceans. New Hampshire had them all.

I had come a long way from the pregnant 17-year-old high school student who barely graduated. I was a wife, mother, and grandmother. I had fallen several times with two divorces and many missteps, but I never gave up. Because of my early poverty years, I had learned to value money and was cautious in how I spent it. I finally had a husband I loved and who loved me. We had our life together planned out. Together we had saved enough money to retire, me at age 50 and him at age 60. We had weathered a lot of difficult family situations over the years but our kids and grandkids were for the time safe and sound. It wasn't always that way, and we knew we were blessed. Despite some troubling times, everyone seemed to have gotten through the worst of it. Or so I thought at the time.

I had a great year with Ryan and would have liked to stay in Massachusetts longer to be near him and Art's grandkids, but we had bought our retirement house in New Hampshire a few years earlier. We used it as a vacation home for a while, but with retirement looming for Art and me not working, we couldn't afford both houses. We sold the Massachusetts house in 2007 and moved to New Hampshire. We had three great years there doing all the things we loved – skiing, boating, hiking, swimming, kayaking, and feeling like we were on a long vacation.

In 2010, things took a turn. My father was diagnosed with dementia and my mother was having trouble caring for him. I and my four siblings held a family meeting. It was decided that since I was the only one of the five who was not working, Art and I would rent out our house in New Hampshire, rent a condo in Hopedale where my parents were living, and try to help my mom. It didn't go exactly as planned.

My dad didn't like anyone being in the house besides my mother. He only wanted to be with her. When I would sit with him so my mother could go to church or run an errand, he would ask me hundreds of times "Where's my wife?" I would remind him that she was at church or shopping and he would say "Oh yes, you told me that," and then ask again a few minutes later. He didn't know who I was or why I was there.

In 2011, we had to move my parents into an assisted living situation. My dad was in memory care and my mom had a small studio apartment of her own on the same campus. She was able to see him every day but didn't have the responsibility of 24-hour care of him.

The most incredible part of this journey through dementia for me and Art, and also my sister, Janet, was that it brought us closer together than we had ever been. Somehow God knew we would need His strength to help my parents through this time. Janet, me, and Art were called to and joined a spiritual community in Framingham, MA named the Order of Christ Sophia; Christ demonstrates the masculine energy of divinity, and Sophia, the feminine. During this period, all three of us stopped drinking alcohol and we all grew closer to God through meditation and prayer.

My father passed away in 2017 at the age of eighty-seven. He had struggled with dementia for seven years. This was the same year that, unbelievably to me, Art was diagnosed with Alzheimer's.

I had watched my father slowly shrink from the confident, strong man I grew up with to a shadow of himself. Now I was faced with the same situation with my husband, a man I loved deeply and who was the other half of my soul.

My Dad was eighty when he began his decline; Art was only seventy and I was sixty. We had both been healthy and active all our lives, so this diagnosis rocked me to my core.

Four years after we received the news of Art's illness, he was gone. Those four years were the most painful of my life. Alzheimer's and Dementia are called "The Long Good-Bye," and truly, it is an agony of despair to see the decline day after day and know the inevitable is coming.

Art passed on December 2nd, 2021. My mother passed on July 7th of the same year, and both losses took a great toll on me. My younger sister, Claudia, also passed away in 2019, two years after my father's death and two years before both Art and my mom. Four deaths in four years were difficult to bear. My mother had been one of nine children, and my dad had two sisters. Our extended family had been large with lots of aunts and uncles who were once close to us as we grew up. By the end of 2021, almost all of them were gone. I had also lost several cousins over the years. The weight of all these lives having ended was heavy on me. I realized how fleeting it all is and how little control we have over the fates. I was feeling pretty knocked around and not sure how I was going to move forward.

What got me through was my remaining family – my sister Janet and my brothers, Dan and Tim; Also my kids, Jamey and Matt, their wives, and my grandchildren. When the chips are down, I know that I can always find comfort in their love.

What also kept me going is my faith that all my deceased loved ones are with God, the creator of the Universe and the loving father of all of us. I was raised a Catholic but I didn't embrace that ideology. I never felt comfortable in the confines of dogma or discrimination. My faith has always been rooted in the belief that to love is to be Godly. If you live in love, you are free to worship as you please, wherever you please, in whatever way you please. My church was the great outdoors and I still marvel at the beauty God has created. I feel closest to God when I am in nature.

In June of 2022, six months after Art passed away, I held a memorial service and laid him to rest. It took me those six months to grieve. I still have moments of intense longing for him, but I am still here, and my time is not done.

I don't think that it was a coincidence that in June of 2022, I was also introduced to a way to serve others who may be struggling with financial, health, or other challenges. What started as a way toward inner healing for me has turned into a way for me to uplift others.

I was introduced to Melaleuca, the wellness company. And that journey has led to The Women's Impact Network. Our mission is to create a movement empowering mission-driven women to live their purpose. We are all co-creators of this world, and by joining together, we can create the kind of world where no one is left behind. God has granted us abundance and it is up to us to embrace and share these gifts with one another.

The major lessons I have learned in my sixty-six years on this planet are these.

- Always be open to learning and growing. Listen to the people who have your best interests at heart.
- Talk to God always and ask for guidance.
- Be open to love.
- Believe in yourself and put effort into getting what you want and giving back what you can.
- Joy comes from living a balanced life.
- Take time to enjoy work, play, friends, and family.
- Be kind to your body and take responsibility for your health and wellness. And always give thanks for the blessings in your life. Even in the darkest moments, God is with you. You never know in what form your prayers will be answered, but if you believe that God is love, you will never be alone.

All along my life path, there were mentors, guides, angels, opportunities, and miracles that appeared when I needed them. If you're in a place where you're looking for the answers to your prayers, I encourage you to join us at the Women's Impact Network. All it takes to realize your dreams is knowing what you want and being brave enough to step into your power. We have been told, "Blessed are those who have not seen and yet believe." Don't stop believing.

Luiara Anderton

Co-Founder of WIN Brazil and
Director of Business Development at LVED.com

https://www.linkedin.com/in/luiara-anderton-3031808a/
https://www.facebook.com/luiara.rego?mibextid=LQQJ4d
https://www.instagram.com/luiara.anderton
https://www.lved.com/
https://winbrazil.org/

Born into an entrepreneurial family in Brazil, I inherited a passion for business and innovation. With a drive to make an impact, I pursued opportunities to expand my horizons, eventually landing a role as Director of business development at LVED.com. This journey wasn't without its challenges, but each obstacle only fueled my determination to succeed. Alongside my professional endeavors, I recognized the importance of empowering women like me to harness their potential in the business world. WIN Brazil led me to dedicate time and resources to providing educational support tailored to developing essential business skills among women. Through mentorship, workshops, and networking opportunities, I strive to level the playing field and foster a more inclusive entrepreneurial landscape. My story is one of perseverance, adaptability, and a commitment to driving positive change, both within the business community and society at large.

UNLEASHING THE POTENTIAL: EMPOWERING WOMEN THROUGH THE JOURNEY OF LEARNING

By Luiara Anderton

1 - Early Life and Challenges

A Symphony of Struggles and Triumphs

In the lively streets of São Paulo, Brazil, my journey unfolds as a testament to resilience and ambition. As a Brazilian immigrant, my odyssey spans continents, woven over 30 years of unwavering entrepreneurial spirit. I faced challenges, dreamed big, and committed myself to carving a path in a foreign land.

Born into humble beginnings, I confronted the stark realities of limited opportunities in my hometown. Fueled by an unyielding desire for a better life, I ventured into entrepreneurship, navigating a labyrinth of uncertainties. With each step forward, I honed my skills—from small-scale enterprises to navigating the complexities of the global market.

Fate took an unexpected turn when I crossed paths with an American entrepreneur, Terry Anderton. Our shared passion for business and mutual respect for each other's ambitions sparked a connection that transcended borders and cultures. Terry and I became partners not only in the intricate dance of entrepreneurship with LVED.com but we got married in 2021, blending Brazilian vibrancy with American tenacity.

Three decades of joint endeavors, triumphs, and occasional setbacks marked my entrepreneurial odyssey. I weathered storms, embraced victories, and learned invaluable lessons that only time and experience could bestow. Yet, amidst personal success, I discovered a new calling – one that would bridge my past and present, my roots, and the land I now call home.

In a world shaped by collaboration and shared wisdom, I became a member of the Women Impact Network and decided to create the Brazilian version of the group to help women from my country develop their businesses in the USA. I founded the WIN Brazil network where women could unite, transcending cultural and linguistic barriers to pursue the American dream. This vision materialized into a collaboration network, a haven for aspiring female entrepreneurs seeking not just financial success but a holistic fulfillment of freedom, health, and wealth.

The subsequent sections will delve into the layers of my life, exploring the challenges I overcame, the triumphs I celebrated, and the transformative impact of my collaboration network on the lives of countless women.

2 - Entrepreneurial Journey

My journey traces back to the heart of Brazil, where I was born into the rich tapestry of an Italian-Portuguese family. From a young age, I found myself immersed in an environment pulsating with an entrepreneurial spirit, all thanks to my father—a visionary entrepreneur and journalist.

My father's impact on Brazil's audio industry was nothing short of revolutionary. He pioneered a groundbreaking technology system for digital audio in trucks used to distribute propane tanks throughout the bustling streets of São Paulo. The resounding success of this innovation not only transformed the audio-marketing landscape of the country but also became synonymous with the famed "ultragaz" jingles— compositions that echoed across every corner of Brazil.

Growing up in this entrepreneurial crucible, I witnessed the dynamic challenges my father faced. The highs of innovation and market success were coupled with the lows of navigating a competitive landscape and overcoming logistical hurdles. These formative years instilled in me a profound understanding of the entrepreneurial journey that would shape my own path in unforeseen ways.

However, life took an unexpected turn when tragedy struck my first family. I faced the heart-wrenching loss of my first husband who succumbed to colon cancer at the tender age of 39, leaving behind a young, ambitious lady with two children who were five and 13 years old. This profound loss became a catalyst for change, prompting me to reevaluate my life and aspirations.

With courage as my compass, I decided to embark on a new chapter. Leaving behind the familiar streets of São Paulo, I set my sights on the United States—a land of promise and opportunity. The decision to move abroad was not merely a physical relocation; it symbolized a profound emotional and spiritual journey of healing and reinvention with no way back.

In the vast expanse of the United States, I sought to rebuild my life and rediscover my sense of purpose. The challenges I faced were not just geographical but also emotional, as I navigated the complexities of grief, adaptation, and the pursuit of a fresh start.

This chapter of my life, marked by the symphony of my father's entrepreneurial legacy, the loss of my first love, and the courageous leap into the unknown, laid the foundation for the indomitable spirit that would define my future endeavors.

3 - Thriving Amidst Challenges

My entrepreneurial journey unfolds against the backdrop of a rich family legacy. Growing up in São Paulo, both my parents worked from home, immersing me in the world of entrepreneurship from a young age. My father's groundbreaking contributions to Brazil's audio industry and my mother's role as a pioneering publisher and organizer of the biggest international bands concerts in Brazil, like U2, RockinRio, Closeup Planet, and Brazilian-famous bands like Racionais and Metallica, shaped my upbringing since I was little. I started working as a receptionist when I was 12 and promoter when I was 13.

Assisting my parents provided me with a hands-on education in business intricacies, fostering a strong work ethic. Additionally, my involvement in non-profit projects instilled a passion for giving back to the community, shaping my values and understanding of entrepreneurship.

Moving to the United States presented cultural and linguistic challenges, but I embraced them as opportunities for growth. Navigating a foreign business landscape was daunting yet my resilient spirit turned every stumbling block into a stepping stone.

Leveraging my diverse skill set, honed as a successful executive assistant, I found my niche in the American entrepreneurial arena. Despite initial struggles, my tenacity and ability to turn challenges into opportunities propelled my emerging success.

This chapter of my journey reflects not only the influence of my parents but also my own indomitable spirit. The synthesis of my early exposure to various industries, dedication to community service, and trials of adapting to a new culture shaped me into a woman who thrives amidst challenges, transforming adversity into fuel for success.

4 - Inspiration to Give Back: Nurturing Dreams Beyond Borders

After years of chasing conventional corporate success, I found myself standing at a crossroads, feeling a deep yearning for something more profound. It was a moment of introspection where I questioned the true purpose of my journey—a purpose that transcended personal achievements.

Enter my husband, Terry Anderton, a seasoned entrepreneur in the American business world. His guidance not only helped me navigate the complexities of the American business landscape but also ignited a belief in shared success.

This revelation shifted my perspective profoundly. I realized that my journey wasn't just about individual triumphs; it was an opportunity to uplift and empower others, especially women with similar dreams.

Recognizing the doors fate had opened for me, I felt compelled to extend a helping hand to fellow immigrant women chasing their aspirations. My experiences, triumphs, and lessons learned alongside Terry became a well of knowledge meant to be shared.

Fueled by this newfound purpose, I set out on a mission to help women with the power of collaboration in the challenging world of business. I understood that unity among women entrepreneurs could spark transformative change, benefiting not just individuals but entire communities.

In the intricate fabric of my journey, I discovered a divine calling—to be a guiding light for those navigating in a new countryside, cultures, and business environments. My commitment to giving back stemmed from the belief that true success is only meaningful when shared, celebrated, and multiplied.

The "Inspiration to Give Back" chapter embodies my evolving purpose, transitioning from personal success to a dedication to empowering others. As I established a collaboration network, I planted seeds of empowerment, guiding women through the threads of the American dream and fostering collective growth and achievement.

5 - Formation of Collaboration Network: Bridging Dreams and Realities

As I observed the struggles faced by countless women (particularly immigrants like myself), I felt an unwavering resolve to create a platform that transcended borders and languages—a collaboration network designed to uplift and empower immigrant women seeking independence and success in the US. The genesis of this vision lay in my shared experiences of navigating a foreign landscape, braving language barriers, and confronting the challenges of finding meaningful employment.

Motivated by empathy and a genuine desire to make a difference, I initiated the formation of a collaboration network that would become a lifeline for many. Recognizing the power of shared stories and the impact of personal testimonies, I decided to communicate with my fellow countrywomen in our native language, creating a space where they could find solace, inspiration, and tangible opportunities for growth.

My journey into establishing this network commenced with a digital outreach strategy. Leveraging the potency of social media, I began by reaching out to women through various platforms, extending heartfelt invitations to join a community founded on collaboration and shared success. The resonance of my call was swift and profound. Within less than a month, hundreds of women eagerly became followers, drawn to the promise of a supportive community and the prospect of meaningful connections.

With the foundation laid, I seamlessly transitioned from a virtual community to a dynamic platform that actively engaged its members. I transformed my vision into action by managing businesses within the network, providing a practical pathway for women to secure job opportunities and regain a sense of financial independence.

Navigating the initial challenges of building a collaborative space, I faced hurdles like language differences, diverse cultural backgrounds, and the inherent complexities of managing an online community. However, my unwavering commitment and the shared determination of the women I gathered fueled the momentum needed to overcome these obstacles.

The collaboration network quickly evolved into a thriving ecosystem where experiences, skills, and opportunities flowed freely. My testimony of success became a beacon of inspiration, guiding others through the intricate terrain of entrepreneurship, job seeking, and personal development.

In this chapter of my story, the establishment of the collaboration network serves as a testament to the transformative power of collective efforts. Through virtual connections and shared ambitions, I turned a vision of unity into a tangible reality, creating a space where women collaborated, thrived, and propelled one another toward newfound independence and success.

Lynn M. Shallow

LMS Coaching Inc.
Business Breakthrough Coach

https://www.linkedin.com/in/lynn-shallow-080362300
https://www.instagram.com/r.e.a.l.confidence_4you
https://realbizconfidence.com

Lynn grew up as a francophone in a small town in Northern Ontario, where she was content with the familiar rhythms of life. Upon young adulthood, she embarked on a path less traveled, later driven by the pursuit of personal growth and professional advancement. This experience instilled in her a deep sense of perseverance and resilience, laying the foundation for future successes. Each step along this path has been marked by continuous learning and growth, shaping her into a confident and highly adaptable professional prepared and eager to confront new challenges. Being a lifelong learner, as retirement from her corporate career approached, she pursued various coaching certifications to complement her diverse professional and life experiences. This combination has empowered her to confidently establish her coaching business leading women to streamline their business model to deliver impactful results for their clients while leveraging their income, and maintaining a fulfilling personal life.

R.E.A.L. CONFIDENCE 4 EMPOWERMENT

By Lynn M. Shallow

Introduction

In a world where we, as women, journey through a maze of pressures, expectations, and conflicting messages, our quest for genuine confidence and empowerment begins in our earliest years and continues through our lifetime. Fueled by our inherent nurturing instincts, I, like many others, have grappled with self-doubt and uncertainty about my aspirations or what I wanted for my future. Yet, within this uncertainty, laid a flicker of ambition - a dream whispering of endless possibilities.

We have all heard stories of women being underestimated, and their potential overlooked, only to rise and exceed expectations. These examples reveal a profound truth: while external perceptions may falter, our inner strength remains unwavering. This underscores the importance of embracing our resilience and unlocking our boundless potential. As women unite confidently in support of one another, we cultivate a culture of empowerment where kindness and fortitude illuminate the path forward - a collective journey toward a more inclusive, equitable future.

During my retirement years, my passion has been to lead women to evolve to confidently create the life and business they truly desire. It's about more than breaking barriers; it's about fostering a culture where kindness and resilience shine as beacons of hope, empowering us all to embrace our true power to impact the collective.

However, it all starts with us individually. Juggling the demands of daily life, work, and a young family, I made a conscious effort to prioritize self-growth over others' opinions by focusing on furthering my formal education. At the same time, I managed to continue embracing traditional maternal roles, cooking nutritious meals for my family, which at the time brought me joy, even when our children didn't always appreciate the healthier options. My husband and I invested and were actively involved in our children's chosen extracurricular activities, aiming to support their development and self-assurance.

In the midst of my career, I encountered a rare occasion for significant personal and professional growth. This opportunity was rare in the sense that I lived outside major urban hubs where career progression opportunities were more readily available. Despite challenges like being away from my family during the week and enduring weekly long commutes of 350 kilometers each way, often in harsh winter conditions, my husband and I knew the importance of seizing this opportunity. We remain incredibly grateful for the abundant familial support we received throughout our periods of transition, particularly from my mother, mother-in-law, and my sister and her family.

As a parent, I deeply understood the importance of balancing family obligations with my personal values while being a wife and mother. This required a delicate equilibrium between addressing family needs and honoring my aspirations and identity. While extending ourselves from our comfort zone wasn't easy, we developed more resilience individually and as a family. Not only did this opportunity push me out of my comfort zone, but it also prepared me for forthcoming transitions, such as our son heading to university the following year. We also viewed it as a potential avenue for our teenage daughter to further develop her artistic talents.

Empowering women doesn't mean having power over others. In a world where competition to be the best is often seen as the main way to succeed, we often forget about the strength found in working together and empowering each other as a collective force. At its core, empowerment means breaking free from competition and realizing that real success comes from collaboration. It shows us a world full of opportunities to work together, learn, and grow, giving us the confidence to celebrate others' success as it enriches our own journey.

An empowered mindset is crucial for reclaiming our inner confidence and creating the life we desire. It requires personal responsibility and tangible actions rooted in resilience, self-awareness, and confidence amidst societal expectations. As Michael Jordan once said, "Some people want it to happen, some wish it would happen, others make it happen." Empowerment is not just about aspirations; it's about making those aspirations a reality through focused effort and action.

A Women's Day presentation on statistics highlighting the prevalent lack of confidence among women, including those who are highly skilled and educated, ignited my passion for addressing this issue through my coaching services. This chapter introduces R.E.A.L. Confidence, aiming to bridge the documented confidence gaps in women. The R.E.A.L. acronym serves as a guide to nurturing inner confidence, laying the groundwork for cultivating outer confidence.

R.E.A.L. Confidence is grounded in realignment with our true selves, fostering evolving confidence, authenticity, and liberation from societal expectations. Through empowerment and collaboration, we create an environment where support and learning thrive and competition gives way to collaboration. As we journey towards empowerment, our collective success uplifts not only ourselves but also our families, communities, and the world.

I also briefly delve into the realms of intelligence and energy, recognizing their profound impact on personal empowerment. Energetic intelligence encompasses our physical, mental, and spiritual dimensions, influencing our thoughts, feelings, and actions. Understanding our energy patterns and emotions enables us to reconnect with our unique gifts and passions to help create a more purposeful and meaningful life. Developing energetic intelligence is a path to personal empowerment as well as a catalyst for uplifting and empowering others in a collective journey toward greater fulfillment, authenticity, and purpose (you will note that 'energetic intelligence' is substituted with 'energy' throughout to minimize repetition).

Reflecting on writing this chapter has led me to look back at how my choices shaped my journey to where I am today: as the CEO of my business empowering women to confidently transform their businesses. Even though my journey has been a rich source of learning, insights, and accomplishments, I confidently navigated through the lack of acknowledgment or interest from my immediate circle without harboring judgment or comparison. This serves as a testament to the inner peace that comes from being aligned and confident in creating one's unique path, showing that validation from others is not required.

Built upon both personal experiences and theoretical knowledge, the principles of R.E.A.L. Confidence guide my goal to illustrate how your journey towards self-realization and empowerment is attainable by embracing your inner strength while also caring for your loved ones. I've intertwined some elements of my personal journey with how I navigated and fostered some facets of R.E.A.L. Confidence in my life and career. These served as a strong foundation for applying the many skills I developed.

This chapter is dedicated to you, the reader, and serves as a tribute to our two remarkable and kind-hearted children and their young families, as well as to my husband for his continuous support throughout our journey.

Realigned Confidence

Realigned Confidence is a key aspect of empowerment, emphasizing the connection between our inner confidence and outer success. In today's world, it's crucial to rediscover our true selves amidst societal pressures. This process involves looking inward, finding the courage to explore our deepest desires, values, and dreams, and freeing ourselves from external expectations to fuel the transformations we truly want to create and experience in our lives. When our energy is congruent with our values and purpose, we experience a sense of confidence and authenticity. By nurturing our energetic intelligence, we gain the ability to recognize and take proactive steps to realign our energy with our true selves. This process fosters a deeper sense of confidence firmly rooted in authenticity.

Success comes from pursuing our aspirations fueled by desire. Embracing desires and gratitude enriches our lives with balance and fulfillment, often requiring us to step out of our comfort zone and embrace discomfort to grow. Being in tune with our energetic intelligence helps us connect with our deepest desires and dreams, guiding us toward authentic and fulfilling goals. Understanding our energy helps us identify true motivations, empowering us to better navigate obstacles with resilience and optimism. Harnessing our energetic potential propels us towards creating our own path to success with confidence and determination. Although I sometimes questioned if my choices were driven by a desire to rebel against norms, I knew deep down that I was creating my unique path. My commitment to living authentically was shaped by both unconscious and conscious choices that often challenged conventional norms.

Knowing our personal values is essential for guiding our life priorities and making intentional choices with meaning and purpose. Being in touch with our energy helps align our values with our choices, bringing integrity and authenticity to our actions to experience greater fulfillment. When our choices resonate with our values, we experience increased positivity and inner harmony. Developing energetic intelligence empowers us to navigate life with more clarity and purpose.

Family and continuous growth are two of my top personal values. I committed to facing challenges and maximizing opportunities for personal and professional development while keeping our family intact, even from a distance. Balancing family responsibilities with a commitment to learning demanded adaptability from everyone in our family. Genuine confidence emerged when I aligned my choices with my values, relieving me from the exhaustion of trying to be someone I was not and allowing me to naturally expand into a better version of myself.

Resilience is vital, providing us with the strength to overcome challenges. Connecting with our energetic intelligence offers valuable insights into our emotional and mental states, guiding us in managing stress and adversity. By tuning into our energy, we gain a deeper understanding of ourselves and our reactions to stress, empowering us to navigate life's challenges with more grace and confidence. In times of uncertainty, resilience empowered me to persevere and adapt, viewing setbacks as temporary lessons that propelled me forward. Despite being exhausted, I remained determined and highly adaptable, learning the true meaning of strength and perseverance.

Self-compassion and self-acceptance allow us to embrace our inherent worthiness and acknowledge our imperfections with kindness and understanding, treating ourselves with the same gentleness and empathy we extend to others. Our energetic intelligence provides valuable insights into our inner landscape including emotions, thoughts, and behaviors. Without this awareness, we may struggle to fully understand and accept ourselves, leading to feelings of self-doubt and criticism. Obstacles such as shame, guilt, and obligation hinder our level of self-compassion. Shame distorts our self-perception while guilt ties us to past mistakes. Obligation often compels us to prioritize the needs of others over our own. As women, we often struggle to overcome these negative energies. By learning to tune into our energy and identify the root causes of these emotional disturbances, we can respond to challenges with clarity and composure rather than reacting impulsively. This emotional resilience fosters a sense of inner strength and confidence, empowering us to navigate life's ups and downs with grace. I refused to let feelings of guilt stop me and remained steadfast in my chosen path, understanding that others' judgments are reflective of their own experiences and perspectives.

With realigned confidence, we recognize that success is not a one-size-fits-all; it's about defining our own paths and celebrating the diversity of experiences and ambitions. This fosters a sense of unity among women as each of our journeys becomes a unique expression of authenticity, inspiring others to embrace their own truths without conforming to external standards. This realignment helps us recognize that each of our journeys is valid and deserving of respect. By promoting acceptance and inclusivity within our community, we create a collaborative environment, uplifting and empowering one another, free from unhealthy competition or comparison.

Evolving Confidence

Evolving Confidence is about understanding that confidence is not static - it evolves over time as we stretch ourselves and encounter new situations, challenges, and goals. Energetic intelligence supports this journey by providing us with insights into our energetic patterns and tendencies to help us identify areas for growth and development as well as recognize when we're resisting change or self-sabotaging. Awareness of our energy helps us navigate the ups and downs of our evolving journey, fostering resilience and adaptability. We can then harness our energy to support our growth and cultivate a sense of confidence that comes from embracing change and evolution.

Courage was a crucial catalyst for cultivating evolving confidence, urging me to take bold steps toward growth. Lack of awareness of our energetic intelligence hinders our courage to pursue dreams. Our energy serves as an internal compass, guiding us towards our deepest desires and aspirations. Without this awareness, we may overlook our true passions and hesitate to take the necessary steps to achieve our goals, missing out on valuable insights that could bolster our confidence and determination. Understanding our energy enables us to overcome self-doubt and fear, embarking on a purpose-driven journey toward realizing our dreams. Each choice made, from stepping out of my comfort zone to embracing new experiences, propelled me forward in developing R.E.A.L. Confidence despite the inevitable challenges. My journey demanded courage and resilience, including lengthy weekly commutes away from my home. Yet, I remained undeterred by external judgments, aligning my choices with personal desires for continuous growth, evolution, and empowerment. It was not easy, but maintaining balance in coping was crucial. This journey taught me the importance of refraining from judgment towards others' decisions, deepening my commitment to approach others' choices with empathy and respect.

Being adaptable is vital for navigating life's uncertainties with resilience and optimism. Our energy provides valuable insights into our emotional and mental states, guiding us in responding to change and challenges. Without this awareness, we may struggle to recognize signs of imbalance in our energy, leading to feelings of overwhelm or rigidity in uncertain situations. We then miss opportunities to adapt and thrive. Embracing adaptability as a key skill for navigating life's ups and downs allowed me to approach challenges with confidence, knowing that I had the resources within me to thrive in any situation. For example, I began my career in an entry-level position, understanding that opportunities would arise despite this position not aligning with my educational background. I subsequently aimed to qualify for a professional role, requiring further education. Juggling full-time work and caring for two small children at the time, I completed my university degree in under two years. This effort paid off when I was offered the professional role I was aiming for, supporting the value of adaptability and perseverance.

With evolving confidence, we embrace challenges as opportunities for personal and professional development, viewing setbacks as valuable learning experiences. This mindset fosters a culture of mutual support and mentorship where we share insights, strategies, and resources to help each other navigate obstacles. As empowered women, we inspire and uplift one another through shared journeys of transformation. Our energetic intelligence provides insights into our resilience and adaptability, guiding us in responding to life's difficulties and challenges with grace and optimism.

Authentic Confidence

Authenticity means staying true to ourselves despite external influences or pressures. Merriam-Webster defines authenticity as being "true to one's own personality, spirit, or character." It's about being genuine, truthful, and transparent in our thoughts and actions. The word 'authenticity' was recently crowned as the "word of the year" by Merriam-Webster. This recognition suggests a growing trend or interest in authenticity in society.

In a world where appearances often matter more than substance, authenticity emerges as a rare and precious trait originating from within. It enables us to embrace and express our genuine selves without pretense or conformity. Cultivating authentic confidence is crucial in bolstering our trust in our abilities, intelligence, and judgment to empower us to pursue our goals with purpose and conviction. Energetic intelligence empowers us to trust our intuition, honor our boundaries, and stand in our power, cultivating a deep sense of confidence that radiates from within. Many women hesitate to embrace their authentic selves for fear of judgment. Over time, I developed greater self-confidence and self-acceptance, which proved vital to believing that others' opinions do not define me.

Unlike superficial confidence, authentic confidence is not reliant on external validation but instead stems from a foundation of self-awareness, self-acceptance, and self-trust. It enables us to honor our unique identity and values. Constant comparison or the need to compete with others detracts from expressing our authentic selves and hinders our ability to fully embrace our individuality.

Our persona, shaped by beliefs, values, experiences, and social pressures, is the external personality we present in various settings. While creating a persona can be strategic in some cases, we must be mindful of its impact on our authenticity. Over-reliance on our persona leads to feelings of inadequacy, as we hide our true selves. Constantly pleasing others hinders our personal growth. Energetic intelligence offers insights into our authentic selves, guiding us to express our true essence rather than conforming. Shedding pretense and embracing our genuine nature fosters deeper connections and greater self-fulfillment.

Maintaining integrity cultivates self-assurance and trust within ourselves and influences our perceptions of others. It's important to recognize integrity in others to discern their sincerity and reliability. Integrity guides navigating challenges with clarity and purpose. A lack of awareness of our energy may lead to compromising integrity and self-assurance for external validation. Throughout my career, I gradually and increasingly prioritized doing what was right despite challenges. Approaching my mistakes with honesty, I took responsibility and learned from them, navigating challenges with resilience.

Authentic confidence fosters respect for others' dignity, leading to avoidance of gossip and judgment. It reflects a secure sense of self-worth, not seeking validation or status elevation through belittling others. Unconscious engagement in gossip and judgment drains energy and harms relationships. Arrogance and extreme shyness often arise from an imbalanced ego, either asserting superiority or shielding from perceived threats. True confidence, however, embraces balanced self-assurance, free from diminishing others or hiding insecurities. Connecting with our energy reveals the impact of our thoughts and actions, guiding us away from negative behaviors. Choosing kindness and positivity creates a supportive environment, reducing negativity's influence. It's crucial to consciously minimize gossip and recognize that other people's stories are theirs and separate from our own.

Financial struggles often act as a barrier to authenticity, causing stress and anxiety that divert our focus from personal growth. Limited financial resources restrict our opportunities for self-expression and exploration of passions. Societal pressure to attain material wealth may also compel us to conform rather than embrace our true selves. Financial insecurity deeply affects our self-worth and identity, leading to feelings of inadequacy. Understanding our beliefs and attitudes towards money guides our financial decisions and behaviors e.g., engaging in patterns of overspending, under-saving, or living beyond our means. By tuning into our energy, we can identify our limiting beliefs or fears around money and work, shifting them to align with our authentic values and goals. Developing a healthy relationship with money based on integrity and abundance allows us to make financial decisions that support our authenticity and overall well-being, contributing to a more fulfilling life.

In a society where predefined roles and expectations persist, establishing and upholding healthy boundaries becomes essential to safeguard our well-being and autonomy amidst life's demands. Genuine empowerment thrives within these boundaries. Our energetic intelligence offers insights into our internal signals and the energy dynamics between ourselves and others. Tuning into our energy enables us to discern when our boundaries are crossed or challenged and communicate them assertively and respectfully to avoid feelings of resentment, frustration, and compromised well-being. Developing self-awareness and self-worth allows us to set and maintain boundaries that honor our needs and values while fostering healthier and more fulfilling relationships. Assertively communicating our boundaries is crucial to prevent overcommitment or allowing others to disrespect them.

Cultivating authentic confidence creates spaces where honesty and transparency are valued, fostering deep connections and meaningful collaborations. Rather than presenting a façade of perfection, we embrace our imperfections as sources of strength and resilience, inspiring others to do the same. This authenticity builds trust and mutual respect, laying the foundation for genuine partnerships based on shared values and goals. We feel empowered to express our true selves, share our stories, and support one another in our quests for fulfillment and success.

Liberated Confidence

Liberated Confidence represents a significant milestone in our journey toward empowerment, marking the culmination of strengthening the three preceding foundations. As we develop in these areas, we naturally progress toward liberated confidence where our connection with our authentic selves deepens and confidence shines through in our interactions. This phase involves prioritizing authenticity over seeking approval from others and breaking free from external judgment. It's about living according to our individual values and beliefs, irrespective of others' opinions.

Energetic intelligence plays a crucial role in this liberation process by helping us identify and release blocks and patterns that hold us back. By tapping into our inner strength and resilience, we can liberate ourselves from fear, doubt, and insecurity, and shed old programming and conditioning. This allows us to step into our full potential with confidence and freedom. Liberated confidence emerges when we embody our true essence without apology or compromise, empowered by the knowledge that we are the masters of our own energy and destiny.

Embracing freedom is foundational as it entails recognizing and asserting autonomy and independence in our choices, enabling us to live authentically and pursue paths aligned with our true selves. Actively pursuing my desires to build experiences and skills was crucial for breaking free from external expectations and fostering a life aligned with my authentic self. Embracing self-acceptance, forgiving past mistakes, and defining success based on my passions, values, and goals were vital in empowering me to move forward, seize opportunities, and live a more liberated life.

A negative mindset can hinder our ability to feel truly confident and liberated. Awareness of our inner energy helps us recognize how our thoughts and emotions shape our mindset and perceptions. Without this understanding, we may find ourselves stuck in cycles of self-doubt, fear, and negativity, undermining our confidence and sense of freedom. Persistent self-doubt and fixation on our perceived flaws lead to a constant search for external validation, preventing us from owning our story and pursuing our own goals with confidence. Identifying and challenging negative thought patterns and replacing them with more empowering beliefs helps us to take aligned action. Developing a positive and resilient mindset empowers us to navigate challenges with confidence, leading to a greater sense of liberation and self-assurance.

Understanding and addressing our beliefs about money is also crucial for building genuine confidence and freedom. Connecting with our inner energy offers insights into our subconscious beliefs and emotions shaping our relationship with money. Without this awareness, limiting beliefs or fears such as scarcity or unworthiness can inhibit our ability to attain genuine confidence and financial freedom. Having enough money provides security, freedom, and confidence, enabling us to fully embrace our authenticity. By embracing abundance and welcoming financial prosperity, we can turn our lives into a playground for growth, inspiring confidence, fulfillment, and goal achievement.

Being liberated means accepting ourselves as we are, including our inherent tendency to make mistakes - a vital aspect of the human experience. Our energetic intelligence helps us recognize our inner dialogue and emotions, including feelings of guilt or shame that arise from mistakes. Without this awareness, we may struggle to accept our imperfections and be overly critical of ourselves, leading to feelings of unworthiness and self-doubt. Embracing our humanity and treating ourselves with kindness allows us to learn and grow from our mistakes, fostering genuine confidence and self-assurance in our personal development journey. It's crucial to extend forgiveness to ourselves and move forward. By acknowledging mistakes without succumbing to shame and guilt, we prevent negative energies from anchoring us in disempowerment. These energies bind us to the past, hindering growth and opportunities. Similarly, refusing to forgive others strips away our empowerment, weighing heavily on our hearts and minds. Forgiving others doesn't mean condoning their actions but letting go of resentment and anger to reclaim our power and move forward with peace and clarity.

When liberated from comparison and competition, we can more powerfully embrace the abundance over scarcity mentality. This freedom fosters collaboration, seeing other women not as threats but as allies in collective empowerment. We celebrate each other's successes as victories for the entire community, knowing our triumphs contribute to progress and possibility. Liberated confidence fosters a culture of empowerment where we support and uplift each other, breaking free from societal expectations to define success and fulfillment on our terms.

Conclusion

In the context of women's empowerment, R.E.A.L. Confidence emerges as a vital element encompassing various aspects of our experiences and aspirations. It embodies the resilience, strength, and beauty inherent in the feminine spirit, offering hope amidst challenges. Embracing the principles of R.E.A.L. Confidence can collectively pave the way for a more promising and inclusive future for women.

These pillars serve as guiding beacons, illuminating the path toward a more empowered and collaborative future. Realigned confidence invites us to embrace our unique strengths and redefine success on our terms. Evolving confidence reminds us that growth is continuous, encouraging learning and adaptation. Authentic confidence empowers us to be ourselves, fostering genuine connections and respect. Liberated confidence frees us from comparison and self-doubt, enabling the fearless pursuit of passions and support for each other's aspirations. Together, these pillars create a supportive and inclusive environment where women uplift and inspire one another, leading to collective success and advancement.

True liberation extends beyond individuals to the collective, nurturing a culture of inclusivity and empowerment for future generations. By connecting with our personal power and confidently creating the reality we desire, we also contribute to the betterment of our families and communities. Personal transformation serves as a catalyst for broader societal change, as the world around us reflects the positive shifts we embody. As women, we can lead more authentic and fulfilling lives while inspiring others to do the same by breaking free from the chains of shame, guilt, and obligation. Together, we pave the way for a more empowered and liberated society.

I am honored to have shared part of my story and insights with you. As you contemplate the principles of R.E.A.L. Confidence, I encourage you to embrace and align with what resonates with you to forge your own path toward your unique definition of success.

In response to the vital need for empowering women, I am committed to making the following 21-day self-guided foundational coaching programs accessible to all women. I invite you to embark on this self-empowering journey to help uplift each other and contribute to the collective empowerment of our society:

1. Developing Authentic Confidence for Personal Empowerment: https://bit.ly/EmpoweredtobeYou

2. Upgrading your Abundance Mindset to Live More Confidently and Succeed in Business: https://bit.ly/MyNewEmpoweredMoneyMindset

Additionally, if you are a service-based entrepreneur, I'm also offering you a self-guided coaching accelerator program to jumpstart your biz confidence so that you can deliver greater value and impact for your clients while also enjoying more income and time freedom. Learn more here: https://bit.ly/TransformingYourServiceDeliveryFramework.

I thank you for accompanying me on this journey, and may you continue to flourish and inspire others in your pursuit of personal empowerment for a more fulfilling life and, if applicable, your business!

Marla Chaffin

Founder and CEO of Marla Chaffin

https://www.facebook.com/marla.mcnichols
https://www.instagram.com/marladchaffin
www.marlachaffin.com

Marla Chaffin grew up in Oregon and has recently moved to the Las Vegas area where she resides with her husband and two (2) fur babies. Marla has two (2) grown children, a son-in-law and three (3) grandsons. Marla has a passion for working with women and has made it her mission to help as many women as possible; who have suffered trauma; to heal and live a fulfilled life. When Marla isn't working, she loves to read, hang out with her husband and puppies, travel and be creative using clay and glass. Marla is always open to conversation.

THE DRAGONFLY EFFECT

By Marla Chaffin

Breaking out of the Resistance

Generational trauma is like an invisible thread that weaves its way through the fabric of family histories, passing down pain, suffering, and unresolved wounds from one generation to the next. It's the lingering echo of past hardships, injustices, and traumas that reverberate through time, shaping the lives and experiences of descendants.

Imagine it as a shadow cast by the struggles of our ancestors, stretching across the landscape of our lives, influencing our beliefs, behaviors, and relationships in ways we may not even realize. Generational trauma can manifest in various forms from emotional scars carried in the depths of our subconscious to patterns of behavior and coping mechanisms passed down through familial lines.

My trauma didn't happen physically; it was all mental. Mental trauma can be as devastating as physical trauma and abuse. My trauma began due to my family being a part of a religious cult. My father was considered a pastor of this Pentecostal organization. It was very controlling and you weren't allowed to think for yourself. You did and acted exactly as they directed. Women were not allowed to cut their hair or wear pants. All dresses had to be down to or below their knee and sleeves close to their elbow. Being able to fit in with my peers was very important, but every day I was laughed at and made fun of. Every day my self-esteem grew smaller and smaller. After a while, I started believing that I was weird. That I had no value.

> *"Out of suffering have emerged the strongest souls; the most massive characters are seared with scars."*
> —Khalil Gibran

Generational trauma operates like a silent force, shaping our worldview, influencing our relationships, and impacting our mental and emotional well-being. It's like an inherited burden, carried in the DNA of our familial lineage, waiting to be acknowledged, understood, and ultimately healed.

Growing up, I never remember either of my parents telling me they loved me. As a small child, I longed to feel that love. I neither heard nor felt this love. Everything was neutral, and because of this neutrality, I grew up thinking I wasn't loveable.

As a teenager my desire to be loved continued to fester. There was a boy a year older than me that was, I thought, the love of my life. Even he turned against me and chose another person.

In high school, I found a new love - computer programming. The computer era was just coming to light, and I could think of nothing else. I begged my parents to let me go to a secular school to get my degree in computer programming, but my parents would not hear of it. I was to go to Bible school, just like my older siblings.

In Bible school, I met and married a young man who I thought would be the perfect person for my parents to approve of. Maybe just this once, I could get their approval. I also knew this was my ticket out of my parents' home. I could finally be on my own, making my own decisions. Not long after we were married, I became pregnant .... after all, isn't that what you were supposed to do?

As a young mother with a small child of eight months, I couldn't take it any longer. I woke up one morning and told my husband that I wouldn't be coming home that night. I was leaving him. I was breaking free from the chains that had me bound. This is where my ultimate healing started, but I still had a long way to go. The dragonfly was now a nymph.

"You are not what happened to you.
You are what you choose to become."
—Unknown

Breaking free from the cycle of generational trauma requires a willingness to confront the past. It takes courage, compassion, and patience. It involves shining a light into the dark corners of your family history, acknowledging the pain and suffering that has been passed down through the generations, and making a conscious choice to chart a new course forward.

I made a lot of mistakes over the next 30+ years. I had a lot of lessons to learn. During this time, the one good thing that came about was my son. With that came new trauma passed down to him from his dad that has affected my son, daughter, and myself.

The dragonfly nymph morphed several more times, growing a little bigger and a little stronger each time.

During this time, I was trying to reclaim my identity. I was trying to unravel the tangled threads of our ancestry with self-discovery and resilience. Reclaiming my sense of identity, agency, and belonging. Finding community and support from those with similar experiences.

Ultimately, healing generational trauma is an act of liberation—a reclaiming of our inherent worth and dignity, untethered from the chains of the past. It's about honoring the resilience of our ancestors, acknowledging their sacrifices, and carrying forward the legacy of healing and hope for future generations to come.

Healing doesn't mean the damage never existed.
It means the damage no longer controls our lives."
—Unknown

In 2023, I had an awakening. I was going to live my life wide open for the rest of my life. At that point, I didn't understand the full aspect of this, but I was open to direction. What does living your life wide open mean? That was soon to be determined.

The dragonfly morphed once again. Are you strong enough yet for this next lesson, little dragonfly?

Living life wide open means embracing every opportunity, challenge, and experience with arms outstretched, ready to seize the moment and extract its fullest potential. It's about shedding inhibitions, letting go of fears, and diving headfirst into the adventure of existence.

Imagine standing on the precipice of a vast canyon, feeling the wind rushing against your skin, and instead of hesitating at the edge, you spread your wings and leap into the unknown, trusting that you'll soar. Living life wide open is about that leap of faith and that unwavering belief in yourself and the universe's capacity to guide you.

It's about saying yes to new beginnings, even when they terrify you; about embracing vulnerability, knowing that it's the gateway to authenticity and connection. Living life wide open is about being unapologetically yourself, embracing your flaws, quirks, and idiosyncrasies, and recognizing that they make you beautifully unique.

It's about being present in each moment, savoring the sweetness of joy, and finding resilience in the face of adversity. Living life wide open is about seeing the world with fresh eyes, cultivating a sense of wonder and curiosity that fuels your passion for exploration and growth.

So, let go of the reins, release the need for control, and surrender to the beauty of uncertainty. Living life wide open means allowing yourself to be fully immersed in the rich tapestry of human experience with all its ups and downs and twists and turns.

By the end of 2023, I had started a completely different journey, full of anticipation and learning. I had started a new business on social media, was being mentored by several different companies, and learned a lot! During this same time, I was opening myself up to learning more about the spirit world and what it was all about. I knew there was something bigger than the rest of us, and I was on a mission to find it. I started listening to multiple podcasts and read books on healing yourself and being aligned with the spirit. It sounded so much like what I was raised with, yet so much more that it intrigued me. I couldn't get enough.

Many people were led to my life, and they have all put their fingerprints on me. The difference between this spiritual journey and the one my parents believed in, is the purity of the journey. It isn't about judgment or criticism but about love and acceptance. The outward appearance doesn't really matter …. It is what your heart is like. The purity of it all is that everything is directly between you and a higher calling.

Feeling worthy of this new life was hard to accept. Rejection was a big trigger for me. I was such a people pleaser. I knew that if I could make everyone happy, they would like me. I would be worthy of their friendship and/or love. I would not have to be rejected. The struggle between the two was real. Everything I needed to complete, that would either show myself having value or the opportunity of being rejected, was hard to accomplish. My thoughts and actions would freeze and everything would go blank. I could sit at my computer for hours trying to complete a task, but it would never get completed. I realized that I would find everything else to do in order to not have to do what needed to be done.

Not too long ago, I was led to a book called *Worthy* by Jamie Kern Lima. In this book, she made such a profound statement. She came up with a motto that said, "If this person rejects me, they weren't meant to be on my team. They aren't part of my calling." When I heard this, it was like a lightbulb moment that went off.

One of the best teachers in my new journey is Kathy Baldwin, author of *Unlearn the Crap*. The universe directed us together one day on social media, and I knew it wasn't just by happenstance that we met. At the age of 21 when I decided to leave my first husband and the religion, I started living with the understanding that my life would never be dictated by a religion ever again. It was between me and the higher power. Now, 40 years later, I was ready to take that next step, and that was to unlearn everything that I had been taught! The journey to unlearning what I have been taught by others has started.

Today, my heart is more in tune with this calling. I am still learning and searching. My heart cries out to be open and in tune with what I am to do. Everyone is on this Earth for a reason. What is my reason? I believe I know, as it is something that has been on my heart for many years. I have had glimmers of it in the years past, but now I am just becoming. I have left the resistance and I will soar like a mature dragonfly!

In the end, it's not about reaching a destination but relishing the journey—the laughter, the tears, the friendships forged, and the lessons learned along the way. So, open your heart, spread your wings, and dare to live life wide open. Fly dragonfly fly!

Resilience Through Trauma

Adversity as a Catalyst for Growth: Trauma can be a catalyst for personal growth and transformation. Through facing and overcoming my challenges, I was able to develop inner strength, wisdom, and resilience that I may not have realized otherwise.

Finding Meaning in Suffering: Resilience involves finding meaning and purpose in the midst of suffering. By being able to connect with others who have experienced similar trauma, and by using my own experiences to help others, I am finding meaning provides a sense of hope and direction in the healing journey.

Coping Strategies and Support Systems: Resilience involves utilizing coping strategies and relying on support systems to navigate the challenges of trauma. This includes seeking therapy, practicing self-care, leaning on friends and family, and engaging in activities that promote well-being and healing.

Embracing Vulnerability: Resilience requires me to be willing to embrace vulnerability and acknowledge my emotions and experiences, rather than suppressing or denying difficult feelings. By being resilient I allow myself to feel and process my emotions in healthy ways, which can ultimately lead to greater healing and growth.

Cultivating Self-Compassion: Resilience involves cultivating my self-compassion and self-kindness, especially in the face of setbacks and struggles. Treating myself with gentleness and understanding will help foster resilience and provide a foundation for healing and recovery.

Flexibility and Adaptability: Resilience requires that I be flexible and adaptable in responding to changing circumstances and challenges. Being able to adjust my mindset, expectations, and goals can help me navigate the unpredictable nature of trauma and find new ways of coping and thriving.

Hope and Optimism: Resilience is fueled by my hope and optimism for the future, even in the darkest of times. Believing that there are better days ahead and holding onto a sense of possibility can provide the motivation and resilience that I need to persevere through difficult times.

Embracing the Journey: Resilience through trauma is not a destination but a journey of healing, growth, and self-discovery. Embracing my ups and downs, setbacks and successes, and uncertainties of the journey is an essential part of building my resilience and finding strength in the face of trauma.

Today, I am so excited to share my story with those who have also suffered trauma. Ultimately, I know that this is what I am here for. There are so many people in this world who are wandering, lonely, looking for someone to care for them. They are scared and broken and in need of positive reinforcement. Until they hear the truth, which is that you must first love yourself, they will continue to wander. Until they are taught the steps needed to take to love themselves, they will continue to live in the nymph stage of the dragonfly and will never be able to feel completely free to soar.

Melissa Cruz

The Locker Room Real Estate Coaching Company
Real Estate Coach

https://www.linkedin.com/in/mcruz19/
https://www.facebook.com/cruzm19
https://www.instagram.com/mcruz.19/
https://melissa-cruz.my.canva.site/

It wasn't long after Melissa moved to St. Augustine, Florida from her home state New Jersey, she embarked on her real estate journey. Discovering her passion for real estate, she pursued further education, attaining her broker's license in 2018, her GRI designation in 2019 and began mentoring agents in 2019. By 2020, she expanded her role to become a respected coach. Melissa's leadership shone through as she served as Director and Secretary in her local BOR, as well as local & state committees and she graduated from The Leadership Academy with Florida Realtors in 2022. Today Melissa is a full time Impact Coach at The Locker Room and is embracing a new chapter in Denver, Colorado. While her professional achievements are noteworthy, Melissa treasures her role as a devoted wife and mother of two. She enriches her life with hobbies like learning, puzzles, and hiking.

FROM SUPPORTING ACTRESS TO LEADING LADY EMBRACING YOUR POWER AND PURPOSE

By Melissa Cruz

You're supposed to be the leading lady in your
own life for God's sake!
—The Holiday

That one line in that movie, which came out back in 2006 by the way, has been something I have thought about for a very long time. I remember hearing that line the first time and I thought, 'Huh, that's interesting. What does that even mean? How do you become a leading lady in your life? How would I know if I was a leading lady? Is that even possible?' For years to come, I would watch these movies with a powerful leading actress, playing these roles of a badassery, and being in awe of them. I wanted to be like those women too!

Now, years later, as I go back and look at my life, I in fact see that woman! That leading lady I've been wanting to be all along. As you read the stories I am about to share, I want you to think about your life. How have your life's experiences shown you that you are a leading lady in your own special way?

ACT I

It was 2005 and I just moved back home from college. You would think it was a happy time but it wasn't. When I went into college, I was seventeen so my parents secured a loan the first year as I wasn't of age. When the second year rolled around, I was now eighteen, I tried to secure a loan for school. I tried all semester and ultimately couldn't secure a loan. They sent me packing. It was not a very fun time for me but there wasn't anything I could do. I moved back home with my parents and got a job.

One day, I was heading over to a friend's house when I saw this guy walking down the road. I thought, 'Hmm, he's cute.' I saw him heading into the house next door to the house I was about to go into Naturally, I said "Hi!". It wasn't long before we were all over each other. I was never with anyone like him and I freaking loved it! I started noticing him doing the same with other girls. I didn't say anything. I thought. 'He keeps coming back to me. Whatever.' One day we both stayed overnight at my friend's house. When I came downstairs that next morning, he was on the couch sleeping with another girl. I was furious and hurt. How could he do that to me?! Especially with me being there?! I left, returning a few hours later and there he was apologizing. Between the apology and some pretty good sex, all was forgiven. Little things like this kept happening. I kept looking the other way. making excuses for his behavior.

In 2006 I moved out of my parent's house and into my very first apartment. I was so happy! Thrilled to have my own place! When I told my mom about it, she encouraged me to take some time and enjoy living on my own while I had the opportunity. I, of course, ignored her advice. I let him move in with me. Everything was great for a while. I had my own place and he was away from all the other girls. I thought 'Yay! I won.' Ha! The joke was on me! Not long after he moved in, things started to spiral. He drank a lot and he was an angry drunk. It started with him getting mad and lashing out over the smallest things. I would just dodge him. That it slowly turned into pushing me and threatening me. He would question what I was doing, where I was going when I left the apartment, what I wore. He would look at me like he wanted to kill me. He would go out drinking, come home and wake me up by punching me in the face. I was really confused because when he was sober, he wasn't like that. The moment he got drunk, he became evil. It was really scary. This continued for a number of years. You might be thinking, why would you stay? Great question. I did try leaving a few times but when I did, he would chase me down the hall, carry me by my throat back to the apartment, and lock me in the bedroom for hours.

I felt trapped. He tore me away from my family and friends. I was isolated and alone. My family had an idea of what was going on but because he was so scary, I didn't want to involve them. I wanted to protect them. By day to the world I was strong, successful, and happy. What they didn't know was, I was screaming on the inside for help. Who was I going to ask for help? My apartment eventually became the place for all of his friends to hang out and get drunk all day. Obviously, he didn't work the majority of the time. My apartment was destroyed. Sometimes, when I got home, they would jump me, hold me down laughing, as they watched me try to squirm my way out of it. I was scared for my life.

I got to a point where I felt like I was living in a twilight zone. In my head, I would constantly be asking myself, How could I let this happen? Who was I anymore? Was this ever going to end? As if things couldn't get worse, I got pregnant. The one thing I promised myself since I could remember was, I would not get pregnant at a young age. As a hispanic woman, I was determined to not be the statistic people saw me for. I felt so alone and disgusted with myself. What was I to do? I did the only thing I thought was right. I decided to have it. I figured, I got myself into this situation. I needed to accept the responsibility. A few months later, I was laid off, losing my health insurance. It took me about a month to find a doctor who would see me. I went into the appointment, to the surprise of the doctor doing the ultrasound, found there was no heartbeat. The baby had died a month prior. He told me had I not come in when I did, I would have died too. Initially, I was so upset. I felt like it was my fault. Like I did something wrong. When I was finally able to wrap my head around what happened, it turned into relief. I was not ready to be a parent. Especially not with him! Goodness! The doctor scheduled a procedure to have the fetus removed and off I went.

In case you've never experienced this, when you are done with the procedure, there is to be no sexual activity for a number of weeks afterwards. This gave me solace. It at least bought me some time to figure myself out. That was until I was forced to have sex much sooner. He said, because he was my boyfriend, that gave him the right to do whatever he wanted with, and to me. Just five weeks later, I found myself pregnant again. I was so mad and again, so disgusted with myself. I know the difference between right and wrong. Why couldn't I just speak up? Just say no? I knew I was better than what I was living. I knew deep down, I deserved better. How was I going to get out of this? I couldn't do it anymore. I was watching myself die in slow motion. One night, I found myself up in the middle of the night, crying on the floor. I just fell to my knees completely broken. I looked up and prayed the hardest I had ever prayed in my entire life. I begged God to help me. To be completely honest, I begged him to take the baby. I know! That sounds horrible! But it was all I knew to do. It was at that moment, I knew if I wanted a different life, I was the only one that could do something about it. I needed help badly. I promised God that night, if He helped me, I would get out of that relationship, get on birth control, and I'd never allow anyone to treat me that way EVER again. I promised Him I would work really hard and I'd make something of myself.

A few days later, out of nowhere, I started to feel really bad cramps. I thought, 'How could that be? I'm pregnant.' Since my partner didn't drive, he couldn't get me anything to help with the pain. I didn't have any medicine or a heating pad. All I had were these hand warmer packets. You know, the ones you put in your gloves when it's cold outside? I put one warmer on the front, on my belly, and one on my lower back. Needless to say, it was a very long night. Thankfully, I was able to get an appointment to see a doctor the next day. I was informed that what I experienced was another miscarriage. They told me that I had another miscarriage because I did not give my body enough time to heal from the first one. Boom! That was my sign! My chance! It was finally time to put an end to this nightmare I was living.

Not long after, he and I went to a barbecue at his parents house. It seemed to be a chill day. He was in a good mood. I, on the other hand, kept thinking 'This was it! Today is going to be the day! We got back home, he was drunk of course, and now not in a good mood. Sitting on the couch, I mustered enough courage to say, "I can't do this anymore. You need to go, today." He yelled at me and smacked me upside my head once last time. I got up from the floor, waited for him to get his things, and I drove him back to his parents house. I was so scared driving him back. It was super quiet in the car. I thought for sure he would push the steering wheel and we would crash. When we got there, I couldn't even look at him. I just wanted him to go so I could run as fast as I could, and never look back.

I went straight to see my family. I told them it was over. They were so happy and relieved. The one person I was afraid to face the most was my sister. I don't know if it's a big sister thing, but my whole life I protected her. I could tolerate people teasing me or being mean to me, but when it came to anyone hurting her, I drew the line. The reason she and I didn't see each other anymore was because one night, while she was at my apartment, she saw the monster come out. Not only did she see it but he was going to hit her too! I did nothing. I was a coward. I just sat there frozen. The look in her eyes when she looked at me was a combination of shock, confusion, and hurt. It crushed me. I had to face her though. When we finally reconnected, she showed me nothing but love. She was so happy to see me well and out of that hell.

After our reunion my family was finally able to come to my apartment. When they entered, they gasped at the conditions I had been living in. I had no carpet in my bedroom, just cement for flooring, the cabinets were falling off in the kitchen walls, it was trashed. They had questions

I didn't care to answer. We rolled up our sleeves and put the place back together. Let the healing begin!

My sister started coming over every night. It was so refreshing to be with her again, laugh and cry, just spend time together. I missed her so much! I felt like I let her down but she showed up and loved me through it.

To be completely honest and transparent, I have never shared this story in this detail with anyone before. For many, many years I felt ashamed and embarrassed about it. I hid that part of my life. I share this story with you now because I now know I am not that girl anymore. I learned that this experience does not define me. While I would never wish for this to ever happen to anyone, it happened to me. It is part of my story. I would not be the woman I am without it.

ACT II

Fast forward to 2008, I reconnected with my old roommate from college. She had since graduated and became a flight attendant. We got to talking and the next thing you know we were planning a trip to Las Vegas. I was so excited to go! I had never gone anywhere that far. After months of planning and prepping for the trip, it was the day before we left when she broke the news to me. She told me she could not get me on the flight. I was stunned and upset. I had already told everyone I was going! How could I not go now? My mom, with her wonderful self, asked if I still wanted to go. I told her, "How the hell am I going to make that happen at the last minute?" Well, never underestimate a determined mother. She bought me a ticket and the stay for five days. I thought, 'Holy shit! I'm really going! Except, I'm really going alone." You see, up until that point in my life, I couldn't fathom doing anything by myself. What would people think? What would I do? Was I safe? Could I actually go on a trip alone? I did the only thing I knew to do. I cried and prayed really hard. The next day my mom took me to the airport. I was off. Here we go!

Once I landed in Vegas, the first thing I saw in the airport were slot machines. That was really interesting. I immediately felt so empowered and proud. I just kept thinking, 'Look at me flying across the damn country alone!' It was so freeing. I felt like I was soaring. I had an incredible five days there. I did a little sightseeing, gambled a bit, caught a show, hung poolside, and boy did I eat! Now, I did play it a little safe, but still I had a lot of fun. When I came back from that trip, I was a brand new woman. No one could say anything to me. From that moment on, there was nothing I couldn't do alone. I no longer needed anyone to have fun or do anything with. I went to the movies, out to eat, shopped, everything! I felt like I could take over the world. I felt so good.

As much as I was growing and learning to love me again, I was still pretty messed up on the inside. Over the next two years, I turned to alcohol. I didn't know how to heal, so I numbed the pain. I soon turned into an angry drunk myself. After a crazy drunken week in Wildwood, NJ, I decided I needed to cool it a bit. I was going backwards in my healing journey. While I was trying to get better and sober, I had landed a part-time job. I became fast friends with one of the girls there. She was smart, fun, and good for me. After a few months of working there, she invited me out dancing. I excitedly said "Yes!". The day we were planning on going out, I was feeling really tired. I contemplated not going at all but I felt bad canceling at the last minute, so I went. When we got there, I was telling myself in my head, 'Ok Melissa, just two drinks tonight. It's your first night out with a good friend and you still have to drive home.' If only I had listened to my own plan. I not only had three drinks, but I was drinking something someone else was having just to fit in. That drink had several different types of alcohol in it. I thought, 'I'll dance it off. I'll be fine.' We danced our butts off having a blast! Soon it was time to go. We went back to her house, I got in my car and headed home. I remembered her asking me if I was ok to drive. I assured her I was fine.

That night I almost died. I fell asleep at the wheel just five minutes from my house. My car flipped a few times, ending up hitting a tree. I passed out. When I awoke, I saw a guy running towards me on the phone. I frantically searched for my phone and dialed 9-1-1. I remember trying to climb out of the window when passed out again. When I awoke that time, I was in the ambulance heading to the hospital. I had no idea what the hell was happening. I thought it was a dream. Everything was happening so fast. Soon after arriving at the hospital, I remember seeing the doors open and my parents were standing there. I will never forget the look on their faces. Their eyes were filled with fear, relief I was alive, and utter disappointment. I could not believe what I just put them through. This was not a dream.

I got a DUI and reckless driving citation that night. Since I had been living at my parents house, I had saved up some money. I spent every dollar I had and more, to take responsibility for what I had done. I did not want to accept any help my parents offered. They taught me better. I felt terrible and extremely embarrassed. I was so lucky no one got hurt. Talk about rock bottom!

ACT III

Once all of that went down, I stopped drinking for a long time. I secured a second job and started working a lot. I worked anywhere from fifty to sixty hours a week. It was a lot, but I really enjoyed it. I was making decent money for myself. It wasn't anything crazy but it was good for me. Once I was done paying for everything concerning the accident, I was able to start saving again. Within a few months, I had saved enough money to purchase some furniture and snag a new apartment. I put the hard times behind. I was ready to move on. I was feeling pretty good. That was until about six months into my lease. A couple of friends of mine were getting cool job opportunities in Florida. I was really happy for them. Don't get me wrong. I was happy for myself too. I just couldn't shake this nagging feeling that I was meant for more. I am a born and raised Jersey girl. I knew since I was a child, I wanted to move when I was old enough. I didn't want to just be born there, live there my whole life, and die there. It seemed daunting, I wanted out.

I quietly started to inquire about moving as well. I figured, if I start this process of moving and God gave me green lights, I'd know this was the right time to take the leap. When I started to get things in order, I kept getting green lights. I sublet my apartment, was able to transfer my second job to a store in Florida, and secured a place to stay for a few weeks. I felt these were all signs from God. It was the push I needed to move forward. All I needed to do now was give my two weeks' notice at my first job and finally tell my parents what I've been up to. I remember it was a Friday when I broke the news. After the initial shock, they were very supportive. With that, the following Monday, I put my two weeks' notice at my morning job. Two weeks and a day later, I left. I moved to Florida by myself, with what I could fit in my car. It was the scariest, yet most exciting time of my life! I, of course, balled my eyes out. For a moment I asked myself, 'Am I sure this is what I'm supposed to do?' My mom kindly reminded me this had been a goal of mine for so long, otherwise I wouldn't have had all those green lights. Once I arrived in Florida, I felt so free and happy. I actually freaking did it!

Now, I didn't have any life-changing goals or intentions when I arrived. None of that was figured out at all. However, over the course of the next year, I received a promotion at my job, found a place to live in St. Augustine, my parents took the trip to FL, driving the rest of my belongings which I had in storage. A guy I was kind of seeing back in Jersey, got serious and he moved down too. I was on cloud nine. Could life actually work out? Could I finally be happy? Answer, yes! For a good while anyway. Not long after my boyfriend moved in, we got pregnant. We were so excited!! In less than two years we had two children. Yes, that fast! Once I had my second child, I made the difficult decision to quit my job. I took a year off. I didn't want to work in retail management any longer. With my boyfriend having a great job, we could afford it. What I didn't expect was postpartum depression. How could I be depressed with these two beautiful children we planned for. I didn't know what to do about it.

The next year after having my second child, I spent every night crying on the bathroom floor while everyone slept. I would wake up and act like everything was ok. I didn't talk to anyone about it. During that year, I started feeling guilty about how I was feeling. On one hand, I was grateful for the opportunity to stay home, on the other I felt I had this inner fire burning for more. For some women, staying at home with their children, raising them gives them purpose and is fulfilling. That wasn't me. I had deep feelings that I had more purpose for my life. That I was meant to do more in this world. Even with all of that, was it possible to have a career and be a mother? The only way I would know is to throw more wood into that fire. Surely other women somehow cracked the code. I suppose I could too.

ACT IV

In 2016, I decided to get my real estate license. I had no idea what I was getting myself into but starting that journey gave me so much to look forward to. I was learning something new. I was finally doing something for myself again. The beginning was incredibly difficult. My children were two and one years old at the time. Our budget only allowed us daycare part-time, which was three days a week. I could have used more time, but I was grateful for what I was able to get. It was time to get to work.

For the first couple of years, my real estate career had been nothing short of a roller coaster ride. There was so much to learn, so much I didn't know…I didn't know. Of all the lessons learned, one of the biggest was, I wasn't just slinging houses. I was in fact building a career. That realization opened my eyes to what was actually possible. I used that as motivation to conquer the world with no barriers. After about five years of working in the real estate industry, my roller coaster which had been going up, came crashing down.

In March of 2021, I lost my only sister unexpectedly. It is a phone call I will never forget. At first I thought it was a joke. I thought, not my sister. No way! She was home, wasn't she? Turns out she was not. After getting off of work one evening, she decided to go out for a bit. She got a ride home from a friend. That friend ran a red light, crashing into a semi-truck. My entire world flipped upside down in an instant. I understood that death is part of life, but I hadn't lost anyone that close to me before. Death became very real to me that day. I was lost, sad, angry, confused, hurt, guilty, the list goes on. Her passing knocked me off my feet. My sister was my person, my cheerleader, my friend, my ass-kicker, my 'live for the day' example, my everything! To save my parents from any more pain, I took on everything concerning her passing. Once she was laid to rest, it was time for me to go back home, back to reality. To what reality you ask? I had no idea. I felt like a piece of me died with her. Who was I without her? How do I live and carry on without her? How was I supposed to leave my parents alone? I was all over the place. The reality was, life did have to go on whether I wanted it to or not. When I returned home, a friend of mine suggested I talk to someone about what I was feeling. She gifted me a few sessions with a grief counselor. I began seeing her weekly. The first few sessions I just cried. I still couldn't wrap my head around it. I was so mad. Why did she have to go? Why couldn't she just go home after work? Why did she leave me? We had plans! Now those plans are gone! What am

I supposed to do now? My lovely and talented grief counselor saved me. Losing my sister opened up old wounds I thought I healed from. She challenged and pushed me to face all of it. To forgive myself, the guilt I had been carrying all these years, let it go. If it weren't for her, I would not be here writing any of this today. To you Katie. I truly thank you.

And the story continues...

Ladies, if you have made it this far, thank you! Thank you so much for taking the time to read my story. I hope it inspires you to share your story as well. It took me a long time to get here. I pray, if you are holding onto baggage, find the courage to let it go. Find someone you can talk to and get help.

Being a leading lady in our lives doesn't look perfect. It isn't getting it right, or having all the answers. It sure as hell isn't a one-size-fits-all outlook! It is, however, having courage through all of the fear. Pushing forward anyway. It's believing in ourselves no matter what anyone else thinks. It is having confidence in your flaws and all. It's being kind and compassionate to others, embracing and celebrating what makes us different and unique. It is understanding that the journey of self-love is lifelong.

What I have learned throughout my lifetime thus far is, cutting out negative people can be hard but it is absolutely necessary. Love hard because tomorrow is not promised. Find what makes you happy and shoot for the freaking moon! Every day we wake up is another opportunity to live life to its fullest. What are you waiting for?!

Nicole Keskula

Founder of BLOOM for Women

https://facebook.com/BLOOMforWomen.net/
https://www.instagram.com/bloom_withnikki/
https://stan.store/BLOOMwithNikki

Nikki Keskula, the visionary founder behind Bloom for Women, has built an empowering online community focused on personal development and growth for women. With a background in psychology, business administration, and digital marketing, Nikki combines her diverse expertise to create a nurturing space where women are encouraged to ditch the corporate grind, redefine success, and climb their own ladders. Through her leadership, Bloom offers a wealth of resources, including insightful content and supportive coaching, designed to empower women in all aspects of their lives. With a deep commitment to uplifting others and a keen understanding of digital marketing strategies, Nikki harnesses her expertise to inspire positive change and cultivate a community characterized by resilience, empowerment, and endless possibilities. Join Nikki and the Bloom community on a transformative journey of self-discovery, and growth.

FROM SHADOWS TO LIGHT: A JOURNEY OF MENTAL HEALTH RESILIENCE

By Nicole Keskula

Looking back on my life now, I see that my struggle with mental health started long before I even knew what it was. Let me take you back to where it all began.

As a kid, I was your typical American girl. School came naturally to me—I aced my classes, sat first chair clarinet in band, belted out tunes in the chorus, and threw myself into drama club and sports. Life felt good, especially when it came to school. I was happy, outgoing, and totally clueless.

But outside of school, my home life was anything but typical. I resided in my grandparent's basement—me, my parents, and my siblings. My dad battled alcohol addiction, though he tried to keep it under wraps. My mom fought her own silent battle with depression and anxiety.

Our house was always packed with my uncle and cousins crashing there too. My uncle's struggles with his own mental health led him down a rocky path of drugs and alcohol. Weeknights and weekends felt like a party, our driveway packed with trucks, my uncle and his friends laughing and joking. To me, it seemed normal, just part of life.

But as I got older, I realized it was more than that. Their partying wasn't just fun—it was a way to cope. Without even knowing it, I was being drawn into their world of hidden pain, laying the groundwork for my own mental health journey.

Transitioning into middle school marked a turning point for me. Initially, I dove headfirst into choir, band, and field hockey, carrying on with the extracurricular activities I loved. But as the year progressed, a shadow crept over me, one I couldn't quite name at the time: social anxiety. I felt like a stranger in my own skin, consumed by worries about others' perceptions of me. Doubt gnawed at my confidence, and I found myself constantly comparing my abilities to those around me.

It was during this tumultuous period that I first turned to marijuana at a mere 12 years old. The sensation of being high offered a temporary escape from my anxieties, a blissful retreat from the constant chatter in my mind. In those moments, laughter flowed freely, and for a while, I could forget about my insecurities and simply enjoy the present. It was intoxicating—no wonder adults seemed drawn to it.

Summer rolled around, and with it came another temptation: alcohol. With the help of a friend's older brother, we scored our first drinks and embarked on a makeshift camping trip in her backyard. Under the stars, we toasted to newfound freedom and guzzled down liquid courage. The night blurred into a whirlwind of laughter, but little did I know it marked the beginning of a downward spiral.

For a while, I didn't give much thought to smoking or drinking again. I promised myself it would only be a weekend thing, a harmless escape from the pressures of teenage life without messing with my studies. But let's face it, being a teenager is no walk in the park. The cliques, the cruelty—it's enough to make anyone feel out of place. As any teenager knows, navigating those formative years can be a minefield of insecurities and peer pressure. I found myself caught in a tug-of-war between wanting to fit in with my friends and staying true to the values instilled in me. Despite having a solid head on my shoulders, I struggled to forge my own identity amidst the chaos of adolescence.

My inner conflict intensified as I gravitated toward a circle of friends whose idea of fun leaned toward the wild side. Soon, our after-school routine became a blur of parties where smoking and drinking took center stage, overshadowing any academic responsibilities. Homework went unfinished, and one by one, I abandoned my extracurricular pursuits, trading them for the excitement of endless partying with my friends.

With each puff of smoke and sip of alcohol, the weight of my anxieties melted away, leaving behind a fleeting sense of freedom. Drugs and alcohol became my escape from reality, a temporary relief from the mounting pressures of teenage life. By the time I hit 15, I had dabbled in various substances, bid farewell to my once-beloved activities, and barely scraped through each school year by the skin of my teeth.

At the time, I didn't see the harm. To me, it was just harmless fun—a rite of passage into the wild world of youth.

Junior year of high school threw me into a whirlwind when I started dating an older guy who lived in the city. Home life was rocky, to say the least, and I craved freedom from any form of authority. So, I made a daring move and moved in with him. But just as I was settling into this new chapter, tragedy struck—my grandfather's sudden passing sent me spiraling into a dark abyss of grief.

Doctors prescribed antidepressants and recommended therapy, but defiance became my default mode. Instead of facing my emotions head-on, I sought solace in the chaos of late-night parties and skipped school consistently. By the time senior year rolled around, academics felt like a distant memory. I drowned my sorrows in a haze of smoke and alcohol, rarely sober even on school days.

Then came another blow: my father's hospitalization due to alcohol-related health issues. The weight of responsibility bore down on me, threatening to crush me under its weight. And just when I thought things couldn't get any worse, reality dealt me a brutal blow in the principal's office—years of missed credits, unexcused absences, and the looming threat of not graduating.

In that moment, conflicting emotions tugged at my soul. Escape or redemption? Despite the urge to flee, a glimmer of determination ignited within me. With grit and sheer willpower, I clawed my way back from the brink, attending every class, juggling night courses, and reluctantly opening up to a school-appointed therapist.

Initially resistant, I scoffed at her diagnosis—a toxic relationship, substance abuse, and mental health struggles—a stranger presuming to know my inner struggles. But looking back now, her words rang with painful truth. With hindsight, I realize she saw through the façade I'd carefully crafted. Graduation became my beacon of hope, a ticket to freedom from responsibility and expectations.

But freedom came with its own pitfalls. College seemed like a distant dream. I didn't even bother to apply, and instead, I reveled in the carefree life of partying with friends. Yet, as the days turned into nights, and nights into a blur, I faced a harsh truth: the lifestyle I was living was slowly consuming me.

As the haze lifted, I found myself adrift, moving from place to place with no direction. It was a wake-up call—a realization that I was heading down a dangerous path. So, I made the difficult choice to return to my grandmother's house, hoping for a fresh start.

But instead of finding peace, I found myself drawn deeper into a world of adult vices and reckless abandon. The spiral was relentless, dragging me down a path I never could have imagined.

The years following my graduation were a blur of alcohol-induced oblivion and drug-fueled haze. Working as a retail associate at Sears, I scraped by, earning just enough to fund my nights of partying. Nothing else mattered—bills and responsibilities all faded into the background.

When I lost my job at Sears, it felt like yet another setback in a string of disappointments. But then, a glimmer of hope emerged. I landed a job at an armored money company, tripling my income overnight. Yet, even with the boost in pay, my priorities remained unchanged—work was merely a means to fuel my chaotic lifestyle.

But amidst the chaos, a moment of clarity pierced through the haze that would alter the course of my life forever. It happened one fateful night, amongst a crowd of older acquaintances at a dimly lit bar. Fueled by a cocktail of pot brownies and whiskey, I found myself lost, staring at the red glow of the clock above the bar.

As the smoke hung heavy in the air and the music faded into the background, I surveyed the room—witnessing lives marked by perpetual struggle and disillusionment. These middle-aged souls shackled to their barstools, offered a sobering reflection of a life unfulfilled, their lives confined to the worn bar stools they occupied night after night. And at that moment, a fire ignited within me. I yearned for more, for a future beyond the confines of this suffocating existence.

With newfound clarity, I made a vow to myself—a pledge to break free from the cycle of self-destruction and chart a course toward a brighter future. I refused to become another face lost in the smoky haze of mediocrity, determined to forge a path of purpose and fulfillment.

So, I made a pact with myself. With New Year's Eve a week away, I decided to make it one last hurrah—a final celebration before turning over a new leaf on New Year's Day. The plan was simple: bid farewell to the haze of drugs and alcohol and embrace a life of sobriety. Little did I know, the universe had other plans in store, and my journey towards clarity would begin sooner than expected. I couldn't forget it even if I tried.

It was January 9, 2013, an ordinary day at my job in Loomis, the armored money company. Surrounded by the hum of office chatter and the strains of Zac Brown Band's "Keep Me in Mind," playing on the radio. I was settled at my desk, counting ATM bags as usual.

Suddenly, without warning, my world lurched into chaos.

My heart raced, my palms grew clammy, and each breath felt like a struggle against an invisible weight pressing down on my chest. Panic gripped me, threatening to pull me under. Frantically, I fled to the bathroom, seeking solace in the cool embrace of water against my skin, fearing I might collapse at any moment.

It was there, in the bathroom, that reality crashed down upon me. My supervisor, alerted by my abrupt departure, approached with concern etched on her face. As I struggled to articulate the whirlwind of emotions coursing through me, she offered clarity amidst the chaos: a panic attack.

Yet, behind the veil of panic lay a deeper truth that I hadn't dared confront until now. Nine days into my journey of sobriety, my body rebelled against the absence of substances, unleashing a torrent of withdrawals. And with sobriety came an unexpected reckoning—years of suppressed mental health struggles clawing their way to the surface, demanding to be heard.

The following weeks were an agonizing blur of physical torment and mental anguish. As the grip of withdrawal loosened its hold on my body, a new battle emerged that waged war within the confines of my mind. Stripped of my job, my sense of purpose crumbled beneath the weight of relentless panic attacks that haunted me from dawn till dusk, leaving me gasping for air and clinging to the peace of sleep.

Each morning brought with it a suffocating wave of anxiety, rendering even the simplest tasks a Herculean feat. I retreated to the sanctuary of my room, a prisoner to the relentless grip of fear that threatened to consume me whole. Never before had I felt so utterly powerless, so utterly lost in the labyrinth of my own mind.

Desperate for relief, I relied on the opinion of medical professionals, hoping for a glimmer of hope amidst the wreckage of my shattered life.

Yet, with each diagnosis—chronic acute anxiety, severe depression, ADHD, OCD—I felt the crushing weight of disappointment settle in the pit of my stomach.

Like a punch to the gut, the reality of my condition hit me with brutal force. I was a mere shadow of the person I once was, a broken shell of my former self. The sting of self-blame cut deep. I believed that my choices had led me to this dark place. If only I had chosen differently, perhaps I wouldn't be drowning in this sea of despair.

But as I grappled with the harsh truth, a glimmer of understanding began to dawn. These diagnoses weren't a consequence of my choices. They were a revelation, a stark reminder of the battles I had waged in silence for years. For too long, I had masked the symptoms with substances, numbing the pain rather than facing it head-on. And now, in the light of sobriety, the true extent of my struggles was demanding to be acknowledged and embraced.

As I grappled with the profound impact of my diagnosis, I embarked on a journey to find relief from the relentless storm raging within. Prescription medications became a revolving door—Zoloft, citalopram, lorazepam—the carousel of pharmaceuticals offered no relief. Frustrated and disheartened, I knew I needed a different approach, one that aligned with my belief in holistic healing.

For me, the path to recovery meant embracing a holistic lifestyle, a commitment to nourishing my body, mind, and soul from the inside out. It wasn't easy. Every day was a battle against the suffocating grip of anxiety, but I refused to let it dictate my fate. Instead, I poured my energy into natural remedies, finding strength in the simplicity of daily rituals.

From maintaining a balanced, nutritious diet to prioritizing regular exercise (sometimes multiple times a day), I immersed myself in self-care, determined to reclaim control of my life. And perhaps the most daunting challenge of all: staying sober. Each day brought its own set of hurdles, but with each small victory, I felt a glimmer of hope.

For the next 10 months, I withdrew from the world as I grappled with my newfound reality. It was a period of profound introspection where I had to come to terms with the seismic shift that had rocked the foundation of my existence. Every moment was a struggle, every day an uphill battle. But amidst the chaos, I started to find my way.

Slowly but surely, as I settled into a routine and nurtured myself mind, body, and soul, the jagged edges of my symptoms began to soften. With each passing day, the weight on my shoulders lightened, and I rediscovered the joy of living—a new chapter unfolding before me, one filled with hope and possibility.

Nothing in life could have prepared me for the gut-wrenching events that unfolded next. December 13, 2013, is a date etched in my memory with unforgettable sorrow. Awakened by a phone call that shattered the fragile peace of my world, I learned of the passing of one of my closest friends. In an instant, everything went numb. Tears flowed uncontrollably as I grappled with the overwhelming weight of loss.

The days leading up to the funeral were a blur of grief-fueled activity. I threw myself into the task of commemorating his life, crafting picture boards, and lending a hand wherever needed. But I was crumbling inside. And then came the morning of the funeral—a day that would mark a devastating turning point.

Consumed by emotional turmoil, I made a fateful decision. Driven by the desperate need for relief from the pain, I reached for the familiar solace of alcohol. In a heartbeat, nearly a year of sobriety vanished into thin air. Despite the countless hours spent navigating the depths of my own anxiety and depression, nothing could have prepared me for the searing agony of losing someone I loved.

I wish I could say that I found the strength to pick up the pieces and move forward, but reality had other plans in store. Just two weeks after the funeral, another devastating blow struck—a dear friend lost to the relentless grip of mental health struggles, his life tragically cut short by suicide. The shockwave of his loss reverberated through me, leaving me reeling in disbelief.

And then, like a cruel twist of fate, another heartbreak followed. Three weeks later, as if the universe was determined to test my resolve, a friend was murdered in a senseless act of violence at a house party, snuffing out a life filled with promise. It was a relentless overwhelm of grief, a series of blows that left me gasping for air.

In the face of such unbearable pain, I found myself tumbling down a dark, familiar path. Nights blurred into days as I sought refuge in the numbing embrace of weed and alcohol, drowning my sorrows in a haze of oblivion. But there was one stark difference—I refused to touch drugs. It was a small glimmer of restraint in the midst of my unraveling, a feeble attempt to cling to a shred of control of my world that was spiraling out of grasp.

Amidst the chaos of my struggles, I found refuge in the arms of an old flame, an on-again, off-again boyfriend who offered an escape from the storm raging within. For a while, it felt like we were navigating the turbulence together, finding comfort in each other's company. But as the months passed, cracks began to form in the foundation of our relationship, revealing a darkness lurking beneath the surface.

It wasn't long before I uncovered a harsh truth: my partner was grappling with addiction, locked in a relentless battle with heroin. Suddenly, the ground beneath me seemed to shift, leaving me standing at a crossroads, torn between my own struggles with alcohol and the harsh reality of his addiction.

Our relationship became a turbulent whirlwind of highs and lows, a rollercoaster ride through the depths of despair. Yet, despite the chaos, I couldn't shake the feeling of being drawn to the madness, the adrenaline rush of trying to save someone else when I could barely save myself. The weight of the world bore down on my shoulders, a heavy burden that threatened to crush me under its weight.

Each day brought a new wave of fear as I watched him slip further away, consumed by the relentless pull of addiction. The thought of losing someone I loved became a constant shadow haunting my every step. And yet, despite the darkness closing in around us, I couldn't find the strength to walk away.

My loyalty became both a lifeline and a curse—a bittersweet reminder of the depth of my love and the toll it exacted on my own well-being. As I grappled with the painful truth that sometimes, love alone is not enough to save us, I found myself caught in a whirlwind of emotions, struggling to find a way out of the darkness.

And then, the unthinkable happened—the very nightmare I had feared most became my reality. One morning, I woke up to a world without him. My boyfriend, my anchor in the storm, was gone, lost to a drug overdose. In an instant, I was plunged into a darkness so profound that words fail to capture its depths. The grief, the despair, the suffocating weight of loss—it threatened to swallow me whole, leaving me adrift in a sea of pain.

The depression, anxiety, and overwhelming sense of emptiness that followed were unlike anything I had ever experienced. I felt as though I were drowning with no lifeline to pull me back to the surface. Desperate for relief, I turned to alcohol, seeking relief in the numb embrace of intoxication. But even the numbing effects of alcohol proved insufficient to drown out the agony of my grief.

After two and a half years trapped in a cycle of despair, I reached a breaking point. I realized that I couldn't continue down this path. To do so would mean surrendering my life to a perpetual haze of alcohol-fueled oblivion. My mental health was at an all-time low, my spirit broken, my very essence drained to nothing. Something had to change.

With a newfound determination, I took the first tentative steps toward healing. Therapy offered a glimmer of hope, but my alcohol abuse served as a barrier to progress. And so, once more, I made the choice to reclaim my sobriety, confront my demons head-on, and forge a new path forward. Alongside my commitment to sobriety, I chose to pursue higher education.

I embarked on a new chapter of my journey when I received the life-changing news of my acceptance into Lasell University to pursue psychology. Securing the highest awarded scholarship was not just a financial boost, but a ticket to a fresh start—a chance to escape the shadows of my past and embrace a brighter future.

As my time at Lasell unfolded, I poured my heart and soul into my studies, driven by a relentless determination to excel. With each passing semester, I found myself rising to new heights, earning the highest honors and maintaining a flawless 4.0 GPA. The pinnacle of my achievements came with my induction into the National Honor Society of Psychology, a moment of validation for all the hard work and dedication invested in my academic journey.

Yet, despite the accolades and triumphs, a subtle shift began to take hold. Senior year brought with it the weight of responsibility as I dove into internships at psychiatric facilities and rehabilitation clinics. While my passion for helping others burned bright, I couldn't ignore the toll it took on my well-being. The environments I found myself immersed in were heavy with the struggles of those I sought to assist, and I felt my own cup slowly draining.

Then, on the anniversary of my boyfriend's passing, the weight of my grief and the burden of my surroundings became too much to bear. As I drove to my internship, anxiety gripped me like a vice, and I found myself pulled over on the side of the highway, tears streaming down my face. In that moment of raw vulnerability, I knew I had reached a crossroads where I had to confront the harsh reality of my mental health struggles.

With each passing week, my anxiety intensified, and the shadows of depression loomed ever larger. It was a sobering realization: the path I had chosen was exacting a heavy toll on my spirit, and I knew deep down that it wasn't sustainable. As I stood on the precipice of uncertainty, I made a courageous decision to prioritize my own well-being, to chart a new course that honored my mental health and allowed space for continued healing and growth.

I made a pivotal choice: to step away from my studies and take a pause to reassess my path forward. But this time, there was a marked difference—I didn't turn to alcohol to cope. For the first time in years, I had power over my relationship with alcohol, a victory worth celebrating.

In the months that followed, I embarked on a new chapter of my personal journey, finding unexpected companionship and stability in a blossoming relationship with one of my closest friends. Together, we ventured into the realm of adulthood, securing an apartment outside the city.

My professional trajectory took a turn as well. Embracing a desk job at a local bank, I seized the opportunity to continue my education, pivoting my focus from psychology to business administration. This shift laid the foundation for a transformative career path where I would spend nearly four years in the banking sector before venturing into the world of real estate development.

In the fall of 2023, fueled by a newfound passion for entrepreneurship, I immersed myself in the art of building an online business. Simultaneously, I embarked on another journey, enrolling in graduate courses in architecture.

However, as my entrepreneurial aspirations took flight, I made the bold decision to pivot away from my graduate studies and fully devote myself to nurturing my online venture. I founded BLOOM For Women—an online platform dedicated to guiding women toward a life of holistic well-being and financial freedom. Here, I blend my expertise in mental and physical health with social media marketing, empowering women to create multiple income streams and prioritize their personal growth. This venture has opened so many doors and provided amazing opportunities. I finally know this is where I am meant to be.

Today, I proudly stand as a testament to resilience and perseverance. Twelve years sober from drugs, and seven years free from alcohol, I've never been more in tune with my mental health. Each day, I embrace the journey of self-discovery, continuously striving to evolve and expand my horizons. As I navigate the twists and turns of life, I remain steadfast in my commitment to growth, always looking ahead while cherishing the beauty of the present moment.

My journey toward optimal mental health is a path I walk with steadfast commitment, knowing that it's a lifelong endeavor. Some days bring more light than others, but through years of therapy, sobriety, and unwavering self-discipline, I've managed to create a life that fills me with joy and purpose. It's a life I eagerly anticipate waking up to each morning—a life where despite the darkest days, I find glimmers of hope and resilience.

As of February 2024, the statistics paint an unfortunate picture: 20.3 million adults grapple with substance use disorders, with a staggering

90% of them also battling untreated mental illnesses. It's a harsh reminder of the intertwined nature of substance abuse and mental health where one often exacerbates the other. By addressing the underlying emotional turmoil that drives individuals to self-medicate, we can simultaneously tackle mental health challenges and alleviate symptoms of anxiety and depression.

My own struggles with drugs and alcohol showcase this complex relationship. The depths of my mental health battles were most profound when I turned to substances for relief. It was only when I mustered the courage to seek help, dive deep into self-discovery, and prioritize my mental and physical well-being that I began to see change. This realization fuels my journey forward—a constant reminder of the transformative power of introspection and self-care.

Over a decade of grappling with sobriety and mental health challenges has been anything but easy. Yet, through sheer intentionality and unwavering determination, I've managed to navigate this winding path without relying on prescription medications. It's a testament to the resilience of the human spirit, and a testament to the fact that with dedication and a genuine desire for growth, anyone can break free from the shackles of mental health struggles or substance abuse.

I stand as living proof that recovery is possible, that there is a light at the end of the tunnel. My journey serves as a beacon of hope for those who may be wrestling with similar demons. We can recover, and the journey toward healing is within reach for anyone willing to take that courageous first step.

Rian Donatelli

CEO of Connect To Elevate

https://www.linkedin.com/in/riandonatelli/
https://www.facebook.com/rian.donatelli
https://www.instagram.com/riandonatelli/
https://www.connecttoelevate.com
https://www.riandonatelli.com

Rian Donatelli is a much sought-after expert on business strategy, specializing in helping startups, growth-focused CEOs, and distressed businesses. She's been seen in AmplifyHER and EmpowerHER communities and listed in Who's Who of Women, recognized as a trailblazer in coaching. Rian started her career in 2001 at a Fortune 500 company, where she encountered a significant challenge in event activation. This led her to found her own agency, Talent Booking Experts, now over 20 years old. As CEO of Connect to Elevate and Connections Consulting & Marketing Solutions & Talent Booking Experts, Rian has started, grown, and scaled numerous businesses, working with over 100 brands. When she's not enjoying reading, writing, yoga, and time with friends, you'll often find her guiding business owners and Brand Ambassadors with their growth strategies. Learn more at Riandonatelli.com or visit connecttoelevate.com for more information.

FROM FOUNDATIONLESS TO CEO

By Rian Donatelli

Zero marketing experience led me to head the marketing division of a small restaurant chain at 19.

By 22, I was managing a nightclub, only to be abruptly fired from a Fortune 500 company by 25.

With zero business education, savings, or investors, I embarked on launching my first business, which has thrived for over 20 years.

While my journey may seem exceedingly successful, it has been far from easy or fair. Now, for the first time, I'm sharing my personal story: the opportunities seized, the mindset cultivated, the deceptive setbacks faced, and the 11 fundamental keys to achieving and modeling success.

Starting, growing, and scaling a business demands a unique skill set, attainable by anyone with dedication and a thirst for knowledge. My entrepreneurial spirit and relentless drive unexpectedly led me to own multiple businesses by age 40, driven by curiosity and an unyielding pursuit of excellence.

Over the past two decades, I've tasted both success and failure, each experience enriching my understanding. Now, I'm breaking down the 11 essential elements I've learned, practiced daily, and wished I had known sooner.

My entrepreneurial journey began early, shaped by a childhood devoid of today's electronic distractions. Back then, entertainment meant inventing my own fun and being home by dark. At just eight years old, I unwittingly launched my first business. From my grandmother's house, I'd gather items she needed, setting up an impromptu store in my doorway.

The routine was predictable. As she searched for her missing office supplies, I eagerly offered them for sale. "Yes, Nana, I have your stapler," I'd cheerfully reply, pricing it at a steep $3, complete with an upsell for staples. Thus began my entrepreneurial spirit, fueled by a knack for anticipating needs and a relentless curiosity.

This resourcefulness extended to my lemonade stand—a not-so-ordinary affair. Alongside the traditional fare, I introduced lemonade snow cones and sugar-coated toothpicks, delighting customers with inventive add-ons. Even at ten, I seized opportunities, becoming my mother's top salesperson for special Avon ornaments, benefitting local families in need during the holidays.

These early ventures instilled in me a strong work ethic and a thirst for trying new things. From making pizzas to lifeguarding, I immersed myself in various roles, driven by a desire to contribute and explore.

What have I learned from these experiences? Throughout my journey, what truly served me?

Success Tip #1: Try everything! Embrace curiosity, confidence, and a relentless dedication to serving others. Always seek solutions, identify possibilities, and remain committed. These qualities are essential for every successful individual, always and in every way!

* * *

At 18, I enrolled at my parents' out-of-state alma mater immediately after high school graduation, as expected. According to their divorce agreement, my father was supposed to cover my college expenses, while my mother was responsible for my sister. However, on my first day, I discovered that my father had devised a new stipulation: my food allowance was contingent upon maintaining a 3.5 GPA and completing 18 credits in my first year. When I fell short of these conditions, my father withdrew his financial support, and I returned to Ohio.

Back in Ohio, I quickly secured multiple jobs, including waitressing at a restaurant. During slow periods, I took the initiative to propose ideas to management on how to boost business. Starting with unpaid contributions, I demonstrated my marketing acumen despite having zero prior experience in the field. By the age of 19, I had leveraged these efforts into the role of head of marketing for a small restaurant chain, all while managing my own apartment and feeling on top of the world.

Transitioning from this role, I expanded my portfolio by taking on local restaurants and bars as clients and devising marketing strategies to drive growth. Simultaneously, I worked weekends as a bartender at a nightclub, observing customer behavior and learning invaluable lessons in consumer interaction.

Success Tip #2: Embrace boldness! Pay attention, observe, and immerse yourself in understanding consumer behavior to craft detailed customer profiles, also known as Avatars. Always remain receptive to learning opportunities and view every encounter as a chance to raise your own expectations and beliefs.

* * *

By 22 years old, I found myself bartending and seemingly living large, but deep down, I was lost. Days were spent idly at the pool, contemplating my true passions. Throughout this introspection, my love for furniture consistently surfaced. I was enamored with the various styles and historical eras they represented. After thorough research, I set my sights on attending the Columbus College of Art & Design (CCAD), a prestigious institution at the time. Bursting with excitement, I eagerly shared my plans with my mom, only to receive a blunt reality check: "If you think I am going to pay $30,000 a year for you to paint pictures, you are out of your mind!" It was a stark letdown. Money was tight, and the stipulations of my parents' divorce left me financially unsupported once again, this time in pursuit of my dream.

Undeterred, I enrolled in night welding classes as a more affordable route to earning college credits. Despite some initial mishaps—fainting in class during the first week and even catching fire in the second—I persevered. By working a few days as a waitress to cover costs, I managed to excel academically, earning straight As and securing a spot on the Dean's list. This academic success was a stark contrast to my high school experience, where the only A I received was in entrepreneurship class.

Throughout my college years, I navigated without a clear game plan. I drifted through the motions of higher education, adhering to the societal expectation of pursuing a degree to secure a "big girl job" after graduation.

After achieving straight As for the first time in my life, I felt compelled to continue my education despite financial constraints. I diligently researched financial aid options and secured loans, allowing me to enroll in Industrial Design at CCAD.

Realizing the need to save money over the summer, a skill I had not mastered, was a challenge. Budgeting and financial limits were foreign concepts, akin to nails on a chalkboard. Despite these hurdles, an eight-week opportunity emerged that would alter my trajectory, revealing a new career path I had never considered.

This experience taught me an invaluable lesson encapsulated in **Success Tip #3:** "You don't know what you don't know!" Embrace openness, continuous learning, and take calculated risks—they often lead to unexpected opportunities.

* * *

The new summer role was an eight-week marketing launch. During a series of interviews, I presented ideas and concepts I believed would succeed in the marketplace, ultimately securing the position. Our project focused on launching an alcohol cordial trio—Apple, Watermelon, and the new Island Blue Pucker—designed to enhance cocktail flavors. Before premade options became prevalent, bartenders used such products extensively in crafting martinis.

I received the program outline, expectations, and tools to kick off the eight-week marketing launch. Among the tools were countertop infusion chambers, test tubes, buckets for shots, flavored mints, and even colored condoms—an eclectic mix aimed at enhancing the product experience. When over 100 boxes arrived brimming with Apple, Watermelon, and Island Blue scents, I found myself sitting on the floor, pondering how these items would actually sell drinks.

As one of the few direct hires from the Fortune 500 supplier, I recognized the greater experience and education of the marketing team. Despite this, I set ambitious targets and executed the plan as designed. However, I also experimented with elements outside the original scope of work, going against the grain to implement Marketing 101 principles and test subliminal marketing strategies in a few accounts.

Next, I realized the necessity of assembling a capable team to execute the program effectively. Turning to friends, both men and women, I outlined the program and asked if they would join me in executing events. I took it upon myself to train the team comprehensively, covering everything from product knowledge to customer service, ensuring they understood how to execute promotions seamlessly— from entering the account to the final stages, leaving a lasting positive impression. This approach aimed to create true Brand Ambassadors, providing eloquent, educated, and talented men and women to act as an extension of a brand sales force; thus creating true Ambassadors.

I then visited several top accounts in the city, pioneering promotional sales in seafood restaurants and steakhouses. Through negotiations, I successfully got the product featured on their drink menus, opting to fund new menu printing rather than purchasing samples. To amplify visibility, I coordinated matching color apparel and booked models to traverse the restaurant, each carrying the signature martini in synchronized attire. Every 15 minutes for two hours, these models engaged in subtle marketing, prompting diners to inquire with waitstaff about the new cocktail. Additionally, I stationed models at the bar, further drawing attention to the drink without overtly promoting it. The bartenders were trained to redirect interest to the menu, emphasizing the new Blue Island Martini.

This strategic approach generated curiosity among patrons, leading them to ask the staff about the models and the cocktails they carried. The bartenders were instructed to highlight the Blue Island Martini, ensuring the focus remained on the new menu addition.

Our program's success catapulted us to the top spot in the national market. This achievement not only solidified our dominance but also opened unforeseen opportunities in the Wine & Spirits industry, a field I had never considered before. After completing the program and achieving exceptional results, I was approached about a sales position at a liquor brokerage firm.

In the liquor industry, gaining experience in sales through a brokerage was a prerequisite for working directly for a supplier. Despite not yet meeting the one-year sales experience requirement or having a college degree, I was eager to pursue this path. I resumed my studies while balancing a full-time career, attending classes at night, and advancing my career during the day. Although I didn't earn a degree from my time at CCAD, I immersed myself in various courses, accumulating four minors and expanding my knowledge base significantly. Despite the financial burden of student loans, I reveled in the diverse experiences that shaped my journey.

Raised without discussions on goal-setting or career direction, I initially pursued marketing for its appeal rather than strategic planning. My college journey lacked concrete goals initially, marked by a persistent drive but without a clear purpose.

Success Tip #4: Always be learning and growing. Setting actionable goals and mapping out a 90-60-30 day plan are essential steps toward achieving success.

* * *

I absolutely loved and had the utmost respect for my bosses during the eight-week role only a few short months earlier. I loved what I did at the time, and all I wanted to do was get through that step, so I could strive toward working directly for them at the supplier in the future. All I had to do was keep exceeding goals, keep growing, and kill it in every role I had, building others up around me every step of the way. I had a plan! Art school was so time-consuming, with all the projects and hands-on homework. I stayed focused. I stayed in school, and I worked 24/7 to reach my goal!

During my time at the Liquor Broker, I was promoted three times in 12 months. I had unmatched sales, nearly all of which set records at the time. Gratitude was expressed with $100 handshakes and inappropriate comments. I sold 45 cases of alcohol for an event, setting a record that surpassed anything ever done before. I faced challenges as a woman in a male-dominated industry, enduring comments like "Who are you dating on that account?" and offers of "I am going to buy you a pair of knee pads." This was what it was like to trailblaze as a woman in a male-dominated industry.

Part of the scope of work was to book models from agencies. The problem was the models I received did NOT look anything like their photos; no one had ever vetted or trained the models prior to hiring. Therefore, upon arrival, they neither fit in their uniform nor knew the difference between bourbon and whiskey. This was unprofessional and careless on the agency's behalf; beyond embarrassing and a waste of money. I let this happen one time, and then I took the responsibility for success into my own hands. I recruited and trained a team of my girlfriends who not only looked the part but also understood the products better than many customers. They could educate and create experiences that left lasting impressions, elevating our brand interactions to new heights.

This initiative continued successfully until a pivotal moment with the broker's owner:

Owner: "Rian, we can no longer pay the team directly."
Rian: "No problem, I will let them go."
Owner: "Rian, we can no longer pay them directly."
Rian: "OK, I will fire them."
Owner: "Rian! We must pay a company!"

And that's when I realized I needed to start my own company. Despite lacking prior knowledge of business operations, I embarked on learning the essentials: from obtaining an EIN to understanding the differences between an LLC and a Corporation. With guidance from an attorney I knew, I navigated the intricacies of legal filings, secured insurance, and established Independent Contractor Agreements. Thus, my own legitimate business was born, vastly different from my childhood ventures.

Success Tip #5: Try things! Keep going! Surround yourself with people who are qualified to give the advice you need, people who have successfully accomplished what you are trying to do.

* * *

I was growing and scaling quickly in the Wine, Beer & Spirits industry. Promotion after promotion, I was focused on landing my dream job with one of the largest companies in my field. I had a plan! Fourteen months in, the day arrived—I was offered a career role with one of the largest suppliers of distilled beverages in the world! It was an opportunity of a lifetime. Despite long-standing requirements, an exception was made due to my stats and résumé, and I was offered a position without a college degree.

I was tasked with running all events and promotions (E&P) in the state. I seized the promotion and left school because the opportunity was too good to pass up. I knew college would always be there for me to return to. Most importantly, I had the chance to grow once more and work for the two men whom I respected and admired from the eight-week program! They believed in me, allowed me space to grow, and supported me without any judgments or accusations, unlike previous experiences. Their professionalism inspired me, and I was determined to make them proud.

We established local teams in every major market to facilitate growth and scalability. We hired locally and trained rigorously, so events could proceed smoothly in my absence. After each promotion or event, we implemented a thorough recapping procedure where models provided sales results and feedback, including images. This allowed me to furnish invaluable data to corporations for analyzing purchased and forecasted channel data. This pioneering process set new standards in the industry, particularly within my supplier's operations.

In that year alone, I orchestrated 385 events across the state, substantially growing our business. I even devised a program that cost the company $40,000 but yielded a remarkable $720,000 profit! I was on fire!

Success Tip #6: Be bold! Set massive goals that scare you!

* * *

The following year, I earned yet another promotion to become the E&P Regional Marketing Manager of the Northwest, responsible for overseeing all events, promotions, and sponsorships across seven states. Without hesitation, I accepted the position based in Seattle, without even visiting beforehand. I was eager to take the leap and ready to excel in this new role. With a company car, a new boss, and state managers to collaborate with, everything seemed aligned for an amazing opportunity—until it wasn't.

As the sole female and youngest member in the division, I approached the role with my usual "anything is possible" attitude. However, challenges emerged swiftly as I found myself working under a supervisor who was not only new to the company but also lacked familiarity with the spirits industry. His incompetence became evident as he struggled to earn the respect of senior sales members, raising questions about his suitability for the role.

I sensed that my success posed a threat to him, leading to a strained relationship. He began withholding crucial information such as dates for regional meetings, attempting to undermine my effectiveness. Despite his efforts, I managed to stay informed through other channels and never missed a meeting. His tactics escalated to withholding budgets and deadlines, aiming to set me up for failure.

Despite maintaining strong relationships across the company, his actions tarnished my reputation with senior management. The situation took a troubling turn when he started sending inappropriate texts, venting about his personal life, and making advances during our travels together. One instance demanded that I meet him in his hotel room for our meeting, to which I firmly declined and suggested a public location. His reaction resulted in me being reprimanded and written up with HR for missing a meeting.

Realizing the severity of the situation, I gathered substantial evidence in a three-inch binder and approached HR for protection. Despite assurances of support, the outcome was unexpected—I was immediately terminated. They offered a severance package contingent upon signing a non-disclosure agreement and agreeing not to work for or with the company ever again.

Despite my affection for the brand, its people, and the family behind our brands, I couldn't bring myself to forfeit my rights. Proud of my accomplishments, I refused to fade away quietly. Attempts to negotiate terms with an attorney proved futile due to the corporation's size and influence. In the end, I stood firm in my decision not to sign the document, resulting in termination and the subsequent erasure of my employment history from their records.

Success Tip #7: Do not be afraid to use your voice and stand up for what you believe in.

* * *

Unable to apply for positions with other suppliers due to my lack of work history or a degree, I found myself at a crossroads. However, necessity proved to be the mother of invention, and I seized the opportunity to launch and scale my own talent agency—an unexpected blessing. In an era predating today's internet tools, armed only with basic resources like email, BlackBerry, and Ask Jeeves (before Google existed!), I faced the daunting task of forging my own path forward. With bills to pay and student loans looming, there was no option but to press ahead.

Success Tip #8: Fail forward! Everything happens for you, not to you!

* * *

My face became my business card as I ventured into networking and sought events where decision-makers congregated. In the alcohol industry, networking with top brass was crucial, so I took a bold step and bought a ticket to the 2007 Super Bowl, knowing it would be swarming with beer industry leaders.

At the Anheuser-Busch Super Bowl party, I made a connection that would alter my career's trajectory. Armed with confidence and a pitch about my agency of vetted and trained brand ambassadors, I struck up conversations and exchanged contacts throughout the night. Before long, I secured my first major contract—a six-figure deal with Anheuser-Busch. This success laid the groundwork for my next venture: launching a marketing and consulting company, offering services similar to those I had excelled in previously, but now for other suppliers.

With this pivotal contract under my belt, I embarked on an entrepreneurial journey, driven by determination, and fueled by the belief that success is born from seizing opportunities when they arise.

Success Tip #9: Get in the right room.

* * *

Fast forward over two decades, and my business stands tall as a nationwide enterprise, celebrating 20+ years of growth and success. Along the way, I've had the privilege of guiding over 100 brands to new heights.

Contrary to what some might assume, my journey has been far from easy. No investors were lining up to support my vision, and I had no family fortune to fall back on. Every milestone achieved was the result of relentless hard work and unwavering perseverance.

I learned firsthand that the path to success is fraught with peaks and valleys. Just when you think you've reached the summit, life throws you a curveball, reminding you of the impermanence of success. But in those moments of adversity, I've discovered the true power of resilience and adaptability.

Indeed, reinvention has been a recurring theme throughout my journey. Whether due to shifting market dynamics or personal growth, I've had to pivot time and time again. Yet, through it all, one thing remains constant: The importance of decisive action.

Above all, my journey has taught me the value of persistence. Success is not a destination but a continuous journey, marked by setbacks and triumphs alike. The key is to keep moving forward, no matter the obstacles in your path.

So, to anyone embarking on their own entrepreneurial journey, I offer this advice: Embrace the challenges, welcome change, and above all, keep going. For it is in the journey itself that true fulfillment is found.

Success Tip #10: KEEP GOING! Analysis paralysis is the enemy of progress. In an ever-evolving landscape, indecision can be crippling. Trust your instincts, make bold decisions, and course-correct as needed.

* * *

Throughout my career, I've had the privilege of working alongside countless celebrities, professional athletes, and iconic brands. Yet, amidst the glitz and glamour, there's one regret that looms large—the mistake of dimming my shine.

As social media emerged as a powerful tool for personal branding, I hesitated to embrace it fully. Raised with the belief that humility and kindness should always prevail, I shied away from self-promotion, fearing it would be perceived as boastful.

In hindsight, I realize that this reluctance held me back from fully leveraging the opportunities presented by platforms like LinkedIn, Facebook, Twitter, and Instagram. By showcasing the creative activations, event executions, behind-the-scenes moments, celebrity encounters, and exclusive experiences, I could have catapulted my career to new heights. People could have known my marketing company, my talent agency, and most importantly, me!

I was always ahead of the curve, blazing trails for women, and achieving unprecedented success at a young age. But by downplaying my achievements, I inadvertently slowed my progress.

Success Tip #11: They can't be into your brand if they don't know your brand!

* * *

So, if there's one lesson to glean from my journey, it's this: Never underestimate the power of self-promotion. Embrace your successes, share your experiences, and never dim your own shine. With perseverance and a willingness to seize every opportunity, you can achieve anything you set your mind to.

Success isn't handed out freely—it's earned through hard work, resilience, and unwavering determination. When faced with doubt or uncertainty, remember your goals. Map out your path forward with a clear 90-day plan, break it down into 60- and 30-day milestones, and tackle each day with purpose and determination.

If success were easy, everyone would achieve it. But the journey is filled with challenges that test our resolve and determination. The key is to keep moving forward, even when the path seems unclear or the obstacles insurmountable. The one thing you must do is KEEP GOING.

So, to every woman on her journey to success, I encourage you: To trust in yourself, believe in your dreams, and never falter in your pursuit of greatness. Embrace the challenges, celebrate your victories, and let your light shine brightly for the world to see.

Because in the end, it's not just about reaching your goals—it's about the journey you take to get there. And with perseverance and unwavering determination, there's no limit to what you can achieve. Keep going, keep pushing, and never forget: Your dreams are within reach if you just keep moving forward.

—Rian Donatelli

Sheila Burrell

FairyTale Parenting
Concious Parenting Coach and Elite Connector

https://www.facebook.com/fairytaleparenting
https://www.instagram.com/fairytaleparenting
https://www.FairyTaleParenting.com
https://www.WinWithSheila.com

Sheila Burrell is a dedicated entrepreneur and parenting coach on a mission to immerse her two daughters in the dynamic world of entrepreneurship. With an unwavering passion for her craft, Sheila brings her daughters along on her entrepreneurial journey, instilling a sense of inspiration and ambition in them. Sheila's influence is reciprocal. She draws motivation from her daughters, spurring her continual pursuit of self-improvement. Devoted to fostering strong parent-child relationships, Sheila extends her expertise to parents and children, sharing the secrets of her incredible bond with her daughters. Known as the "great connector," Sheila's impact extends beyond her immediate family. She effortlessly weaves connections wherever she goes, cultivating a network that uplifts everyone involved. Sheila Burrell is not just an entrepreneur and parenting coach but a catalyst for growth, inspiring others to forge meaningful connections and reach new heights in their personal and professional lives.

HOW TO BE AN EMPOWERED PARENT AND YOUR CHILD'S SUPERHERO

By Sheila Burrell

She was becoming a statistic, and she was only five!

She was getting the labels and becoming defined by her behaviors. She was a problem child. The parents at her school were complaining about her. She was falling into depression and distancing her emotional connection at home. Her anxiety rose, and I saw that I truly needed to help my little girl. At first, I just thought, "Why can't she be normal?" She was so unreasonable about everything. It brought up thoughts of the distorted relationship I had with my parents as a child. Why can't she just do the things that needed to be done? I was angry. Things needed to be done a certain way. It was so simple. She was so bright, why wouldn't she just do it, or was she just defiant? The more she pushed, the more I pushed. This caused so many tears, sleepless nights, hurt feelings, disappointment, and horrible feelings. I felt so helpless and alone, abandoned and unsupported. I knew I wanted her to be different, so I set out on an journey to "fix" my kid.

Have you ever felt like your child couldn't or flat out wouldn't do what needs to get done to have a positive outcome?

That's how I felt just a few years ago until I realized that my kid was not broken, She wasn't "something to get fixed."

In this chapter, I am going to guide you to test some common beliefs around parenting and lay seeds of awareness and thought that will sprout into the support that our youth is in dire need of today.

In the intricate tapestry of parenting lies a profound truth: 10-20% of children and adolescents worldwide grapple with mental health disorders. These eye-opening statistics underscore the critical role of nurturing environments in shaping children's emotional well-being. Within this narrative, anxiety emerges as a prevalent concern with 75% of mental health disorders surfacing before the age of 24.

Learning about conscious parenting is what saved my child from becoming another statistic. Its core is rooted in empathy, compassion, and mutual respect - ideas that were far from what I experienced in life. My mom sent me away as a teenager because of my defiant behavior. She did the best that she knew for the time. Back in the 1980s, resources were not readily available like they are with technology today. Most cultures were taught to raise obedient children and provide them with food, clothing, and shelter, that's it.

What happens when the child doesn't stay in the box?

I was the one who always wanted more. I was curious. I would take things apart, but never be able to reassemble them back to the way I found them because my mind was only focused on "hows" and "whys", not "what if I get caught?"

Conscious parenting is about recognizing that children are unique individuals with their own needs, emotions, and struggles. Rather than viewing their behavior as a problem to be solved, conscious parenting invites us to see it as a form of communication, a way for our children to express their needs and emotions, however imperfectly.

Armed with this understanding, I embarked on a journey of self-discovery and growth, a journey that would challenge me to confront my own biases, triggers, and preconceptions about parenting. I truly had to empty my cup to be able to take in these new potential beliefs. There was lots of resistance in my head. I learned about regulating my own emotions so I could respond with patience and understanding, and to create a safe and supportive environment in which my daughter felt seen, heard, and valued. It is still a work in progress, and it takes daily effort and focus. We still experience lots of reflection and repair, but I am my daughter's safe place to learn and grow.

My ploys for attention as a child were extremely unhealthy and usually caused someone else emotional suffering at the expense of my pleasure. I have two brothers, one who is almost 10 years older and the other almost two years older, the one I grew up spending the most time with (hence the main target of my acts for attention).

One time in particular in our childhood, I remember that I pretended to sleep as he wanted me to be awake for something. He tried to put a lamp very close to my face hoping the bright light would get my attention to wake me up. He knew I wasn't sleeping and our egos took over to see who would "win." I was determined to keep my sleeping act in full character.

The lamp was a small plastic one-piece structure that looked like a traditional lamp with a base and shade. On a different occasion, we had used the lamp turned upside down to attempt to hatch a small bird's egg that we found on our walk home from school. We weren't successful at hatching the egg, but we were successful at deforming the lamp. When we had turned over the lamp to get the heat from the bulb closest to the egg, the lamp melted slightly leaving the bulb raised above the top of the shade-shaped structure. The heat from the bulb was very intense. This was before the technology of the cooler light bulbs today. So there we had this deformed lamp that my brother was using to try to wake me up with, its bright light super close to my face.

Then it happened!

The fiercely hot bulb just ever so slightly touched my forehead, sizzling my skin. My eyes opened instantaneously because of the pain. He was successful! I woke up! He won! OR did he?

Wait until Mom got home!

My mom worked at a factory doing typical hours, leaving us a few-hour gap from when we got out of school until she got home. We were left to our devices, being curious kids with plenty of outdoors to explore. I was crying in pain, and my brother felt awful, or so that's the way I remember it. Then my vengeful side came out. He's going to pay for this! I'm going to get him in so much trouble! I milked it for all that it was worth. I wore that scar on my forehead like a badge of honor. My trophy. I WON! It was captured in history as we got our classic Olan Mills family pictures done with this scar on my forehead. My cries for attention and connection were less than considerate, but actually quite age-appropriate for my unguided mind. Yet, I had feelings of guilt that made me feel ashamed, but not ashamed enough to stop "getting my brother in trouble."

One of the fundamental principles of conscious parenting is the importance of **connection** and a world that often prioritizes productivity and achievement over human connection. Conscious parenting reminds us of the profound impact that a deep, authentic connection can have on our children's emotional well-being. By cultivating a strong bond with our children, built on trust, empathy, and mutual respect, we create a foundation for resilience that will serve them well throughout their lives.

As I used my newfound knowledge to comb through my childhood, I realized that my childlike ways were completely in alignment with my development. I had to re-parent myself so I could fully get in the saddle to take my daughter down this path of co-regulation and connection.

Communication is another crucial cornerstone of conscious parenting that is not just about the words we say, but how we say them- the tone, the body language, and the intention behind the message. Conscious parenting encourages us to listen deeply to our children, validate their feelings, and respond with compassion and understanding, even in the midst of challenging moments.

This can certainly be difficult, not only to do but to perceive in the heat of a parenting challenge. Some feel that giving your child the opportunity and assistance to regulate their nervous system with a hug or a pause demeans the point of the situation to prove a point or to learn a lesson. Many times we are stuck in a thought process that says we need to take care of a problem immediately and fix it. It may seem quite counterintuitive to take a moment to co-regulate because we were never taught this growing up. This was another super new concept for me also because my household growing up was full of "doing" not "saying" or "being." Any type of talking most likely ended in conflict.

Essentially, with a greater understanding of how the body works, the foundation of clear thinking comes from a regulated nervous system, and if we don't slow down to take time to get our brains back online to do logical thinking, then we are destined to continue to widen the gap of safety and connection, ultimately leading to the diminished confidence in ourselves and our kids, crippling the ability to accept new challenges to grow in the world.

Through conscious parenting, I learned to see my daughter not as a problem to be fixed but as a precious individual with her own unique strengths and struggles. I discovered the power of **validation**, truly listening to her without judgment or criticism, and responding with empathy and compassion. I realize that I need to reparent myself to recognize this for my own inner child who was longing to be validated. As I embraced the principles of conscious parenting, I witnessed a profound transformation in my relationship with my daughter. Now, understanding and connection deepen our bond immeasurably, and I am constantly amazed by the resilience and strength she demonstrates in the face of life's challenges. It's not a magic switch. We still have tense moments and frustration, but now I am the harbor where she can find safety as we navigate the rough times. We get through the rough times much quicker and are able to enjoy more time being present with each other. Conscious parenting also taught me the importance of

setting boundaries with love and respect. In the beginning, I felt like I had to be numb, so I didn't react. My daughter was 10 at the time, and we had been in a battle for years. Our nervous systems were conditioned to be dysregulated. My reactions at the moment, in my eyes, justified how much I cared about the situation. If my reaction was off the charts, then that meant that I was really putting lots of effort towards the situation. My daughter felt if I didn't react, then I didn't care which meant I didn't love her. I had to learn to respond and set healthy boundaries that met both of our needs.

My daughter has been able to take advantage of some amazing opportunities because of the support she feels from our newfound connection. She has presented business ideas in a room full of adult entrepreneurs and spoken on global virtual stages, yet she still has behavioral issues in school. She continues to amaze me each and every day as we learn this new way of thinking together. She can feel safe with me even though some of the communities around her still don't completely understand how to help her shine her superpowers.

Self-care and the recognition of its importance are other aspects of conscious parenting. I grew up believing that self-care was selfish. The more you could do symbolizes your strength and worth, even if it did completely deplete you.

Suck it up buttercup.

Move on.

There are much worse things in the world. You shouldn't need all these extra things and time to yourself to get your things done. As parents, we cannot pour from an empty cup, and it's essential that we prioritize our well-being in order to show up fully for our children. A common example is when you're on an airplane and the flight attendant lets you know even if it is a small child, you must put your oxygen on first in the case of an emergency. Conscious parenting encourages us to cultivate practices of self-care and self-compassion, recognizing that by taking care of ourselves, we are better able to take care of our children.

Yet another key component of connecting with our children is being **playful**. Kids experience things through play and need time to be kids to be able to blossom to their full potential.

Children are naturally inclined to explore and play, shaping their early learning experiences. Simple games like peek-a-boo foster crucial developmental milestones from forming bonds with caregivers to understanding object permanence and social interaction.

Recognized by experts, play is essential for children's physical, social, and emotional growth. It's through hands-on engagement, both self-directed and guided by caregivers, that children truly absorb knowledge, take risks, and hone their social skills.

Moreover, play offers a unique insight into a child's world, revealing their learning and understanding beyond what traditional assessments can capture. By embracing playful learning, caregivers can lay a strong foundation for lifelong development.

Research from Harvard's Center for the Developing Child underscores play's role in fostering resilience and essential skills like problem-solving and communication. Amidst today's challenges, nurturing play not only supports children's well-being but also equips them for the future.

Despite its importance, play has been sidelined in many educational settings, a focus on academic rigor overshadowing play's benefits. Yet, in times of heightened stress and uncertainty, prioritizing playful learning is more crucial than ever to support children's holistic development. This exhibits another reason why it is beneficial for parents to be playful when they are with their kids.

Also, a NASA study's findings were startling: 98% of five-year-old participants fell within the "genius category of imagination," a figure that dwindled to 12% among 15-year-olds and further plummeted to 2% among adults.

Many are busy multitasking through life, and we sometimes forget that our children's likes, dislikes, problems, and issues are just as meaningful, if not (in their eyes) superior to anyone else's in the household, including your adult responsibilities and problems. Their stress shows up in their body over a broken toy the same way that stress over an unpaid bill shows up in an adult's body. Just because it is not an apples-to-apples type of comparison, we commonly have these over-expectations of our children that dim their confidence and full potential. If we take a deeper look, this is often the case of our own selves.

What does your inner dialogue look like?

What do you expect of yourself?

Is it really realistic?

When was the last time you asked your child what they like or what they think of something?

When was the last time you involved them and the decision-making process, no matter how small or large?

We know physical fitness is important to keep our bodies healthy, but we also need to work out our brain with quality questions so we can keep the thinking muscle fit and ready to be used at will. We can focus on grades and what society and the world seem to want us to be, but grades without guidance are nothing. I am a testament to that. Graduating with Straight As and getting all the awards, getting all the things defined as successful growing up having the degree, having a house at 22, and being the first in my family to have these things. But I never was able to explore my own identity.

Kids are naturally curious, and it is our duty as parents to nurture those seeds of curiosity so they can blossom fully and boldly. Parents need to build their own confidence to realize they are the best guides for their children. Being a parent is one of the most miraculous gifts ever and it should be treated with the profound respect and effort that it deserves. We have the precious seeds of the next generation at our fingertips, and we get to choose what to do with them.

Through conscious parenting, I have witnessed firsthand the transformative power of empathy, compassion, and mutual respect. I have been challenged to define what this looks like in our family and our values and create healthy boundaries to stay in alignment with these intentions. My daughter is no longer on the

brink of becoming another statistic in the world of mental health struggles. Instead, she is on a vibrant path as a confident Individual taking life challenges with curiosity and taking on all the bumps and bruises along the way to build her resilience, no matter how much she doesn't always realize how incredible she is. It's little by little.

Our journey is far from over, but with conscious parenting as our guiding light, I am confident that we will continue to grow and thrive together as a family. I am deeply grateful for the lessons I have learned and for the profound impact that conscious parenting has had on our lives. I hope that by sharing my story we can inspire other parents to embrace this transformative approach and create deeper connections with their children.

It has truly been with the power of community that I have been able to get to the level of understanding and growth that I am. I am proud to be a member of the Women's Impact Network, linking arms with other ladies who are on a mission to better humanity. I am passionate about sharing my knowledge and supporting other families through my Fairy Tale Parenting program so that every family has the resources available to deepen their connection and confidence to take on all our worldly encounters.

My daughters have been my savior, my greatest teachers! My oldest has initiated an adventurous learning journey that I am obsessed with. She helped me find a map for our journey. I'm so grateful because her sister has her own unique characteristics that I need to learn to navigate now. Let the next chapter begin…

How can you disrupt some of your beliefs around parenting and perhaps go back and reparent yourself or do a do-over in your own household to get your connection and align more with your values?

How do you believe your parenting style impacts your child's long-term emotional development?

Have you considered how your approach to discipline aligns with your child's individual needs and personality?

What values and principles do you want to instill in your child, and how does your current parenting style support or hinder that?

Have you explored alternative parenting philosophies like conscious parenting and how do you think you could benefit your relationship with your child?

How does your current belief system encompass the points I have made and discussed?

By exploring these questions and reevaluating your belief systems, you can also start your journey to be a more empowered parent, and along the way, you will become your child's Superhero.

Tabitha Litke

CEO of High Ticket Sales

www.linkedin.com/in/tabitha-litke
www.facebook.com/tabitha.litke
www.instagram.com/tablitke

Tabitha Litke, Successful business owner, CEO, and mentor, is driven to help women gain time and financial freedom. Tabitha coaches clients, guiding them down the fast track success path. She is on a mission to help women break free from the poverty mindset and make their dreams a reality. Tabitha is also a first time published author. Aside from her entrepreneur roles, she is a wife, boy mama to two, and above all else loves Jesus. She also homeschools and helps her boys run two successful businesses of their own. It is her desire to not only help others regain their health and finances, but to first and foremost let Jesus' light shine through in all she does. "For I know the plans I have for you," declares the Lord, "plans to prosper you and not to harm you, plans to give you hope and a future." Jeremiah 29:11

A JOURNEY TO FREEDOM

By Tabitha Litke

Take me back to my childhood for just a minute. Waking up to the warm sunshine beaming through the windows and the sound of the birds chirping, was always so tranquil. The days felt like weeks, and months felt like years. Life was easier, full of outside adventures and imaginative play. Cruising with my best friend in his two-passenger Power Wheel fire truck made me feel like I was on top of the world. The simplicity of life is something I dream of now.

Born into a loving, supportive, Christian home, I was blessed with the most amazing parents in the world. Both so selfless, caring, and loving. Always such great examples of Christ's love, care, support, and forgiveness. It wasn't about religion in our home, it was about having a relationship with Jesus. Living out our faith daily, in everything we thought, said, and did.

At the age of five, I accepted Jesus as my personal Savior. I clearly remember that night, sitting in our living room at family devotions, feeling the Holy Spirit moving me to invite Jesus into my heart. My oldest sister took me aside and led me in prayer, asking Jesus to forgive my sins and acknowledging He died on the cross for those sins. I then welcomed Him into my heart that night. That evening I was forever changed, and I praise the Lord He chose me to be His daughter. A daughter of the one true King. The best gift I have ever been given.

Let's fast forward a bit to my teenage years. Although I was naive to a lot of things in life, I loved life, my family, and my friends. As most would say, life was going great. Little did I know that ninth grade would mark the year that would forever turn my whole world upside down. I woke up one day experiencing horrible intrusive thoughts. No matter what I did, there were more intrusive thoughts. I didn't know what was happening or how to make it stop. It was frustrating, overwhelming, and terrifying. I felt completely trapped in my own mind. It was as though I had become a prisoner in my own brain. I couldn't control my impulses which led to compulsion after compulsion. It all led to stress and anxiety as though my brain had been removed, and a completely malfunctioning one was placed in my head. To say the least, this was a very difficult time in our lives learning to treat and navigate this new "normal."

It's difficult not to get emotional writing this because nearing the age of 40, I still struggle with diagnosed OCD, anxiety, and depression. I would be lying to say I didn't often wonder, why me? Why haven't I been healed when I cry out to God, laying it all at His feet? At times I wanted to give up because it was too much on top of life, but God! He is so good and gracious to me. He has brought me so far through these issues stemming from chemical imbalances in the brain. I've worked hard through endless counseling sessions and am now utilizing active tools to aid in slowing those thoughts. I am realizing I am NOT my thoughts. I've learned that compulsions do NOT help, they actually feed the brain monster aka the chemical imbalance, and make it so much worse. I am learning to stop, take a deep breath, and go to God. God is my strength through it all.

You may wonder why I felt the need to share that part of my life, and it is simply because I want you to know no one's life is all roses. Not one person has it all together. Not one person doesn't struggle with something. I want each and every one of you to know that mental health issues do NOT have to define you. Yes, it may be a daily struggle. It may make you feel less than par. It may beat you up. It may feel like it is winning more than you are winning, but it DOES NOT DEFINE YOU. I want you all to know what IS still possible in life when you make goals for yourself and your family. I want you to know you are more than capable of pushing through to do the hard things, even when you want to curl back into bed and cry. Even when you feel as though you can't leave the house that day. Even when you feel you have made progress, then bam, you take 10 steps backward. Even when you are misunderstood or when others knock you off your feet and try to destroy you. Even when nothing feels like it's going right. I want you to feel inspired to keep going, knowing you are NOT alone. I encourage you to get the HELP you need. I encourage you not to do this alone! Invite Jesus into your life. It is life-changing. He is always with you, cares deeply for you, loves you, and wants nothing but the best for you. Surround yourself with people who genuinely love and support you.

There has been so much growth in my life as well as valuable lessons learned through these difficult seasons in my own life. Not just the mental health trials, but the trials that come with life in a broken world. Sometimes we ask why we have to go through these struggles. Or how long do we have to suffer? What should we do next? Sometimes we get angry. Sometimes life feels so unbearably unfair, but we must trust God has a great plan for us even when we can't see it. He completely understands, and He truly gets me through my own big emotions and struggles.

I am so thankful for all He has done and continues to do in my life. He is leading me to freedom and healing in so many ways. I've learned so much through my suffering. So for those lessons, I am so grateful.

You see, 2023 was a year that nearly broke me. I was betrayed and hurt deeply. Words and actions crushed me in a way I didn't know possible. Those scars are deep, and I am still healing from the trauma that took place. I am still learning how to truly forgive like Jesus because I know no one is perfect, and we all need forgiveness. I am still grieving the loss of someone very much alive, a pain that I never experienced before. A pain that is currently still a bit raw, welling up tears in my eyes because I still love this person. I pray for this person. I have so many questions, but God. He is the healer of broken hearts. He is the healer of mental wounds. And even as I've endured trial after trial, He has taught me to trust in the Lord like I never have before. Everything was stripped away to open my eyes for the better. It's taught me He is the ONLY one who will ALWAYS be there. He will never leave me or forsake me. He is the only one who truly knows everything about me and cares about me. He will never give up on me! He will NEVER fail me. He sees the best in me and holds His loving hands out to me. Jesus is accessible at all times. He's molded me to be more empathetic and sympathetic towards others. He allows me to try to see the best in every circumstance. It isn't always easy, and I am still a work in progress, but I am forever changed.

Now that you have a background glimpse into my own life and journey, I want to transition and talk to you about dreams. I have been a dreamer for as long as I can remember. I am an optimist and see big visions that excite me. Even as a young girl, I remember having big dreams. I'm not sure they were your typical children's dream; however, for me it was fun and something I thought of often. There was an innocence and excitement that would build inside me as I allowed my imagination to run freely. Oftentimes, I miss the simplicity that came from my childhood when things were easier. There's a sweet innocence in childhood that you don't understand till you're much older.

One of my childhood dreams was to build a house filled with many levels and rooms. I can envision the exact kitchen seat I sat in as I put my dreams on that blank piece of paper. Drawing out each room and thinking about the many details and how badly I wanted an upstairs in my house. Better yet, multiple levels. I wanted to build a mansion. Although many of the other specific dream home details have slipped my memory, I do recall how happy and excited envisioning that home made me feel. I remember going over all the important details with my mama explaining why I needed and wanted each space. She chuckled and said, "You better keep on dreaming." My parents have always been my biggest supporters, so admittedly, I remember thinking to myself, "O you wait! I WILL build my own house one day!" Like most kids, I wanted to prove her wrong. Even from that young age, I saw a vision bigger than many ever allow themselves to.

I'm aware my mom wasn't trying to discourage me from my dream. But, as an adult, she understood what it would take to accomplish that massive dream. It wasn't that she didn't believe in me but rather that she was thinking of the "unrealistic" aspect. I'm sure when she looked at the mansion on my paper she was thinking, "Yeah right, that's gonna cost an arm and a leg." She probably didn't want me to set myself up for disappointment in the future. However, that never stopped me from continuing to dream. It only lit a fire under me to build that dream house one day.

Maybe this vision came from vacationing each year in the Outer Banks with my family. We'd rent a beautiful beach house every summer, and oftentimes it was multiple levels, and it was magical. It felt like a beach house mansion, and we always had the best times. We made so many unforgettable memories that I will forever cherish.

Don't get me wrong, growing up, we had an amazing one-story home. I was actually quite content, yet still loved to dream and set a bigger vision for my future. I enjoyed the home I grew up in, and there were lots of unforgettable memories made there as well.

The hope of building my dream home has been carried into my adult years. Although, over the years, what that looks like has definitely changed. I'd like to say it has become something more practical and more realistic. But I love saving Pinterest ideas and pictures of what I envision, from the many storage spaces to the outside exterior with its various paint colors and rustic front porch columns.

For most of us, building a house is not an easily attainable goal. It costs a small fortune and takes time and patience. The reality is many don't ever get to fulfill that dream due to the financial aspect. There's a lack of money, never seems to be enough. Many individuals are stuck in poverty, stressed to the max, and burnt out. It's a never-ending cycle that I personally have no desire to be stuck in any longer or have my loved ones stuck in. Trust me, I am speaking from experience.

I want to take a minute to clarify something. Dreaming big does not always mean you have a lack of contentment. My interpretation of dreaming is seeing a bigger vision in some aspect(s) of your life and applying yourself to fulfill certain goals to make those dreams a reality. I see a lack of contentment as not being thankful for what you do have, all the while chasing more and more, yet never feeling fulfilled. That can be a super unhealthy place to be. I'm not speaking for everyone, but it's often true we want what we don't have. And that's not necessarily wrong, as long as it doesn't cause jealousy or cause us to lose our grateful hearts for what we have been blessed with. If it empowers us to work towards something bigger and aids us in setting goals for our future, we can use it for good.

I'm constantly learning contentment. It's a lesson most of us need to learn, no matter our age. In Philippians 4:11-13, Paul says, "Not that I was ever in need, for I have learned how to be content with whatever I have. I know how to live on almost nothing or with everything. I have learned the secret of living in every situation, whether it is with a full stomach or empty, with plenty or little. For I can do everything through Christ, who gives me strength." Paul was going through trials and was still content and trusted He could do all things. Not in his strength, but in God's strength.

If you haven't figured it out by now, I obviously believe in allowing yourself to dream. To think outside the box. Don't limit yourself or your mindset solely to what you're textbook taught. For example, life often looks like the following: Finish high school, go to college, get a 9-5 job, pay off thousands in college debt, work hard, buy a home, go into 30 years of more debt, and repeat until you may be able to retire at the age of 67 with no extra funds to travel or enjoy not working.

Don't misunderstand my point here; we all know working hard is great. We should work hard; however, we often get so caught up in the mundane that we don't realize or dig into our fullest potential. We're often conditioned to believe our 9-5 job is all we are capable of until retirement. We just don't know what we don't know. There are certain things we aren't taught because they are not the norm.

There is often this mentality that struggling financially is normal and is a part of life. And yes, that is true for a lot of us; however, how would it feel to break those chains and no longer have to sacrifice all the time? How would it feel to not have to go without? How would it feel to not have to work multiple jobs? How would it feel to no longer have limited time for the rest of the life God has gifted you? How would it feel to spend as much time as you wanted with your kids and family?

For many years, I've felt God calling me to something bigger. Oftentimes I jokingly say, "I don't know what I want to be when I grow up." It's quite comical as a 39-year-old wife and mama, with a college degree. I would think to myself, "How do I still not know my entire 'purpose'?" It's very tough at times and can actually be very defeating.

Of course, I know God has called me to be a wife and mama. I know one of my greatest jobs is being a mom, and I love it so much. It's such a gift and a blessing to have this treasured role of not only being a mom but also their teacher as we begin our seventh year homeschooling. I wouldn't trade it for the world, but this makes the financial struggle more stressful. Knowing you need to help provide for your family and relieve some of the stress from your spouse but also not wanting to leave your kids.

It's also tough when year after year you find your finances struggling more and more. Losing out on experiences, vacations, and time with the kids because there's never extra money. And can we talk about the guilt that can come along with a lack of finances? It's a sting knowing you're the reason for the debt. Yes, I'm admitting I have debt. I will be even more honest and vulnerable with you - some of this debt is from investments I previously made into low-ticket sales businesses. A lot of the debt is due to a lack of sticking to a budget. And let's face it, life is darn right expensive. Money definitely does not grow on trees, although we all wish it did.

My hubby works four-plus side hustle jobs on top of his demanding 9-5 job. And let's be honest, his 9-5 is more like a 7-7 job. Can I add he does this all without complaint and because he takes his role as a leader and provider for us seriously? His work ethic is truly unmatched, and I am so thankful for him. Unfortunately, like many other couples, finances can cause a lot of stress in a marriage. Life can be challenging enough, so of course, I never want to add more stress, but definitely have.

Time is a thief and not slowing down. Knowing we can't get back time with our precious kids is hard. My husband and I want to take them on more trips to see the world and get away from the daily grind throughout the year. That all comes with a great price tag. The economy most certainly does not help with the price gouging making it nearly impossible to make ends meet for many of us, let alone allowing us the freedom to travel or enjoy life more.

I don't know about you, but I knew I needed to make a BIG change to better help our family. I knew it, yet I felt so stuck. I tried so hard to figure it out and lean into God's plan, but I felt like I was failing in so many aspects. And if you have ever experienced those feelings of defeat or failure, you know it can feel like you're drowning with no way out. It can feel like you are worthless in most ways. But guess what? You're not worthless! You are valued! You are loved! You are blessed! You keep on keeping on! God has great plans for your life! Always lean into Him.

I have been in the entrepreneur world for over 15 years now. I have had many highs and some lows with it. I get passionate and love learning about health and wellness and clean living. I have done many low-ticket sales businesses and have enjoyed them. I have sold everything from cookware to clothes, from essential oils to green cleaning products, and more. There is something wonderful about being your own boss. I love being my own boss and not stressing about the 9-5 job. I love the freedom to make my schedule and work when I can. I love not having to call off when I am sick or when my kids are sick. It is such a stress reliever for me to own my business and do what I love.

This entrepreneurial passion has faded in and out over the years because I would work so hard and then get a bit burnt out or frustrated when things were not working out how I envisioned. Most of the time I was making way less commission than I was investing out for the businesses. Overall, I was not making the much-needed full-time income, oftentimes putting us in the negative instead of providing for our needs. I was starting over each month. It was a bit of a hamster wheel.

I had been struggling, feeling like I was a disappointment to my husband and family because I couldn't seem to hold a job out of the home anymore. Struggling with mental health issues was definitely playing a role in this "as well as" being complacent right where my comfort was at home. This made me question myself and at times feel horrible, especially since I always thought I'd have my breakthrough with a business I was running. It was my dream to be a successful businesswoman. I wanted my husband to retire early. It was my dream to prove to him I could follow through with something and break the way we were living. My dream was to have us set for life, so we could enjoy life more. I desired time and financial freedom for us! I wanted to be able to help others in need. I wanted to show my hubby I could do difficult things and follow through even when it got hard. I dreamt of a breakthrough to change our finances for the better, to change my children's future, so they do not have to struggle in the ways we have.

I knew for years that there was so much potential in the network marketing world yet always seemed to fall short. Not to mention network marketing companies sometimes get a bad rap from others (mostly those who are uneducated on the subject). At times, that would upset me and even hurt my feelings. I was trying to provide for my family. How could others be harsh or unsupportive? Thankfully, I always had more support in my arena than not. Sometimes I look back over the years and feel as though I had "given up" right before my breakthrough. I am thankful for my optimism, which allows me to always try to look at my endeavors as learning and growth experiences.

The truth is I really did learn so much and wouldn't be where I am today without the knowledge that led me here. I am so thankful for my entrepreneurial endeavors in low-ticket sales over the years. I still love low-ticket sales, and I still use and promote many of the products. Nonetheless, I needed a big change to fast-track me to financial freedom.

Let's fast forward to just a couple of months ago when God laid high-ticket sales in my lap. Keep in mind, I had no idea what the high-ticket world was either, but I could feel it was something amazing. I was a bit skeptical at first. I prayed and reluctantly talked to my husband who isn't typically in complete alignment with my entrepreneurial endeavors. However, he was different and didn't give me the automatic no. That was a breath of fresh air for me because I was expecting a big fat no. Don't get me wrong, he supports me in his own way; however, he doesn't always see the vision like I do. And that's ok. I fully believe God gives us all different desires and visions for a reason.

This is definitely an area where I have grown over the years. I used to find it difficult when others did not share in my excitement or support me. But I realize now not everyone will understand why we choose certain paths. They won't always support us, and that's ok. Let them go because God has the right ones who will support you and want you to succeed. It is OK to have the vision alone. As long as God gives you peace about it, go for it. Don't wait for the perfect time because there is no perfect time. Do it afraid. Do it inexperienced. Do it with all your heart. Don't give up!

So, you are probably wondering what the heck high-ticket sales are and why you should jump in. It's essentially the sale of a product(s) valued over $200. High-ticket sales offer a distinct set of advantages for businesses, allowing them to thrive with a different strategy than low-ticket sales. Here's a breakdown of the great value in high-ticket sales. First, this means the need for fewer sales to reach your revenue goals. It also means a higher profit margin, allowing you to reach your financial goals a lot faster. It means a deeper focus on clients. We are able to invest more time in tailoring to their needs and better serve them on their journey. This gives them not only satisfaction but also loyalty to you. The premium service perception means the higher the price tag on the product can position your offering as exclusive and valuable, attracting clients who seek premium experiences. Lastly, high-ticket products can elevate your brand image and position you within a luxury or high-quality category.

When God laid this high-ticket opportunity before me, I was beyond thankful. He is already doing great things. I am telling you, high-ticket sales are the place to be. It is changing lives for the better. I have no doubt it is leading me and my family to time and financial freedom, and the products are the icing on the cake. They are absolutely needed and aligned with health and wellness.

I love helping others, and it truly is my desire to serve as many of you as I can. I would love nothing more than to support you and help you reach your goals and dreams. Let's free your time and reach financial freedom together!

You will be blown away by the business compensation plan as it is truly unmatched and patented. You will NEVER de-rank, but you WILL rank up quickly. You can make up to $7,700 per sale. It is like nothing I have ever been a part of before. The like-mindedness, support, and training are nothing short of amazing. You don't need experience as the training is all set up for you and the system is duplicatable.

Remember, no matter what happens, do not compare yourself to other people's journeys. Do not compete with others because we are all in this life together. Life is hard. It is beautiful. It is sometimes a bit messy. Sometimes, it is a bit like a roller coaster. Each season of life is another chapter in our book. Every chapter is different and unique. We learn and grow. We gain wisdom and knowledge.

It's my desire to honor and serve Jesus above all else through this chapter and throughout my life. If you take nothing else away from this chapter, I pray if you don't already have a relationship with Jesus, you will accept His free gift of Salvation. John 3:16 says, "For God so loved the world, that he gave his only Son, that whoever believes in him should not perish but have eternal life."

Tishana Eason

Brooklyn Beauty Bar
Owner and Self Love Coach

https://www.linkedin.com/in/tishana-eason-92912761/
https://www.facebook.com/BrooklynstylistTishana
https://brooklynbeautybarga.com/

Tishana also known as Brooklyn was born and raised in Brooklyn, New York. Her parents came from Panama in search of the American dream in order to provide for her and her siblings. She attended Bushop Laughlin memorial high school. At the age 19, she became part salon owner, where she began to counsel women behind the chair. Once Brooklyn became a wife and a mother, she put her career on hold. 37, was a turning point for her, life as she knew it changed. This was a fresh start for her. Brooklyn opened a salon, started a fashion line business and took her life experience and became a life coach.

EMPOWER HER

By Tishana Eason

I'm that Coach who will push you to the limit. Get ready because change starts today. "I had the power all along," is what I had to learn at the age of 45 years old. No more faking it til you make it. It had to become a lifestyle. One may think that this is easy, but with the weight of the world on your shoulders, it can be very challenging. I wanted to activate the best version of myself.

You see, I was a people pleaser, putting everyone and everything before myself. This made it hard for me to move forward with my goals and inspiration. I had to hit rock bottom in order for me to get what God was trying to show me - self-love. And, oh, did I hit rock bottom. I was able to feed my kids but I ate ramen noodles many nights. Self-love may not sound like much, but it's everything. One can't survive without it.

Let's look at the definition of self-love. Self-love is having a high regard for your own well-being and happiness. Taking care of your own needs and not sacrificing your well-being to please others. How can you function without loving yourself? This alone empowers you to be great. With that being said, how do show up for you? Are you taking time throughout the day to better your life? Or are you helping someone else better their life? This is what I kept doing over and over.

Starting over after the divorce was so hard for me. No one was there for me. Mentally, I had to deal with the fact that I was there for others, but I couldn't find anyone to help me. By then, I didn't know who I was. Self-love is also about knowing your worth. I knew nothing about that. If you keep putting so many things before you, you can lose and devalue yourself. I had to make so many hard decisions that made me uncomfortable because I didn't know how to say "No."

I began with thirty- and sixty-day goals. Sometimes I didn't see results right away but I kept going. I started to seek a coach, and she said power comes from within yourself. You have to learn to tap into your inner strength to defeat any insecurities you may have that will stop you from greatness, and I had many insecurities. After all, I was getting a divorce after 19 years. I knew where it was coming from; I just didn't know how to control it.

Sometimes, we need to ask ourselves what is going on internally and what we have to face that is holding us back. For me, it was my childhood trauma and divorce. I looked for validation from my dad. It was like he had to approve before I did something. Seeing my mom looking for his love, I guess I was too. This was just me trying to please him instead of myself. There is no way my goals were his, so why did I do that? I realized I didn't want to be in a confrontation with him. It was my life. I had to be happy, right? Standing up for myself is a must. Sadly, I didn't understand that then, so I got into my marriage and repeated the same behaviors while looking for validation. That was the worst thing I could ever do. I spent so many years in a box. I had so many ideas and visions. We all have to be careful about what example we're setting for our kids and the people we influence.

Let's start with daily affirmations. My favorite one is, "I can do all things with God who strengthens me." I had to reprogram my brain about the way I look at things. Like if the glass is half full instead or half empty. Here are more that might help you. "I am what God says I am." "I have the power within to move mountains." "I will fulfill my goals." "I will keep going even when I get distracted." Come up with some of your own so that we can be great.

I would start my day with prayer. I would ask God to wake up whatever is dying inside of me. To give me wisdom on how to use it. You have to understand that our old ways of thinking are always going to creep up and attack us. I had my good days and bad. But I was willing to see the fight through. I wrote down the things that I was great at doing versus the areas I needed help in and figured out how I could get better in those areas of my life. Do the same so that you have a plan.

God blessed me with more clients and widened my territory. I started getting clients from across town, passing by salons near their homes to come see me. I started my own clothing brand in the midst of the pandemic, leading me to enter fashion shows. I was doing at least five shows a year. I started to feel empowered and saw the evidence of my hard work. When in doubt, think about a time you put in the work and saw the fruits of your labor.

You have to start aligning yourself with people who are already where you want to be or going there. Once I started changing my circle, doors that I thought wouldn't be open, opened. Like-minded people will encourage you and help you get to the top. Do what makes you happy. You should always be you and be comfortable doing so. I even started taking classes for fashion design as well as extra classes for my business.

Remember, each one teaches one. Never just keep the gift to yourself. There is someone who needs your wisdom. But always be careful who you tell your dreams and feelings to. Not everyone is worth your while. So, walk in your destiny. The more power you have, the more you're able to help others. I was a wife following her husband who became a boss lady. I'm here to tell you that dreams do come true, and you have the power to do anything. Never give up. I'm now a coach helping other women like myself. I have a podcast on Spotify - Diving Deep with Brooke.

JOIN THE MOVEMENT!
#BAUW

Becoming An Unstoppable Woman
With She Rises Studios

She Rises Studios was founded by Hanna Olivas and Adriana Luna Carlos, the mother-daughter duo, in mid-2020 as they saw a need to help empower women worldwide. They are the podcast hosts of the *She Rises Studios Podcast* and Amazon best-selling authors and motivational speakers who travel the world. Hanna and Adriana are the movement creators of #BAUW - Becoming An Unstoppable Woman: The movement has been created to universally impact women of all ages, at whatever stage of life, to overcome insecurities, and adversities, and develop an unstoppable mindset. She Rises Studios educates, celebrates, and empowers women globally.

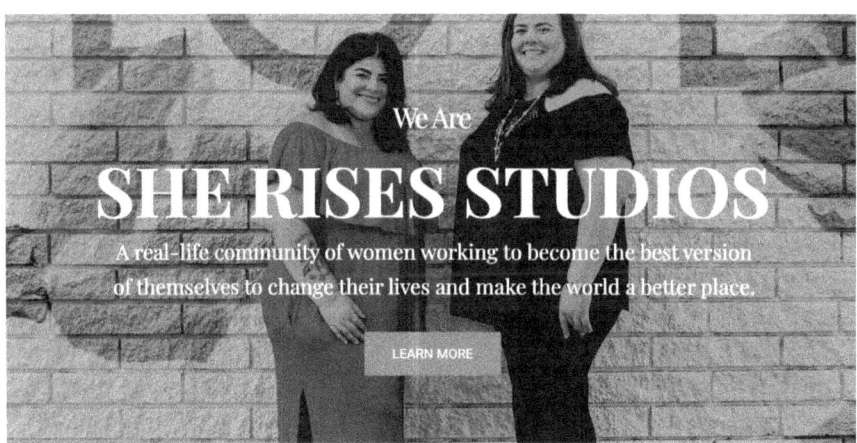

Looking to Join Us in our Next Anthology or Publish YOUR Own?

She Rises Studios Publishing offers full-service publishing, marketing, book tour, and campaign services. For more information, contact info@sherisesstudios.com

We are always looking for women who want to share their stories and expertise and feature their businesses on our podcasts, in our books, and in our magazines.

SEE WHAT WE DO

OUR PODCAST **OUR BOOKS** **OUR SERVICES**

Be featured in the Becoming An Unstoppable Woman magazine, published in 13 countries and sold in all major retailers. Get the visibility you need to LEVEL UP in your business!

Have your own TV show streamed across major platforms like Roku TV, Amazon Fire Stick, Apple TV and more!

Learn to leverage your expertise. Build your online presence and grow your audience with FENIX TV.
https://fenixtv.sherisesstudios.com/

Visit www.SheRisesStudios.com to see how YOU can join the #BAUW movement and help your community to achieve the UNSTOPPABLE mindset.

Have you checked out the *She Rises Studios Podcast?*

Find us on all MAJOR platforms: Spotify, IHeartRadio, Apple Podcasts, Google Podcasts, etc.

Looking to become a sponsor or build a partnership?

Email us at info@sherisesstudios.com

www.ingramcontent.com/pod-product-compliance
Lightning Source LLC
Chambersburg PA
CBHW070908120626
46546CB00001B/176